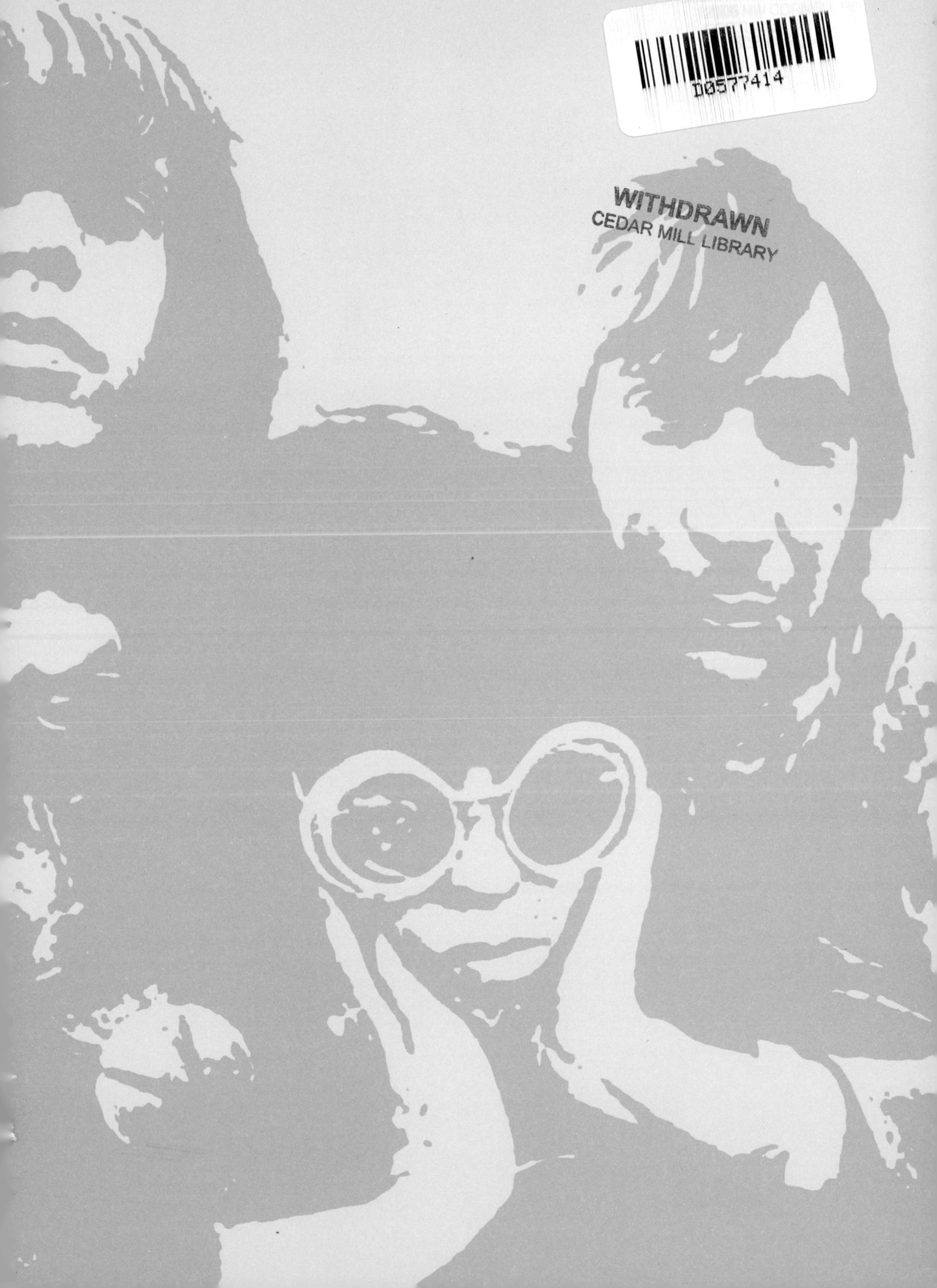

The ROLLING STONES
in Comics

Text: Céka
Cover: Bast

nbm GRAPHIC NOVELS

Nantier • Beall • Minoustchine
NEW YORK

The ROLLING STONES in Comics

ISBN 9781681121987
© 2017 Editions Petit a Petit
© 2019 NBM for the English translation
Library of Congress Control Number: 2018965122
Translation by Montana Kane
Lettering by Ortho
Layout design by Mary Delavigne

Printed in Korea
1st printing March 2019

This book is also available wherever e-books are sold

Unless the publisher is mistaken, all photos in this book belong to the
public domain or are free to use, taken from Wikemedia Commons platforms.
U.S. publisher disclaimer: most of the quotes in this book are translated from the French
edition, and are therefore not phrased exactly like the original quotes in English

nbm
COMICS BIOGRAPHIES

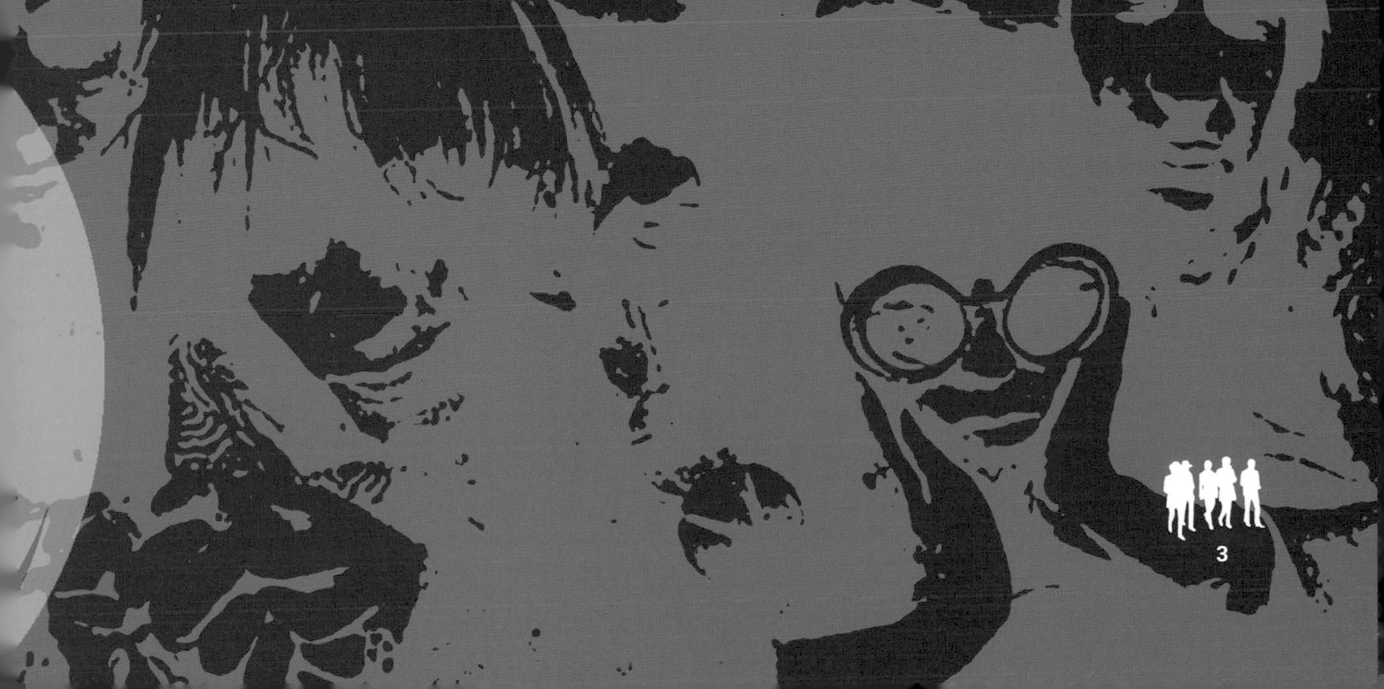

1965 ©Olavi Kaskisuo Lehtikuva

"TRUTHFULLY, I THOUGHT MICK WOULD BECOME A POLITICIAN. HE WAS ALWAYS THE LEADER, EVEN IN SCHOOL. "
Eva Jagger, mother of Mick Jagger

"HE NEVER REALLY DID MUCH IN CLASS AND SPENT MOST OF HIS TIME TALKING ABOUT CHUCK BERRY."

Dick Taylor
TALKING ABOUT KEITH

1965 ©Kevin Delaney CC BY-SA 2.0

The Stones,
Before the Stones

Two geniuses coming together is a rare event. **But five is downright miraculous.**

And yet that's exactly what happened in the early '60s. Hailing from different geographical, social and musical backgrounds, the future Rolling Stones were nothing like your typical garage band buddies. But chance and circumstance have a funny way of making things happen...

Michael Philippe Jagger was born on July 26, 1943, in Dartford, Kent, to a middle-class family. His father was a gym teacher who wrote the first guidebook on basketball in England, which was published in 1962. Mick Jagger demonstrated a propensity for rebellion at an early age. Though not very studious, he ended up in business school—which would prove useful later on. He was forced to wear a uniform, so he added his own personal touch to it: tennis shoes. A class act from day one... And when he eventually drifted toward music, things got pretty heated in the family household. **But the kid was determined.**

————————————

Keith Richards was born on December 18, 1943, in the same hospital as Mick Jagger; he lived in the same town and went to the same grade school as well. But they didn't live in the same neighborhood and didn't know each other yet. Thanks to his grandfather Gus and his mother, he got into music at an early age. As a teenager, he was crazy about Chuck Berry and spent all his time playing guitar and all his money on albums... a sign of things to come... He later enrolled at the Sidcup Art College on a "welcome" grant **so he could play even more guitar.**

"I ALWAYS TOLD MY CHILDREN THAT IF THEY PLAYED AN INSTRUMENT, THEY WOULD ALWAYS FIND A WAY TO EARN A LIVING."
Kathleen Perks, mother of Bill Wyman

"BRIAN LOVED MUSIC EARLY ON: HE STARTED TAKING PIANO LESSONS AT THE AGE OF SIX OR SEVEN, THEN HE JOINED HIS SCHOOL ORCHESTRA."
Louisa Jones, mother of Brian Jones

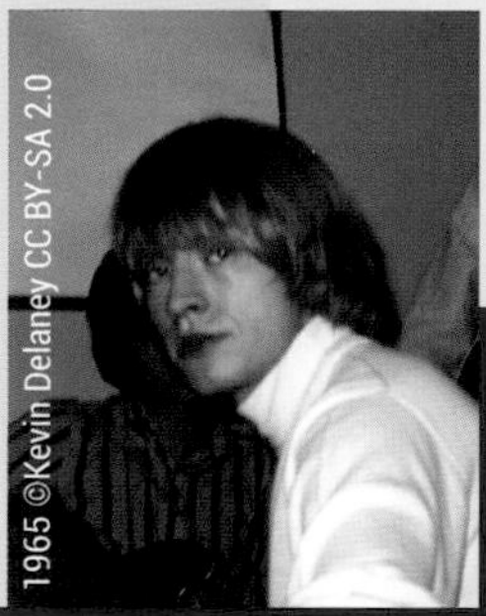
1965 ©Kevin Delaney CC BY-SA 2.0

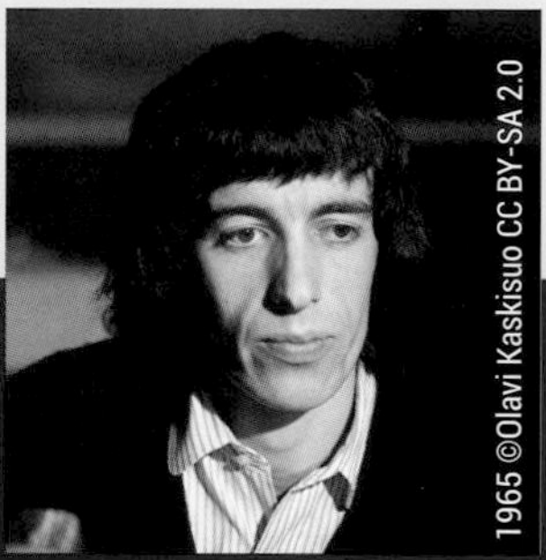
1965 ©Olavi Kaskisuo CC BY-SA 2.0

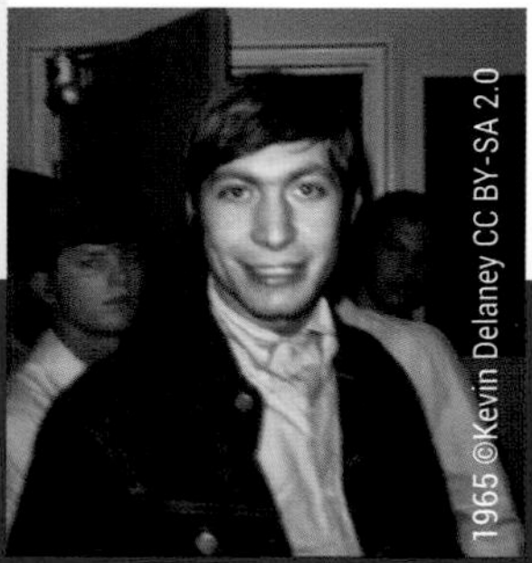
1965 ©Kevin Delaney CC BY-SA 2.0

"WHEN I WAS TWELVE, I HEARD AN EARL BOSTIC ALBUM CALLED *FLAMINGO* AND RIGHT THEN I KNEW I WANTED TO BE A SAX PLAYER. THEN I HEARD ANOTHER ALBUM TITLED *WALKING SHOES*, BY GERRY MULLIGAN WITH CHICO HAMILTON ON DRUMS, AND I DECIDED TO BECOME A DRUMMER." **Charlie Watts**

The strikingly handsome **Brian Jones** wasn't born in Dartford but in Cheltenham, Gloucestershire, on February 28, 1942. His father, the son of a piano player, worked in aeronautics. Brian's parents were supportive of his musical calling. He learned to play the clarinet and he sang in his church choir. He was a little volatile, constantly changing schools and musical instruments. A restless soul? Perhaps, since he dropped out of school as a teenager to hitchhike across Europe. He came back determined to make it in the music biz... **playing the blues!**

Bill Wyman, real name William Perks, claims he was born in Lewisham, a suburb south of London, on October 24, 1941. He was in fact born on October 24–but in 1936. (Vanity? Age related insecurity complex? Being older than his bandmates?) He was the son of a mason and also got into music at an early age. He was particularly drawn to the piano, the organ and the clarinet. **At the tender age of thirteen, he already wanted to conduct his own orchestra!**

He was an avid record collector, with eclectic taste that ranged from jazz to blues to rock.

Charlie Watts was born on June 2, 1941, in Islington, just north of London. His father was a truck driver with British Railways. Though not exactly a star pupil, the kid was a born drummer. At the age of twelve, anytime he heard a song on the radio, he would start beating out the rhythm, using anything he could get his hands on until, presto, his parents bought him a little drum set—just a very basic one, but it was still better than banging on plates and trash cans. Like many young people of his generation, he went to art school—in Harrow, in this case. **He wasn't into R&B but jazz. Real jazz!**

Now that we've introduced the band, except for Ian Stewart, the famous sixth Stone, a nagging question remains: **how did these little rocks meet?** Well, it was in June 1960 at the Dartford train station, that the mythical encounter between Mick and Keith took place. Mick was carrying Chuck Berry, Little Walter and Muddy Waters albums under his arm. Upon discovering that they were both passionate about the blues, the two men became fast friends.

The Stones' story can now begin... hit it!

Blessed Be the Vinyl

Artist: Marin Trystam

The Unlikely People
One Meets on a Railway Platform...

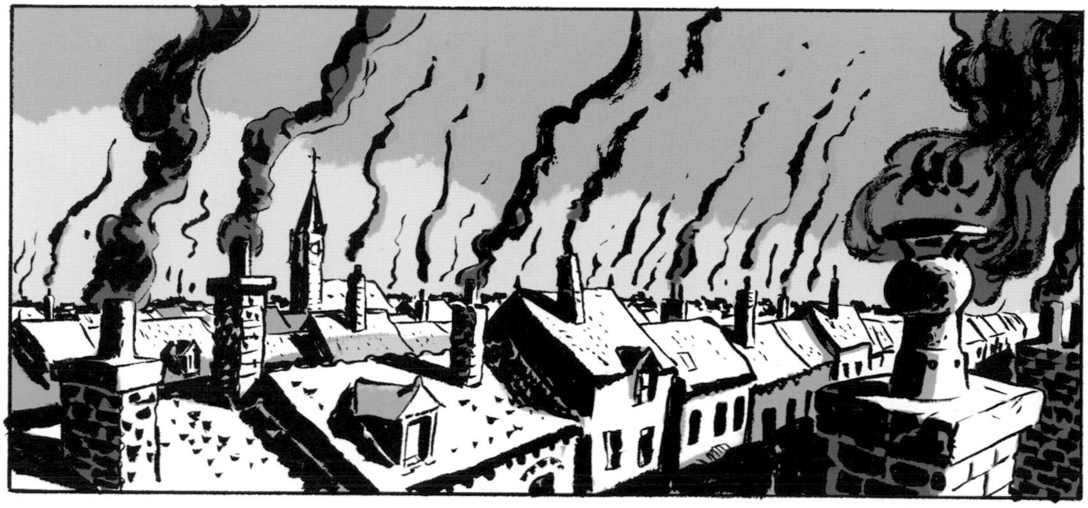

DARTFORD, KENT, JUNE 1960. A PEACEFUL VILLAGE SOUTHEAST OF LONDON.

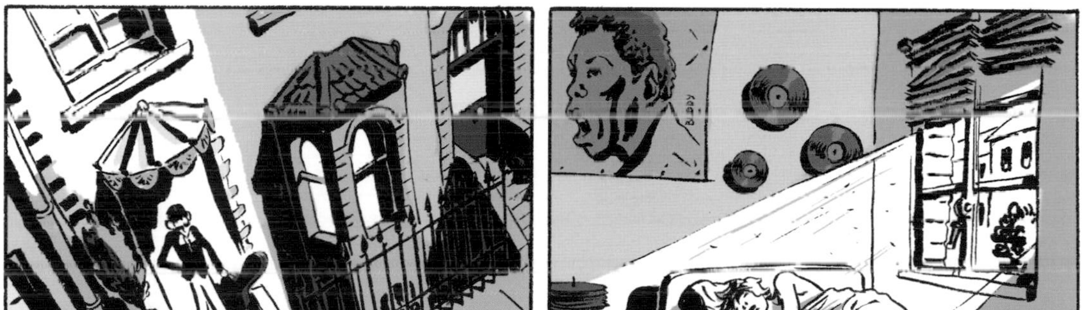

EVER WONDER WHAT IT TAKES TO MAKE A LEGEND?

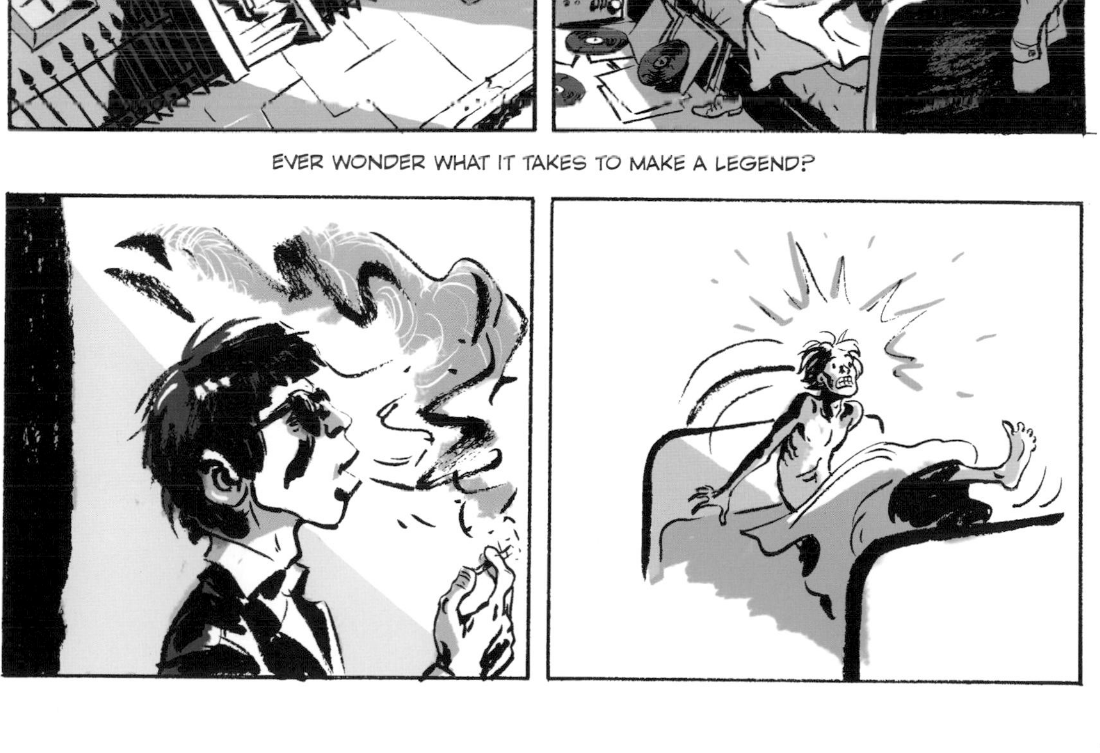

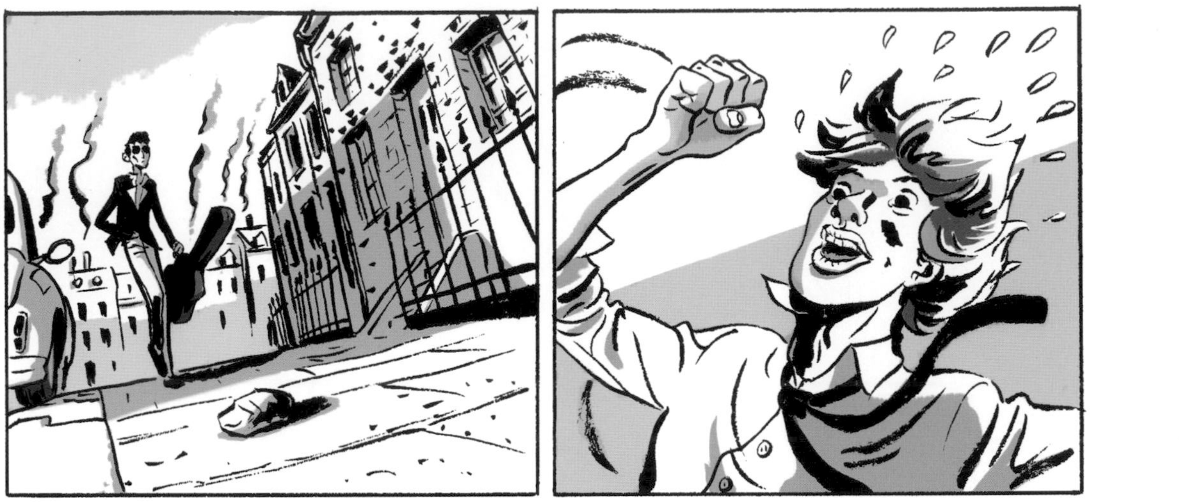

TWO GUYS WHO LIVE IN THE SAME TOWN?

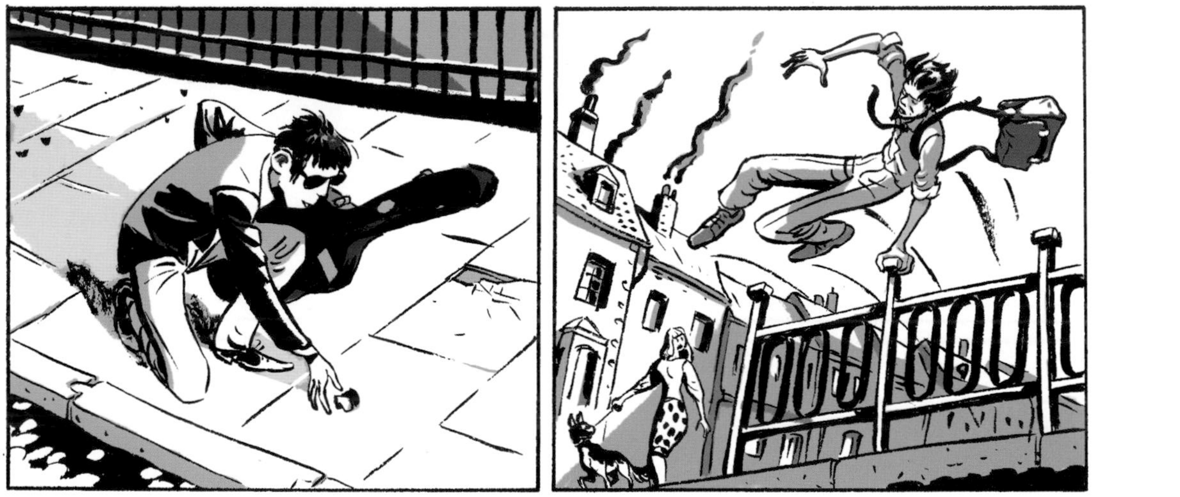

THAT'S PART OF IT, OF COURSE.

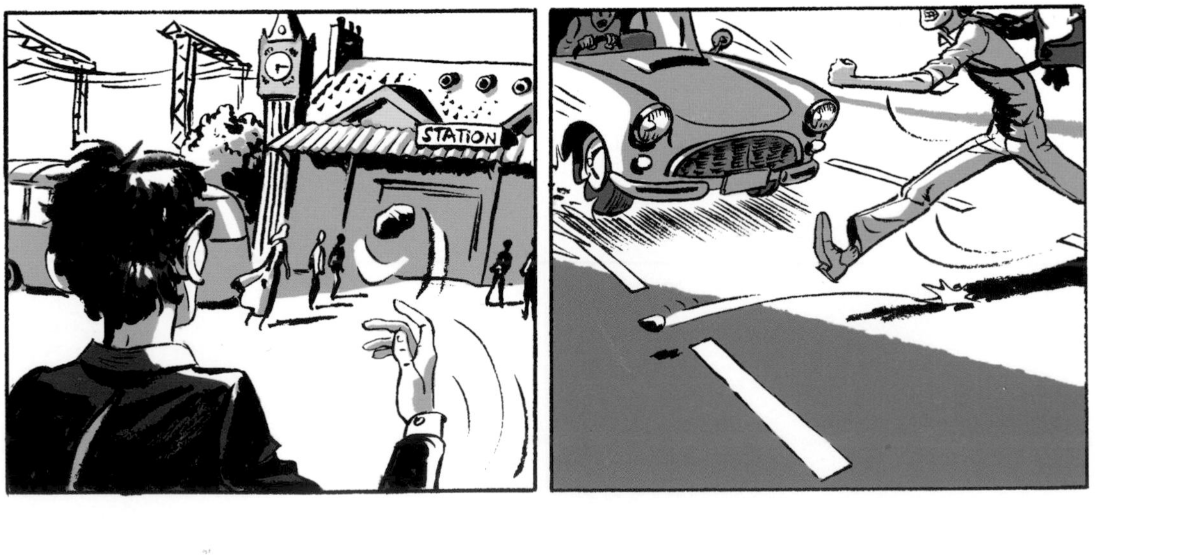
STATION

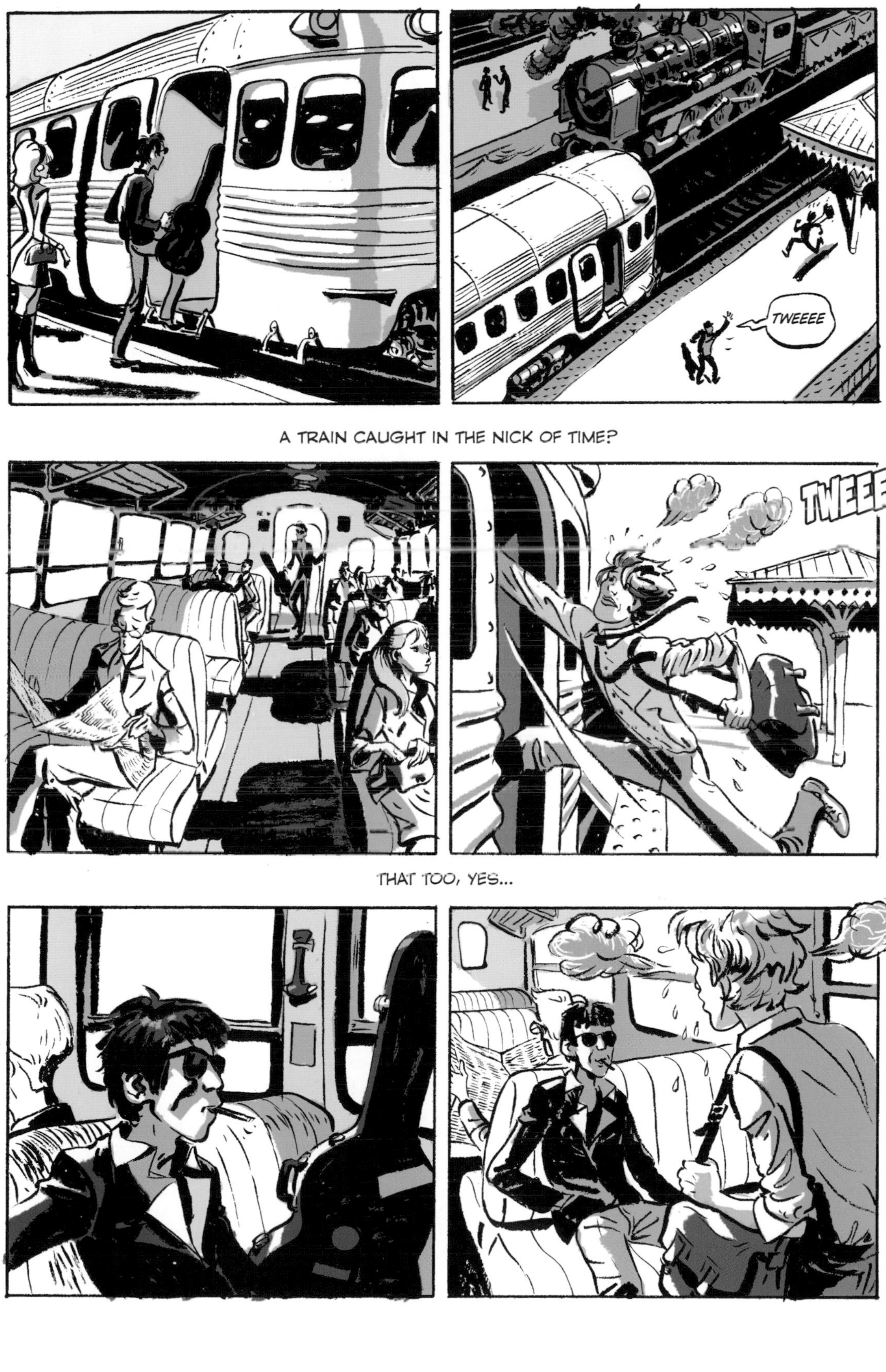
TWEEEE
A TRAIN CAUGHT IN THE NICK OF TIME?
TWEEEE
THAT TOO, YES...

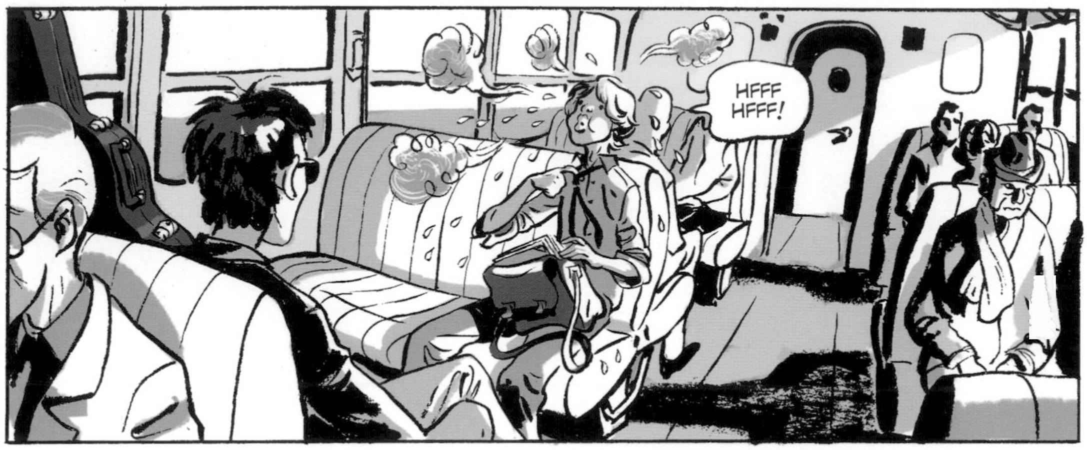
HFFF
HFFF!

A FEW BLUES VINYL ALBUMS? DEFINITELY!

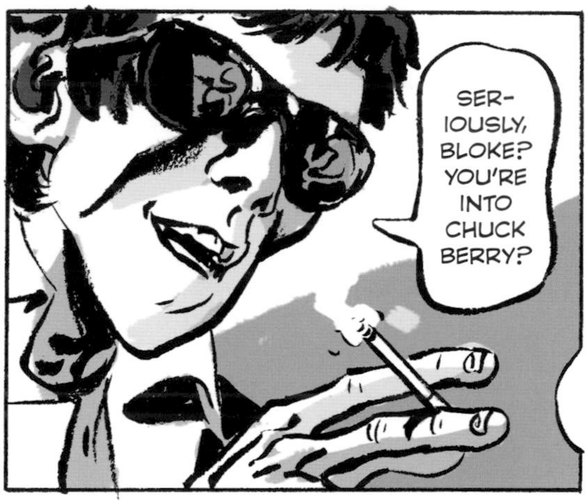
SER-
IOUSLY,
BLOKE?
YOU'RE
INTO
CHUCK
BERRY?

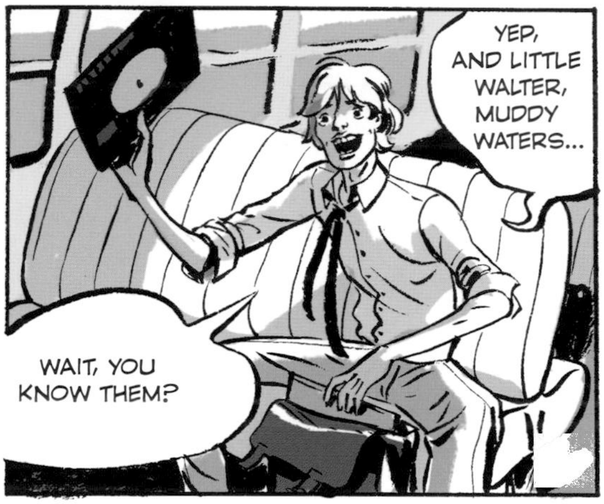
YEP,
AND LITTLE
WALTER,
MUDDY
WATERS...
WAIT, YOU
KNOW THEM?

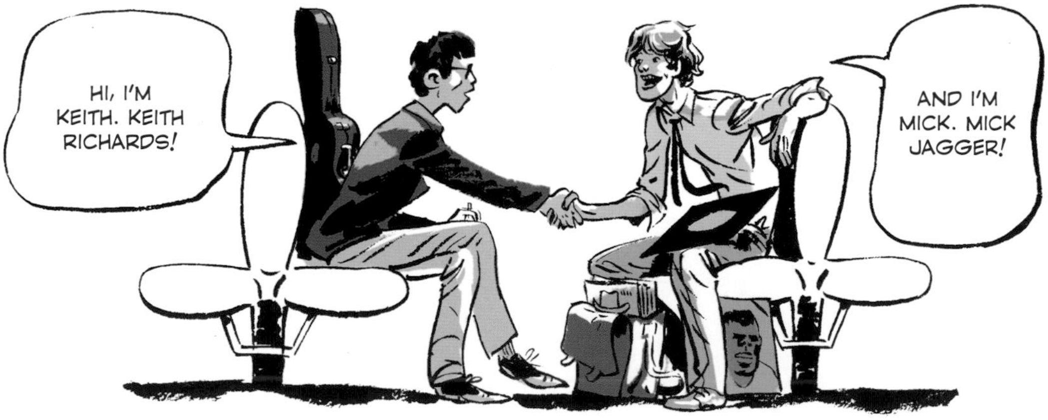
HI, I'M
KEITH. KEITH
RICHARDS!
AND I'M
MICK. MICK
JAGGER!

BLESSED BE
THE VINYL!

NOW THE LITTLE STONES
COULD START ROLLING...

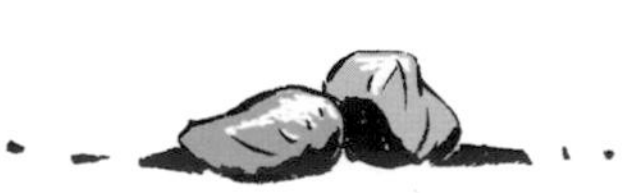

Make Way, Here Come the Blues Boys!

Playing R&B in the early '60s? What a silly idea! In those days, white guys playing black guys' music was unheard of. But the Rolling Stones weren't afraid of anything, especially not of shocking people. To them, conventions were just something to thumb their noses at!

At a time when the Internet didn't exist yet and blues lovers weren't that common in England, it took a while for that musical genre to make its way to Europe. There were only a few pieces occasionally played over the air waves, little bubbles of oxygen in an England still recovering from the war. Keith Richards, now Mick Jagger's friend, joined his band, which was called Little Boy Blue and The Blue Boys. Jagger was the lead vocalist and sometimes played guitar. As he used to say, "We did a little of everything. That's how you learn."

Keith's arrival helped the band crank things up a notch: he brought with him a sound they hadn't heard before. Mick Jagger could feel that and gradually left the guitar to Keith so he himself could focus on vocals and the harmonica, an instrument he would excel at over the years.

Muddy Waters

Increasingly self-confident and certain that music was his calling, Mick Jagger decided to dive into the deep end of the London R&B scene...

What could newbies possibly do but imitate the originals?

They had no idea, but one thing they did know was that music, and nothing else, was their thing. Right about that time, something happened that would turn out to be pivotal: Mick Jagger made the acquaintance of major London R&B supporter Alexis Korner and his Blues Incorporated. The famous band was sort of like an open lab in which all kinds of future rock-and-roll greats played, including Jack Bruce, Ginger Baker, Graham Bond, Eric Burdon, Long John Baldry, and Lee Jackson. And there was another musician who played with the band, as their official drummer: Charlie Watts... **another stone added to the foundation!**

Mick Jagger made his debut as a vocalist with Blues Incorporated in April 1962 at the Ealing Club, the palace of R&B in West London. This first performance turned into a regular gig, as his flashy attitude was already getting attention. Sometimes Keith Richards would join him on guitar. On one of the evenings when the club opened up the stage to young musicians, Mick and Keith heard Brian Jones for the first time, who was going by the moniker Elmo Lewis then—after Elmore James, his idol, who inspired his slide guitar.

Even though he was more into jazz than Mick and Keith were, the latter quickly became friends with the man who would go on to become the founder and the soul of the band. For Brian Jones was obsessed with having his own band. The little stones were finally all together, but that wasn't the band's final composition. Their debut show on July 12, 1962, at the Marquee as the "Rollin' Stones (the spelling would change later) featured the following lineup:

Jagger on vocals, Richards and Jones on guitar, Dicky Taylor on bass, Ian Stewart on keyboards and Mick Avory—future member of The Kinks—on drums. The show went so well they were asked back to the Marquee. **The Rolling Stones had finally come into existence.** All that was left to do was to make the equally pivotal acquaintance of Bill Wyman...

> "WHEN I WAS YOUNG, THERE WAS THIS FEELING IN THE AIR THAT THINGS WERE TRULY CHANGING."
>
> **Keith Richards**

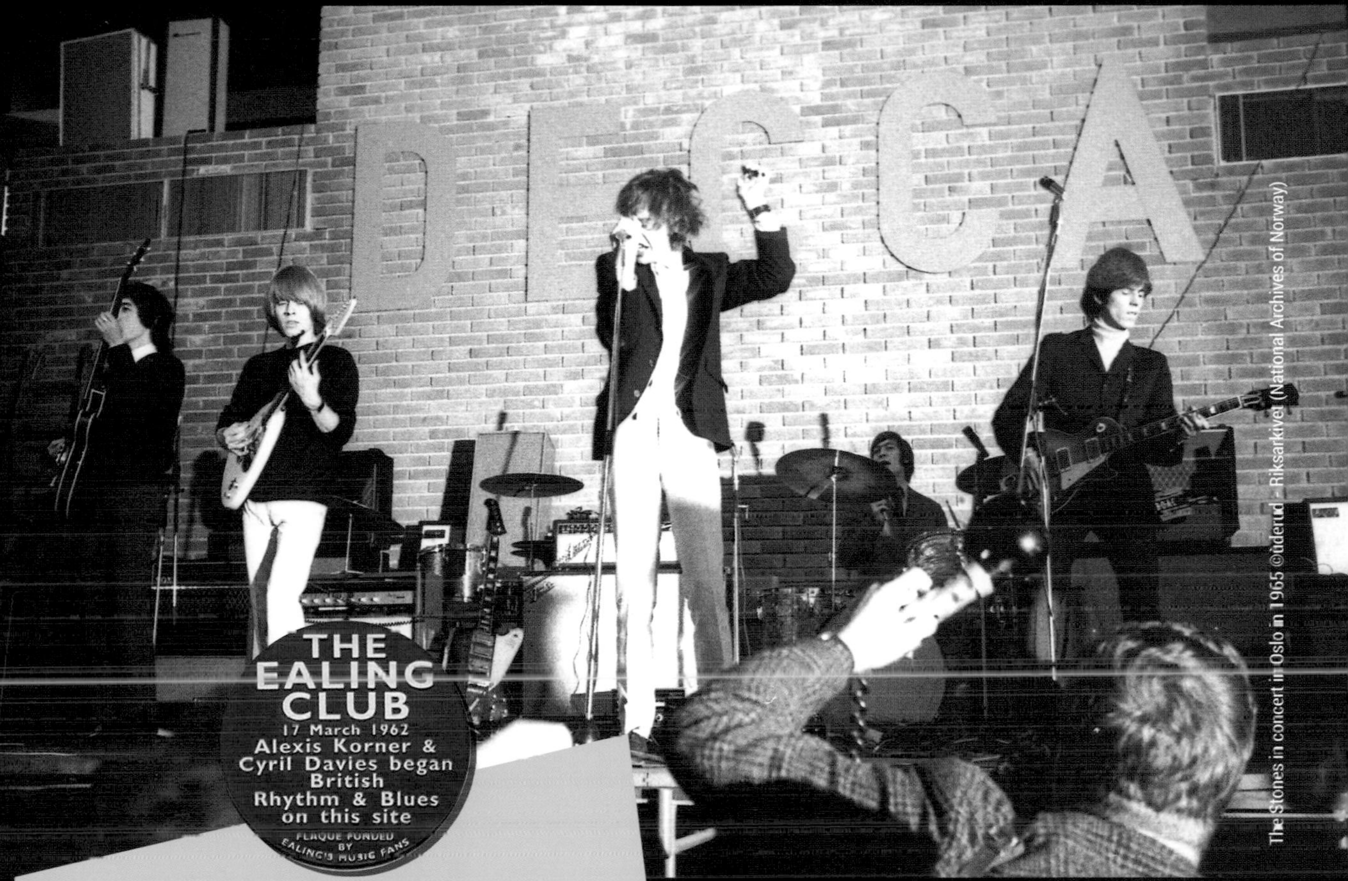
DECCA
THE EALING CLUB
17 March 1962
Alexis Korner & Cyril Davies began British Rhythm & Blues on this site
PLAQUE FUNDED BY EALING'S MUSIC FANS

The Stones in concert in Oslo in 1965 ©Iuderud - Riksarkivet (National Archives of Norway)

What is R&B exactly, otherwise known as Rhythm & Blues?

It's music that uses twelve measures just like its ancestor from black American music, the blues. But the blues can come across as sadder and more repetitious, while R&B is more energetic and coarser-sounding. Generally speaking, R&B replaces brass sections with a more compact formation that emphasizes guitars. American R&B musicians in those days were Bo Diddley, Jimmy Reed and Muddy Waters, who will be showing up again in this tale.

"WE WERE SO SURE THAT OUR MUSIC WAS THE BLUES THAT WE NEVER LISTENED TO ANYTHING ELSE."

"IN BOTH ENGLAND AND AMERICA, THERE WERE SOME PEOPLE WHO ONLY LISTENED TO A CERTAIN TYPE OF JAZZ."

Mick Jagger

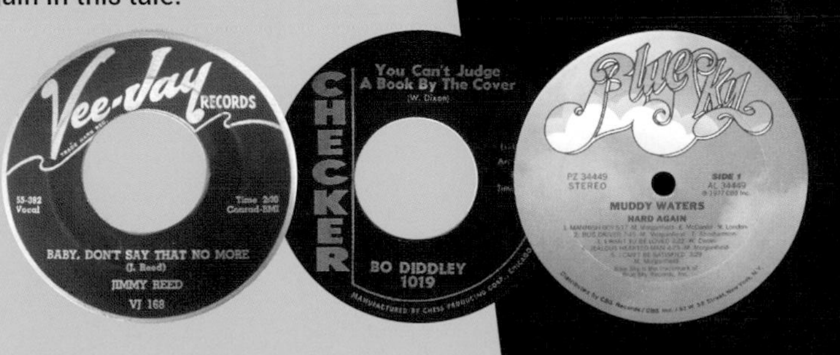
Vee-Jay RECORDS
BABY, DON'T SAY THAT NO MORE
(J. Reed)
JIMMY REED
VJ 168
CHECKER
You Can't Judge A Book By The Cover
(W. Dixon)
BO DIDDLEY
1019
Blue Sky
MUDDY WATERS
HARD AGAIN

Rollin' Stones Blues

Artist: Patrick Lacan

Why Stones That
Roll, Incidentally?

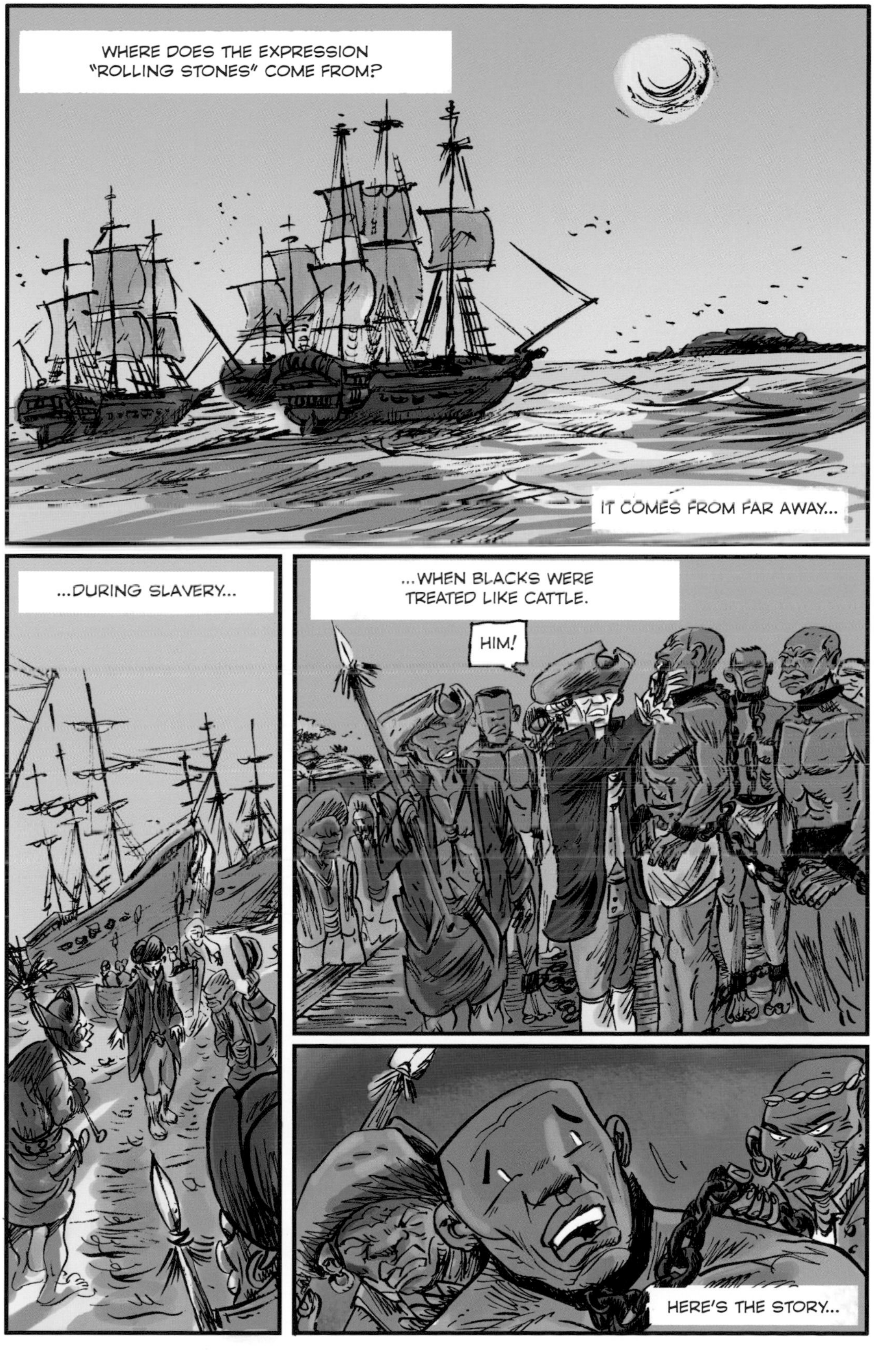
WHERE DOES THE EXPRESSION "ROLLING STONES" COME FROM?
IT COMES FROM FAR AWAY...
...DURING SLAVERY...
...WHEN BLACKS WERE TREATED LIKE CATTLE.
HIM!
HERE'S THE STORY...

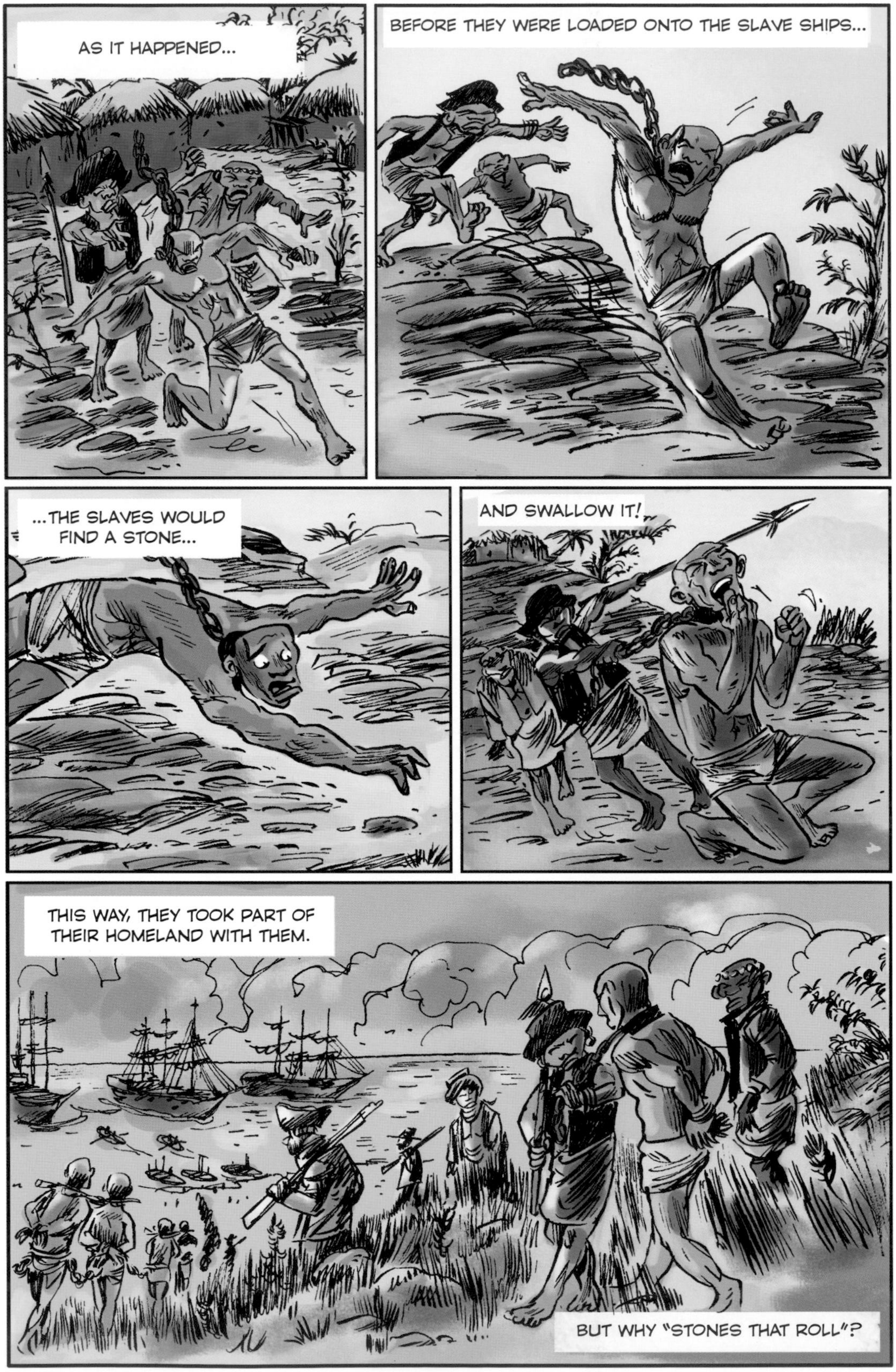
AS IT HAPPENED...
BEFORE THEY WERE LOADED ONTO THE SLAVE SHIPS...
...THE SLAVES WOULD FIND A STONE...
AND SWALLOW IT!
THIS WAY, THEY TOOK PART OF THEIR HOMELAND WITH THEM.
BUT WHY "STONES THAT ROLL"?

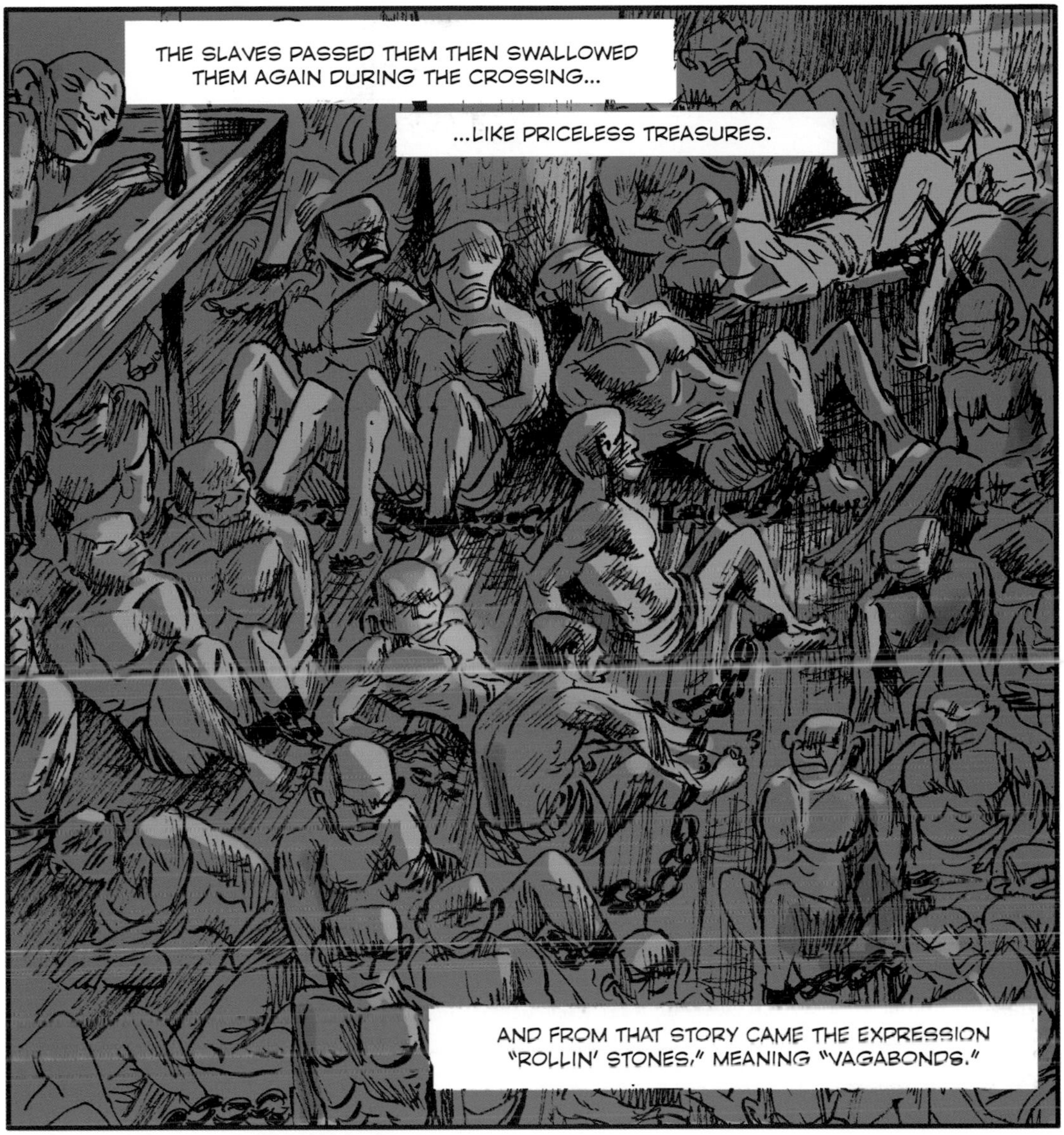
THE SLAVES PASSED THEM THEN SWALLOWED THEM AGAIN DURING THE CROSSING...
...LIKE PRICELESS TREASURES.
AND FROM THAT STORY CAME THE EXPRESSION "ROLLIN' STONES," MEANING "VAGABONDS."

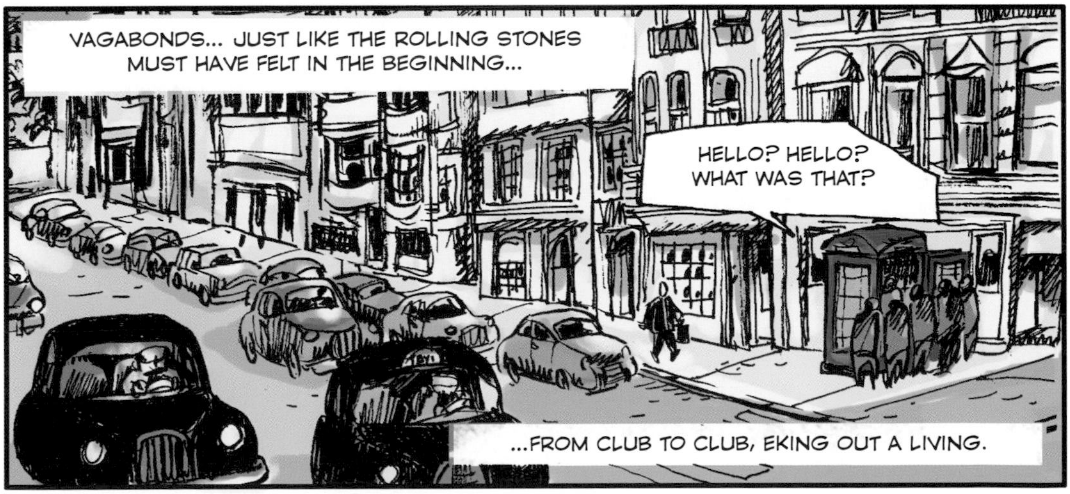
VAGABONDS... JUST LIKE THE ROLLING STONES MUST HAVE FELT IN THE BEGINNING...
HELLO? HELLO? WHAT WAS THAT?
...FROM CLUB TO CLUB, EKING OUT A LIVING.

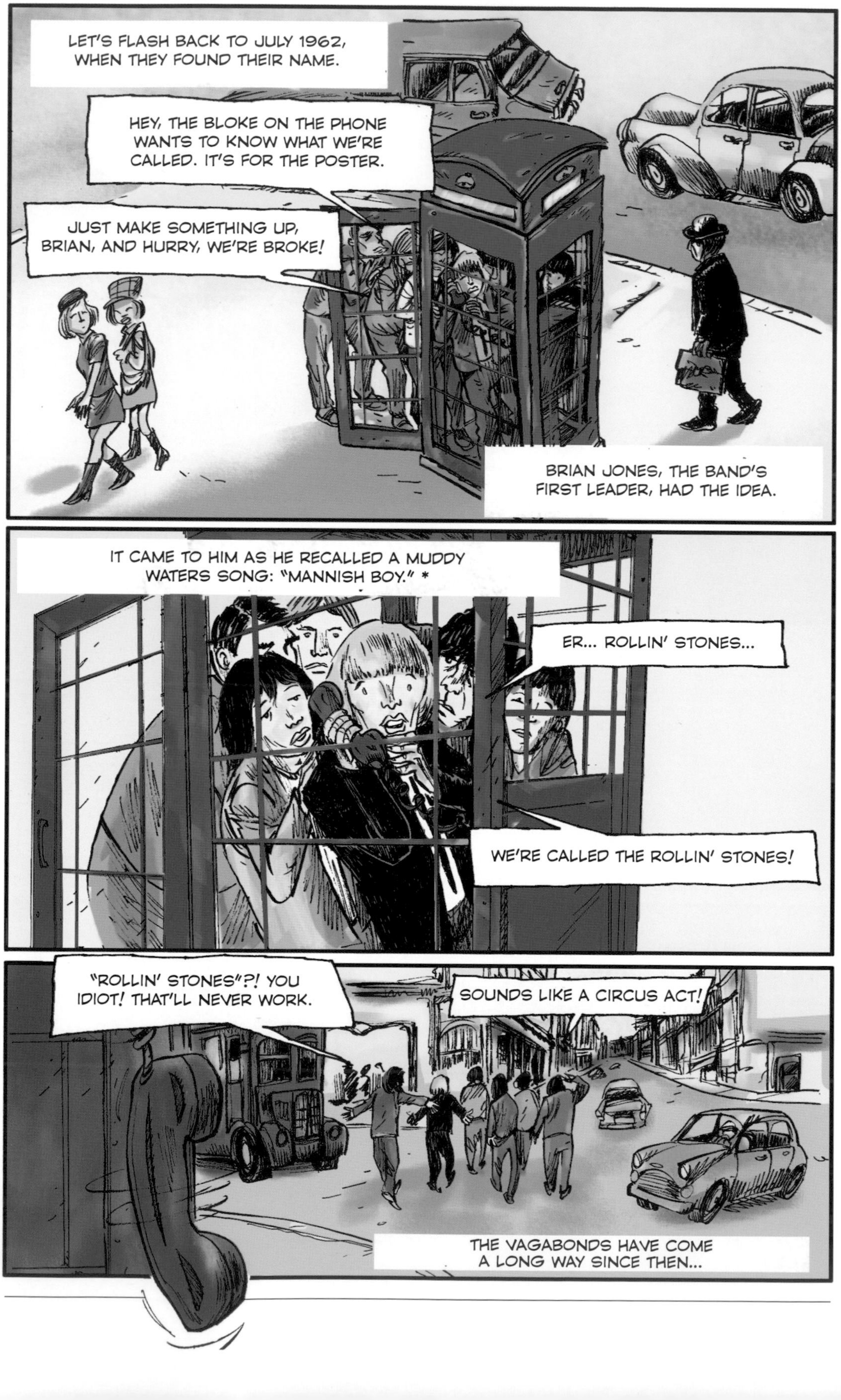
LET'S FLASH BACK TO JULY 1962, WHEN THEY FOUND THEIR NAME.
HEY, THE BLOKE ON THE PHONE WANTS TO KNOW WHAT WE'RE CALLED. IT'S FOR THE POSTER.
JUST MAKE SOMETHING UP, BRIAN, AND HURRY, WE'RE BROKE!
BRIAN JONES, THE BAND'S FIRST LEADER, HAD THE IDEA.
IT CAME TO HIM AS HE RECALLED A MUDDY WATERS SONG: "MANNISH BOY." *
ER... ROLLIN' STONES...
WE'RE CALLED THE ROLLIN' STONES!
"ROLLIN' STONES"?! YOU IDIOT! THAT'LL NEVER WORK.
SOUNDS LIKE A CIRCUS ACT!
THE VAGABONDS HAVE COME A LONG WAY SINCE THEN...

Rags Before
Riches

Pat Andrews ©The Sun

In the month of August 1962, Mick Jagger and Brian Jones moved into **102, Edith Grove** in Chelsea, along with Pat Andrews, Brian's girlfriend, her son, and Keith Richards. They lived in squalor there, sharing their meager earnings, clothes, food, rooms, girlfriends. But most of all, they shared the music. **That shabby apartment turned out to be a fantastic incubator that gave birth to the Stones!**

R&B from the MARQUEE

ALEXIS KORNER'S BLUES INCORPORATED

Mick, Brian and Keith wanted to put a real band together, live off their music, be independent: perfectly normal for young men approaching their twenties, hence the two-room pad in Chelsea. Still, it meant shelling out 16 pounds a week for rent... not a paltry sum for them, since playing the music they wanted meant fewer gigs.

"IT WAS HARD CONCENTRATING ON OUR MUSIC WHEN WE WERE SO HUNGRY WE COULD BARELY THINK."

Brian Jones

Brian Jones in 1965 ©Olavi Kaskisuo CC BY-SA 2.0

BOROUGH OF CHELSEA
EDITH GROVE
S.W. 10

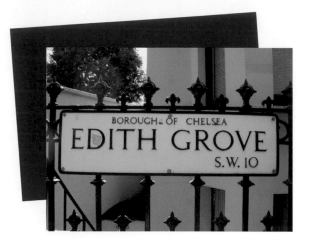

"SINCE WE DIDN'T PLAY OUT MUCH AND DIDN'T REALLY HAVE ANYTHING ELSE TO DO, BRIAN AND I STARTED PLAYING INTERLOCKING GUITARS."

Keith Richards

And so they lived in squalor and total deprivation. They put up with things only passion makes tolerable. What kind of prophets of new music would they be without paying their dues? Luckily, Pat was there, and able to help out a little financially, since she actually had a job. She was also on kitchen duty whenever she was there. Keith's mother, Doris, would send them care packages so they didn't starve to death—not money, as it would have promptly been spent on cigarettes, alcohol, or guitar strings. There was also Mick's university scholarship, food people gave them or food they stole from their neighbors. They did what they had to do! Of course, there were conflicts at times... like when Mick went out alone for fish and chips at the pub next door while the others were starving upstairs. Sure, it was his money, but didn't they say they would share everything?

But wait, there's more. There was Brian, insisting that, as bandleader, he should get a larger share of their performance fees. There was Mick, getting it on with Pat Andrews, Brian's girlfriend... behavior that would become a habit... **But hey, this is the kind of stuff memories are made of. Memories and scars!**

What did it matter, being cold and hungry? That was the price to pay to play music, which as far as they were concerned, was worth all the sacrifices in the world. First and foremost, they wanted to learn! And so they played night and day, listened to the masters and tried to unravel their secrets. As Brian Jones would later say: "We were so deeply immersed in our music that anything and everything we did had to be connected to rhythm & blues somehow."

Living in such close quarters led to the guitar style that became so characteristic of the Rolling Stones: "In English bands, there was usually a good lead guitar and a rhythm guitar, and no attempt to produce a matching sound between the two guitars," Keith Richards later said. He and Brian Jones developed a sound of "interlocking" rhythm guitars that they held on to throughout their career, except with classical guitarist Mick Taylor.

Back then, they all spent every pence they had on equipment worthy of the professionals they aspired to become. Brian Jones tossed his secondhand Gibson and splurged on a brand-new Gretsch. Keith was now playing an Epiphone electric guitar thanks to money from his mother. Mick added an amp to his Reslo microphone. Now, there was only one thing missing: gigs that paid well so they could start actually living instead of merely surviving... **Easier said than done...**

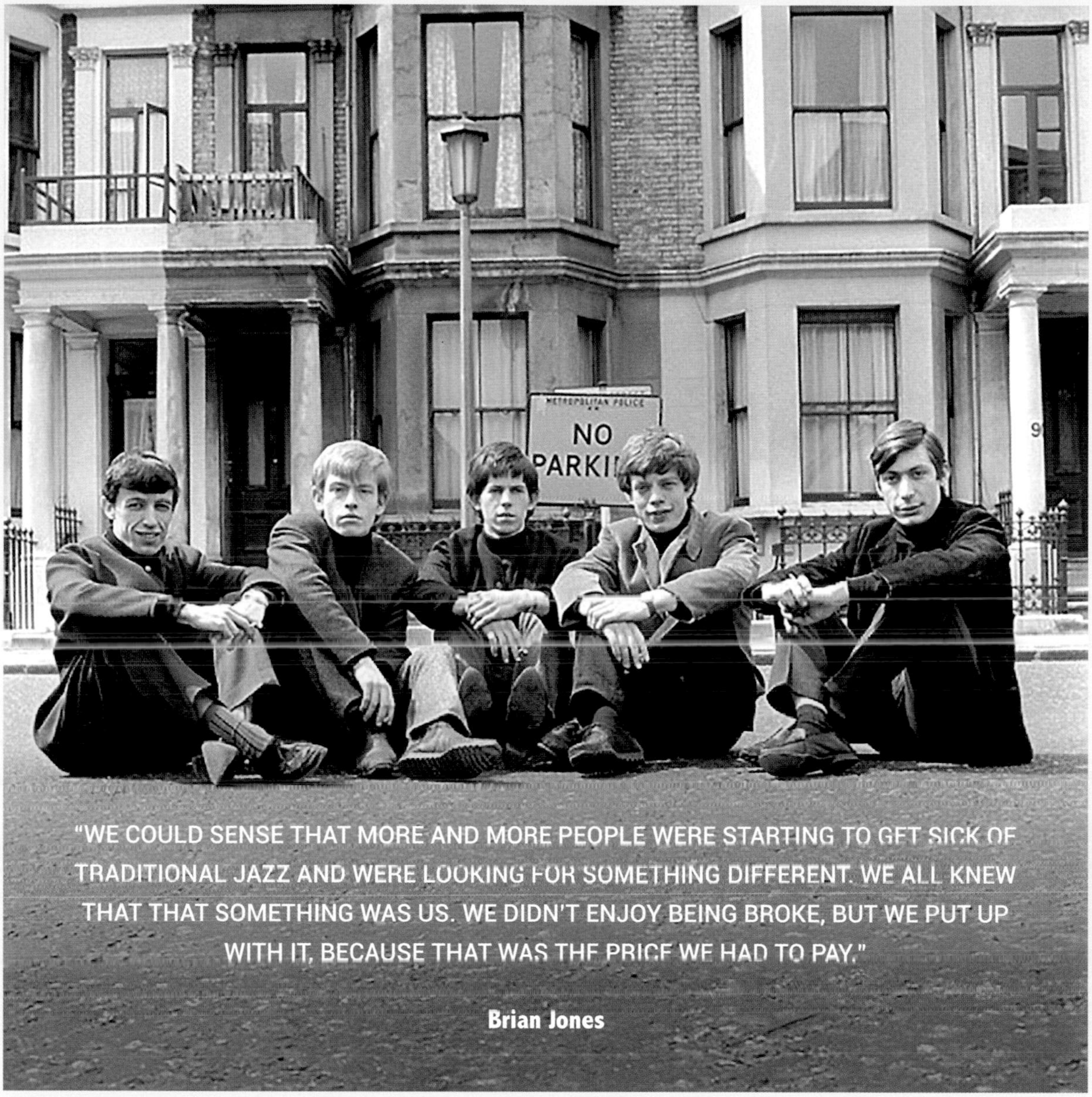
METROPOLITAN POLICE
NO
PARKI

"WE COULD SENSE THAT MORE AND MORE PEOPLE WERE STARTING TO GET SICK OF TRADITIONAL JAZZ AND WERE LOOKING FOR SOMETHING DIFFERENT. WE ALL KNEW THAT THAT SOMETHING WAS US. WE DIDN'T ENJOY BEING BROKE, BUT WE PUT UP WITH IT, BECAUSE THAT WAS THE PRICE WE HAD TO PAY."

Brian Jones

The Rolling Stones in front of 102, Edith Grove

"EDITH GROVE. AH, WHAT A PIGSTY THAT WAS. WHAT A FABULOUS PIGSTY! IT WAS SUCH A PAIN GOING BACK AND FORTH BETWEEN LONDON AND DARTFORD, WE FIGURED THAT TOGETHER, WE COULD SCRAPE UP ENOUGH DOUGH FOR RENT. THERE WASN'T MUCH TO EAT, BUT AS LONG AS WE COULD AFFORD TO BUY A FEW ALBUMS... I THINK IT'S BECAUSE WE ALL SPENT THAT WINTER THERE THAT ALL OF A SUDDEN, WE REALLY FELT THAT WE WERE A BAND."

Keith Richards

102, Edith Grove

Artist: Dimitri Piot

It's Important to Have
a Sound, Creative Environment.

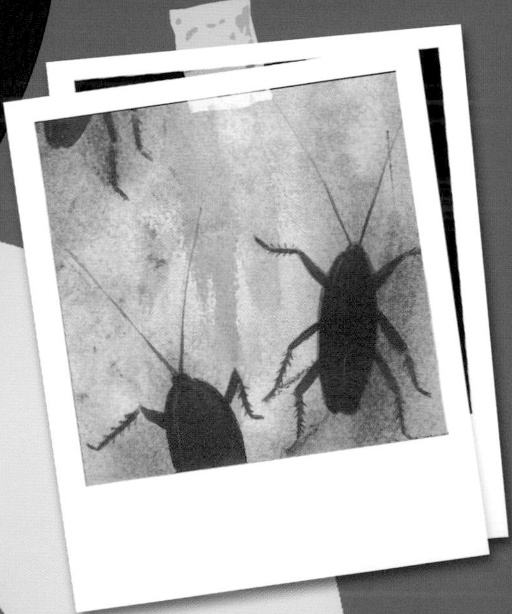

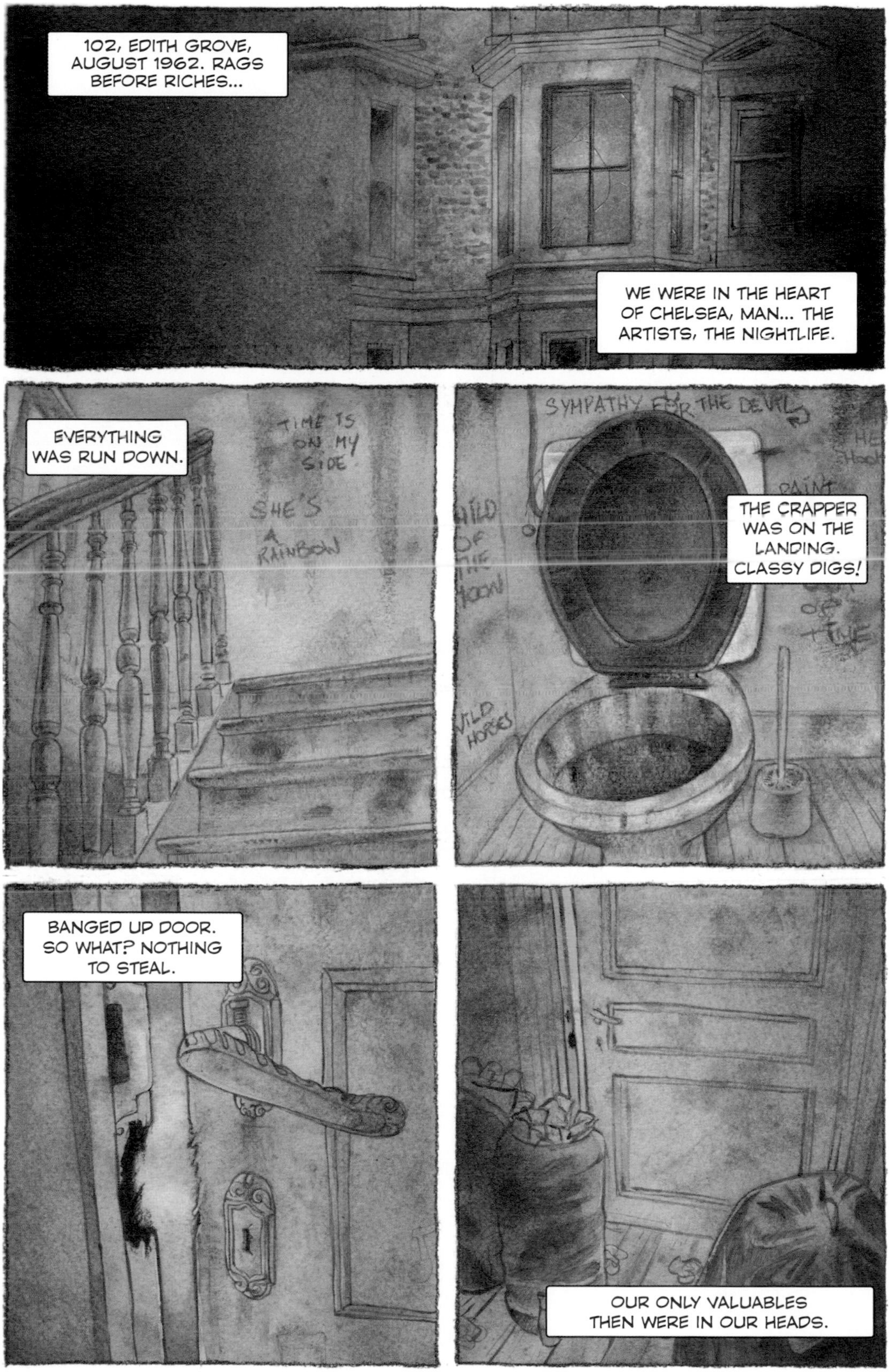
102, EDITH GROVE, AUGUST 1962. RAGS BEFORE RICHES...
WE WERE IN THE HEART OF CHELSEA, MAN... THE ARTISTS, THE NIGHTLIFE.
EVERYTHING WAS RUN DOWN.
TIME IS ON MY SIDE
SHE'S A RAINBOW
THE CRAPPER WAS ON THE LANDING. CLASSY DIGS!
WILD HORSES
BANGED UP DOOR. SO WHAT? NOTHING TO STEAL.
OUR ONLY VALUABLES THEN WERE IN OUR HEADS.

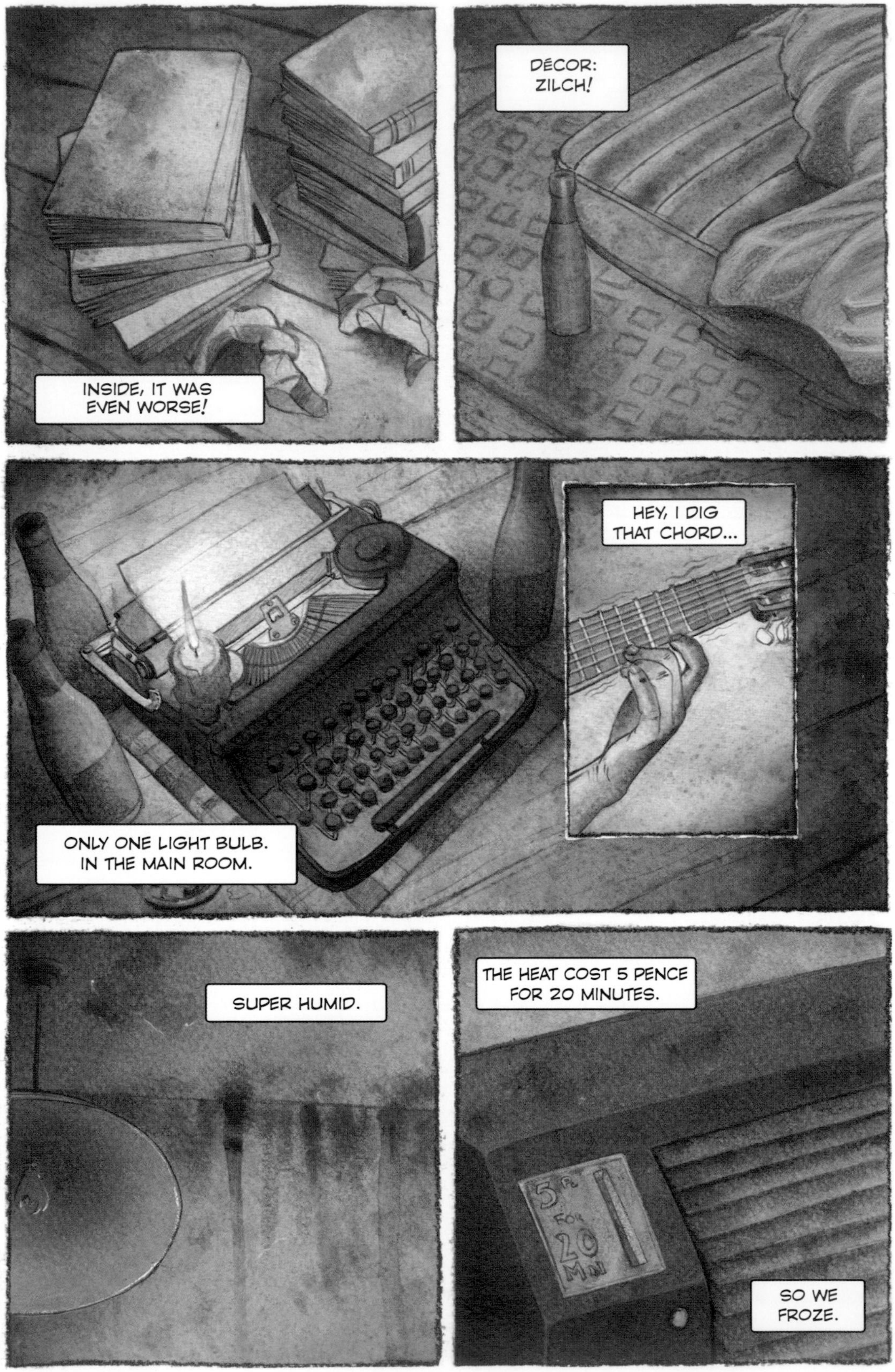
INSIDE, IT WAS EVEN WORSE!
DÉCOR: ZILCH!
ONLY ONE LIGHT BULB. IN THE MAIN ROOM.
HEY, I DIG THAT CHORD...
SUPER HUMID.
THE HEAT COST 5 PENCE FOR 20 MINUTES.
SO WE FROZE.

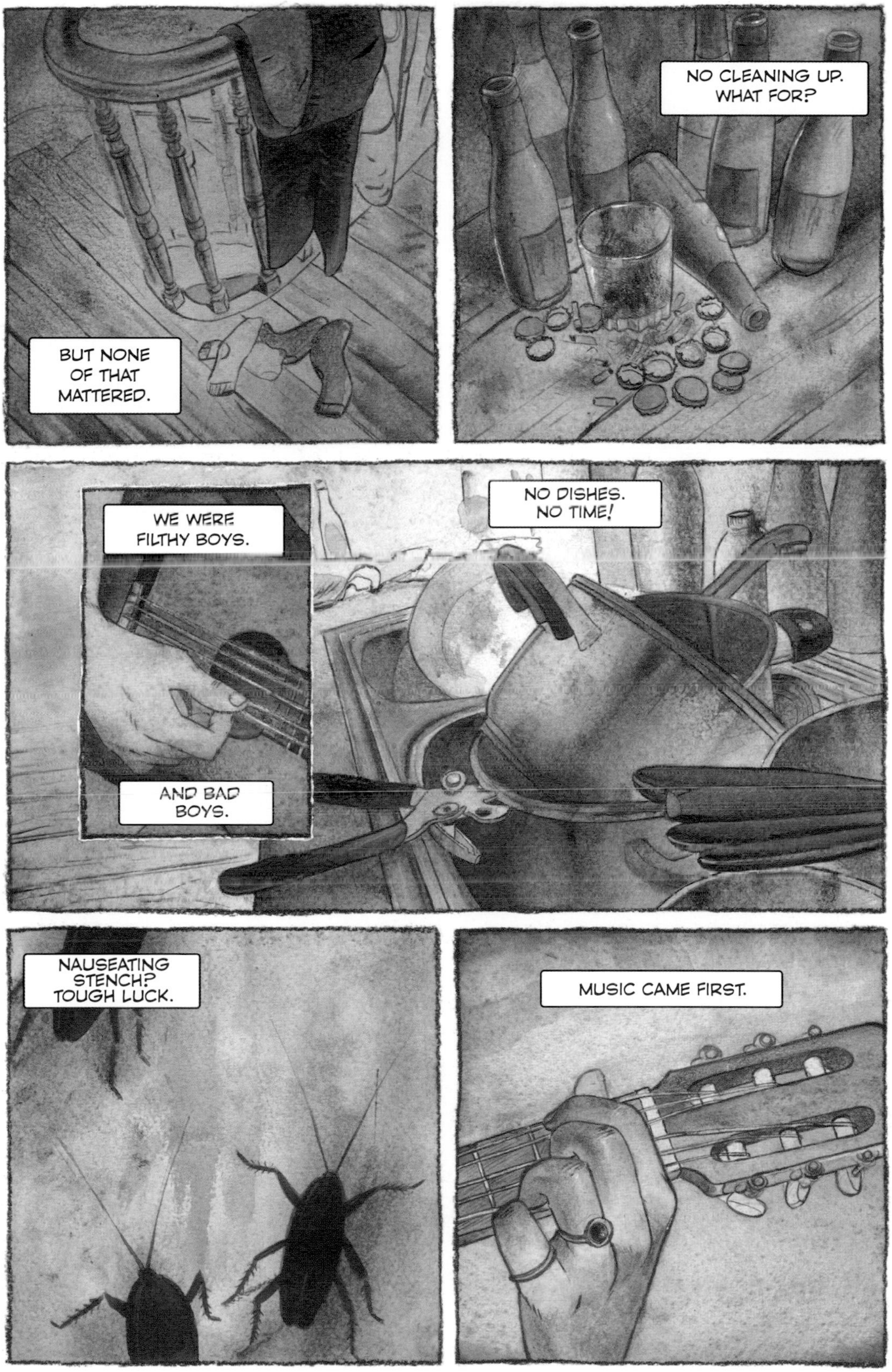
BUT NONE OF THAT MATTERED.
NO CLEANING UP. WHAT FOR?
WE WERE FILTHY BOYS.
AND BAD BOYS.
NO DISHES. NO TIME!
NAUSEATING STENCH? TOUGH LUCK.
MUSIC CAME FIRST.

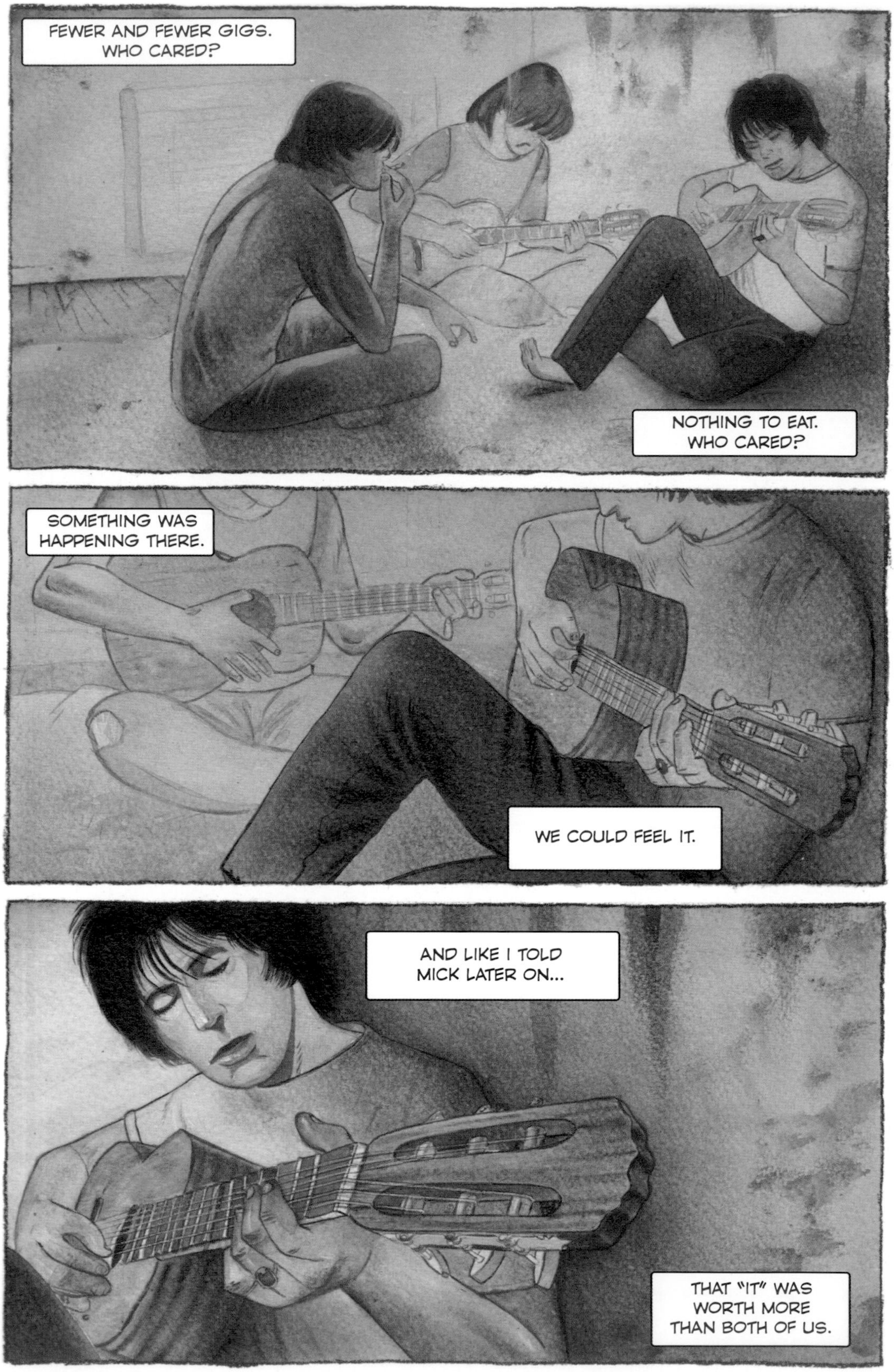
FEWER AND FEWER GIGS. WHO CARED?
NOTHING TO EAT. WHO CARED?
SOMETHING WAS HAPPENING THERE.
WE COULD FEEL IT.
AND LIKE I TOLD MICK LATER ON...
THAT "IT" WAS WORTH MORE THAN BOTH OF US.

Crank Up the Amp!

The Rolling Stones were having a hard time carving out a place for themselves on the London scene when two things happened that changed things for the better. First, Bill Wyman joined the band, bringing with him his experience as a bass player and his professional equipment.

The second fortuitous change in early 1963: Charlie Watts joined the band for good. **The Rolling Stones sound could NOW finally blow up.**

The learning period on Edith Grove bore its fruit; Keith Richards made incredible progress. The Keith–Brian guitar duo became the main attraction in the nightclubs. Never before had people heard two guitars play in unison like that. Alexis Korner encouraged them to keep going down that path. And yet, while a few jazzmen understood the new direction their music was taking, many of them rejected it, starting with the nightclub owners. As they got closer to the kind of music they wanted to play, the Rolling Stones gradually shifted away from traditional jazz. Jagger used to play with Korner, he could get in the door. Brian Jones was playing à la Elmore James, that was borderline acceptable. But Keith Richards? That was a no go.

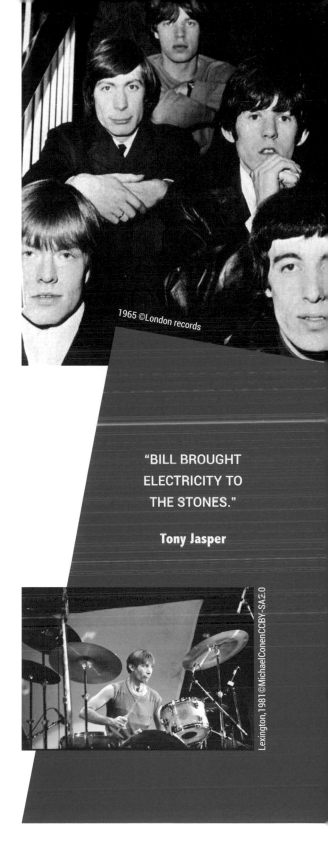

1965 ©London records

"BILL BROUGHT ELECTRICITY TO THE STONES."

Tony Jasper

Lexington, 1981 ©MichaelConenCCBY-SA2.0

Marquee club owner Harold Pendleton felt that their sound was too much of a departure from rhythm & blues. It was too electric, loud and urban for his taste, and so the Marquee became the nightclub that kicked out the Stones! For the first time, the Rolling Stones, who saw themselves as playing jazz, were forced to position themselves with respect to rock and roll. Mick Jagger famously said, "I hope they don't take us for a rock-and-roll band!" Brian Jones even wrote a long letter to *Jazz News* to explain that their urban blues was still jazz. But the band was getting fewer and fewer gigs. They had the fans but not the venues. That was about to change, though...

Forever searching for THE sound, the Rolling Stones recorded a demo on October 6 in the studio of jazz guitarist Curly Clayton, Mick Jagger, Brian Jones, Keith Richards, Ian Stewart and Tony Chapman recorded three titles along with covers of songs by their masters: Muddy Waters, Bo Diddley and Jimmy Reed. They sent it out to record companies around town but only got one response, from Decca Records: "You'll never go anywhere with that vocalist."

But they were determined and tried their luck recording a new album in March 1963 with George Clewson. The response was hardly any better. They were told that their type of music was "not commercial enough." However, good news came like a ray of light in the fog during that same time period: first, they made the acquaintance of Bill Wyman and his Vox amps! Even though he had more of a rock background and was older than the others, the kids were impressed by his experience in dancehalls. The other fortuitous event was the decision that Charlie Watts, Korner's official drummer, made to join those starving wretches for good—a

brave decision, seeing as he had a job in an advertising agency, a good gig with Korner and growing notoriety on the more traditional jazz scene. The first concert of the now-assembled Rolling Stones took place on January 12, 1963, at the Ealing Jazz Club.

> "THERE WERE ONLY SIX PEOPLE AT OUR FIRST TUESDAY CONCERT AT THE EALING CLUB. IT WAS SO COLD THAT WE KEPT OUR COATS ON."
>
> Mick Jagger

The Rolling Stones' real breakthrough came shortly afterwards; while looking for a venue they could play more regularly, they made another key acquaintance: Giorgio Gomelsky who agreed—informally, unfortunately for him—to become their manager. He liked their style and got them booked as the house band at Station Hotel, in Richmond, twenty kilometers outside of London. The nightclub was soon re-baptized The Crawdaddy Club. Audiences liked the Stones' radically different sound, and young people were drawn to their long hair and scruffy look.

They were starting to make conservative England feel uncomfortable... fame was just around the corner.

"ART STUDENTS FROM THE KINGSTON COLLEGE OF TECHNOLOGY STARTED COMING TO THE STATION HOTEL PUB. IT WAS QUITE A SHOW."

Giorgio Gomelsky

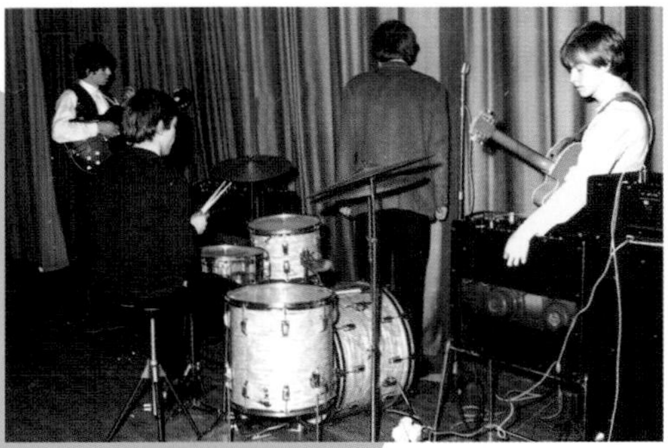

London, 1963 ©Paul Townsend CC BY-ND 2.0

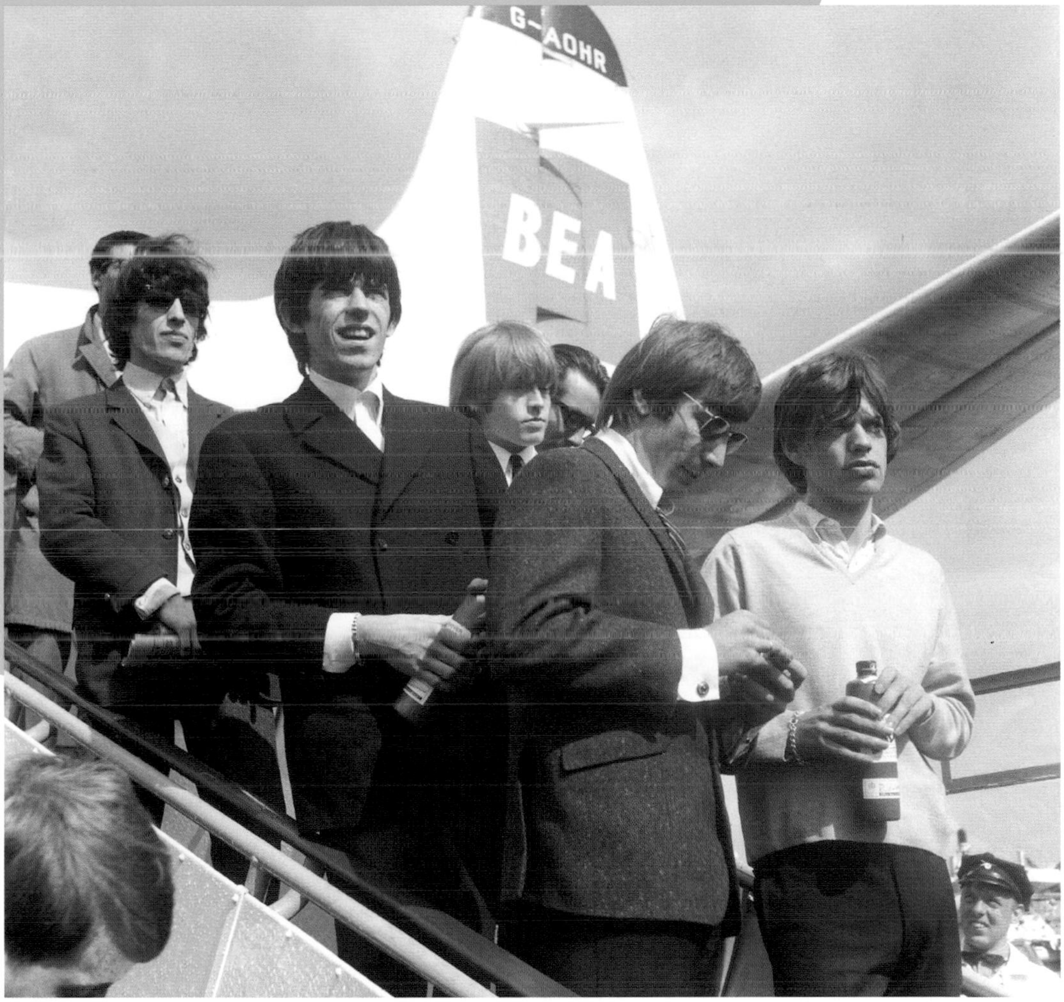
G-AOHR
BEA

Bill Wyman, Keith Richards, Brian Jones, Charlie Watts and Mick Jagger in Amsterdam in 1964 ©Hugo Van Gelderen CC BY-SA 3.0

"THE JAZZ MAFIA WAS GIVING US A BAD REPUTATION AND PROBABLY EVEN PREVENTED US FROM PLAYING CERTAIN VENUES."

Bill Wyman

Screw You!

Artist: Kyung-Eun Park

Or How to Negotiate
a Raise... and End Up
Getting the Can!

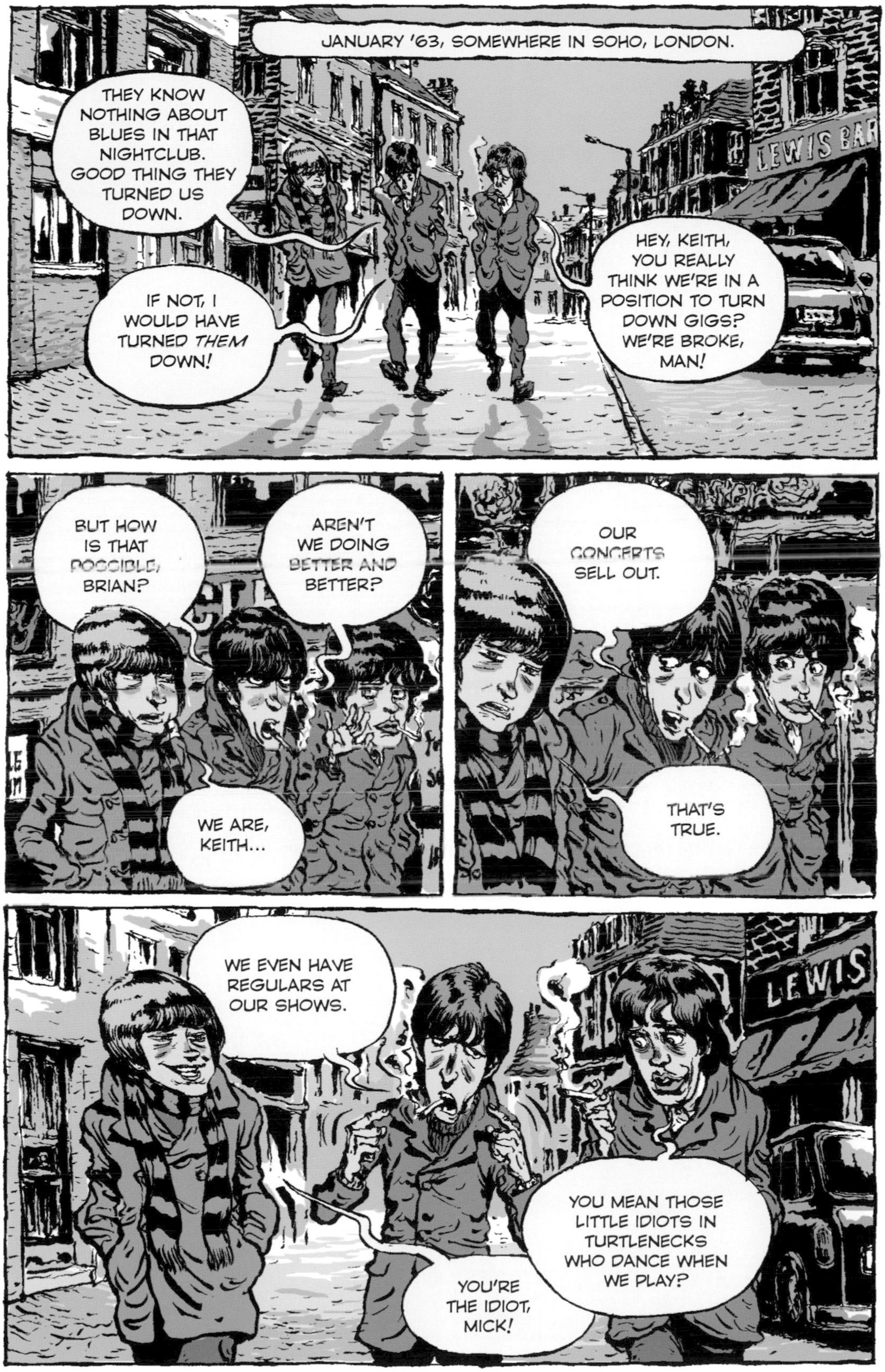
JANUARY '63, SOMEWHERE IN SOHO, LONDON.
THEY KNOW NOTHING ABOUT BLUES IN THAT NIGHTCLUB. GOOD THING THEY TURNED US DOWN.
IF NOT, I WOULD HAVE TURNED *THEM* DOWN!
LEWIS BAR
HEY, KEITH, YOU REALLY THINK WE'RE IN A POSITION TO TURN DOWN GIGS? WE'RE BROKE, MAN!
BUT HOW IS THAT POSSIBLE, BRIAN?
AREN'T WE DOING BETTER AND BETTER?
WE ARE, KEITH...
OUR CONCERTS SELL OUT.
THAT'S TRUE.
WE EVEN HAVE REGULARS AT OUR SHOWS.
LEWIS
YOU MEAN THOSE LITTLE IDIOTS IN TURTLENECKS WHO DANCE WHEN WE PLAY?
YOU'RE THE IDIOT, MICK!

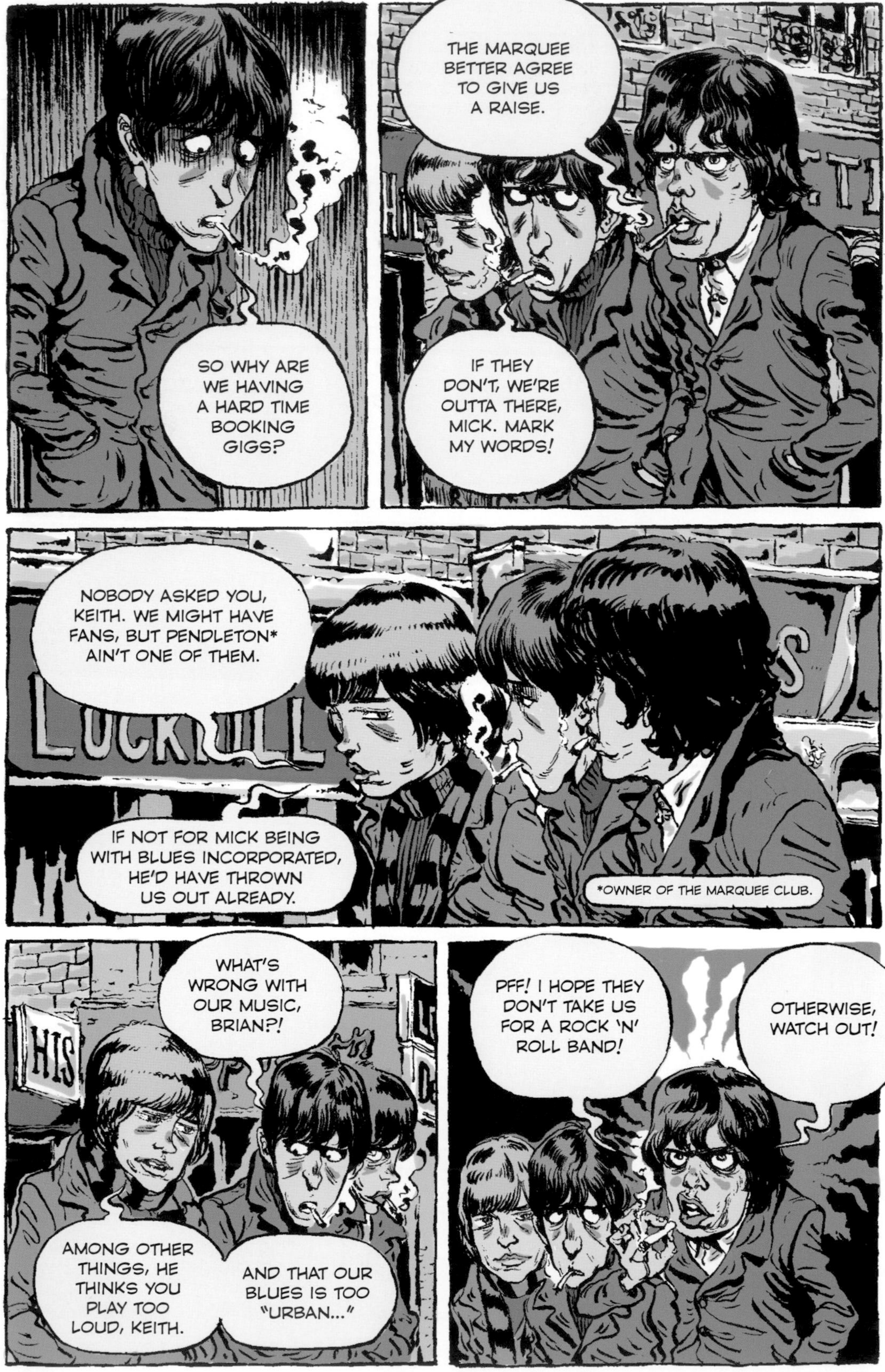

THE MARQUEE BETTER AGREE TO GIVE US A RAISE.
SO WHY ARE WE HAVING A HARD TIME BOOKING GIGS?
IF THEY DON'T, WE'RE OUTTA THERE, MICK. MARK MY WORDS!
NOBODY ASKED YOU, KEITH. WE MIGHT HAVE FANS, BUT PENDLETON* AIN'T ONE OF THEM.
IF NOT FOR MICK BEING WITH BLUES INCORPORATED, HE'D HAVE THROWN US OUT ALREADY.
*OWNER OF THE MARQUEE CLUB.
WHAT'S WRONG WITH OUR MUSIC, BRIAN?!
AMONG OTHER THINGS, HE THINKS YOU PLAY TOO LOUD, KEITH.
AND THAT OUR BLUES IS TOO "URBAN..."
PFF! I HOPE THEY DON'T TAKE US FOR A ROCK 'N' ROLL BAND!
OTHERWISE, WATCH OUT!

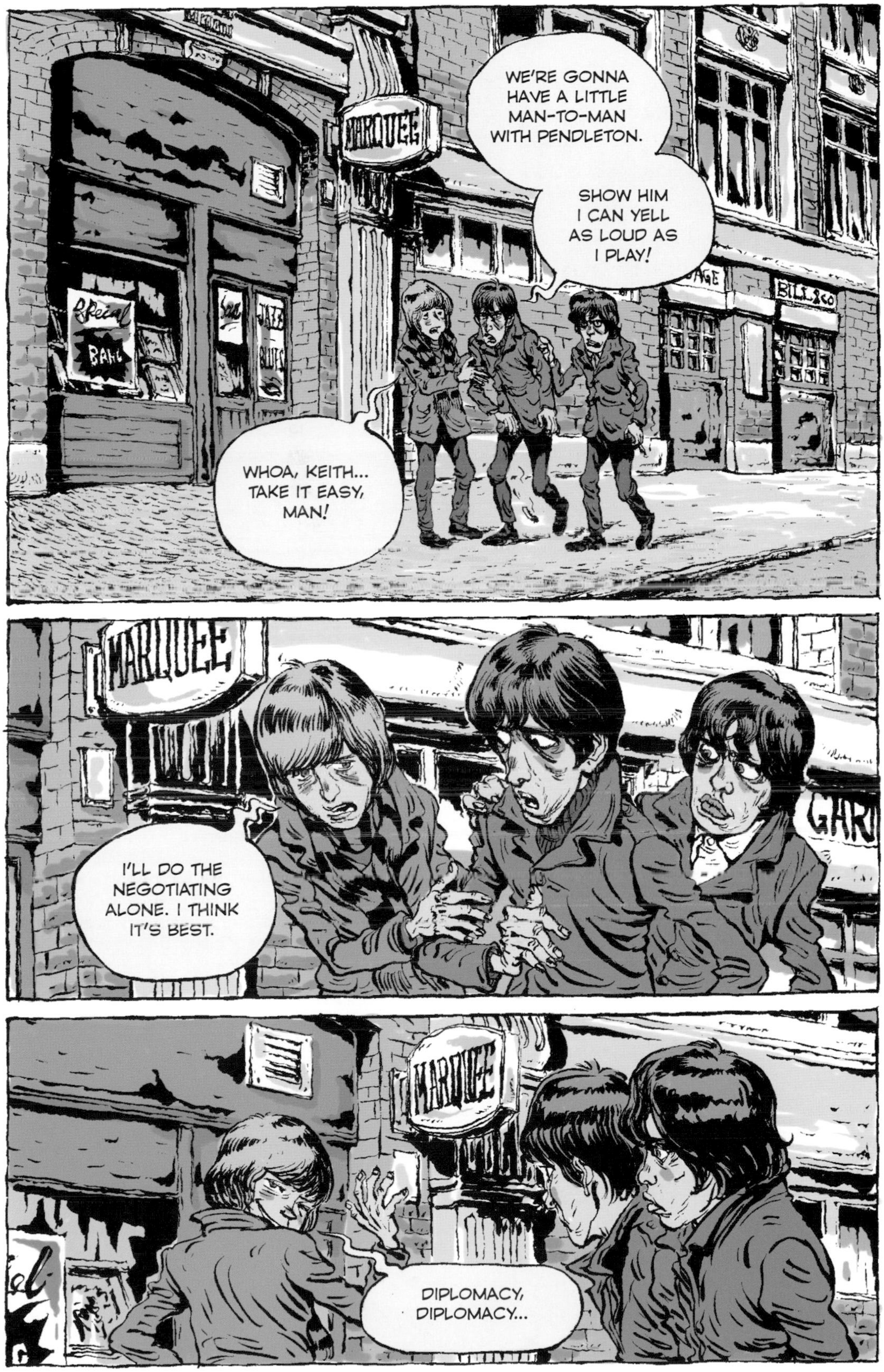
MARQUEE
WE'RE GONNA HAVE A LITTLE MAN-TO-MAN WITH PENDLETON.
SHOW HIM I CAN YELL AS LOUD AS I PLAY!
WHOA, KEITH... TAKE IT EASY, MAN!
I'LL DO THE NEGOTIATING ALONE. I THINK IT'S BEST.
DIPLOMACY, DIPLOMACY...

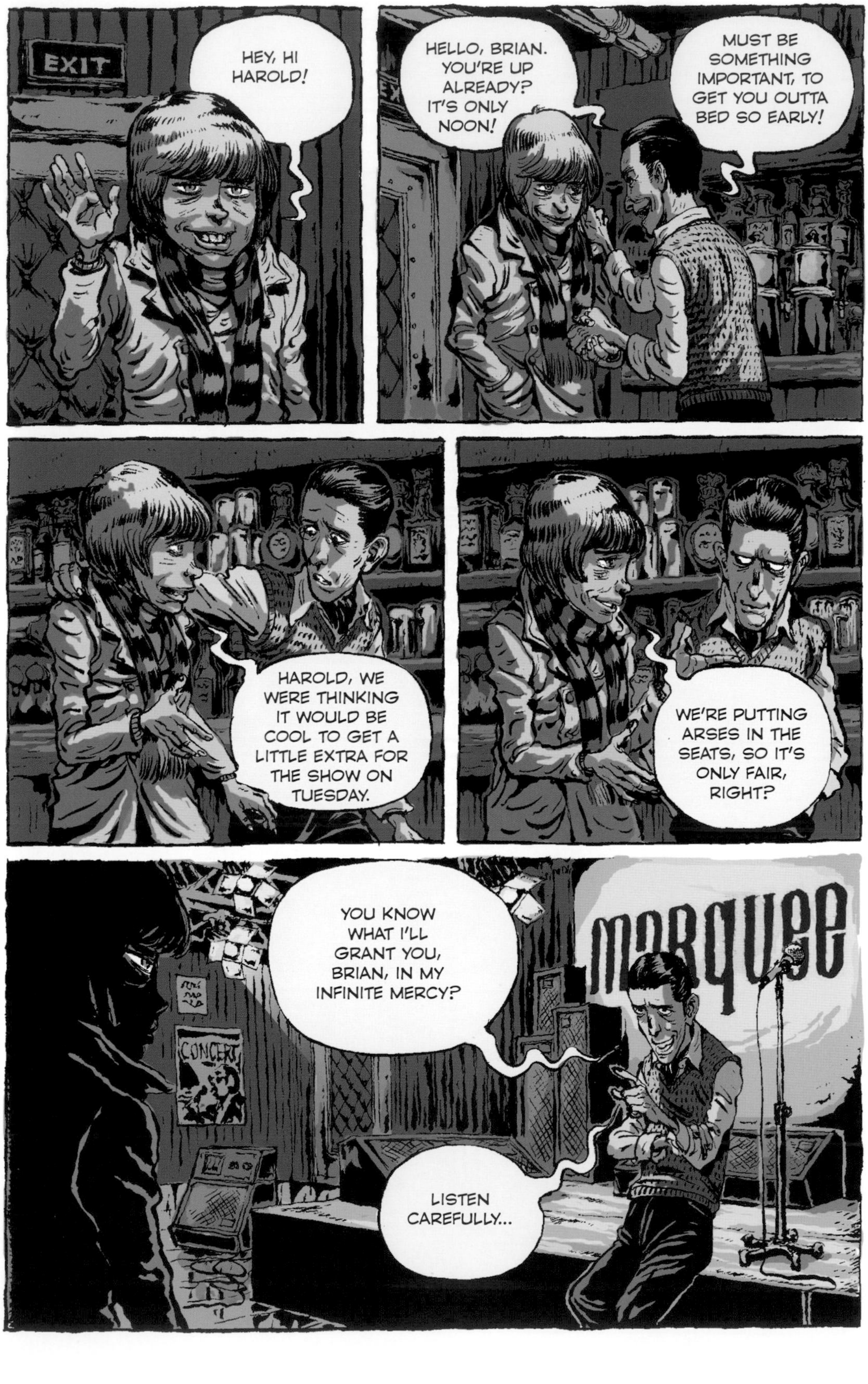
EXIT
HEY, HI HAROLD!
HELLO, BRIAN. YOU'RE UP ALREADY? IT'S ONLY NOON!
MUST BE SOMETHING IMPORTANT, TO GET YOU OUTTA BED SO EARLY!
HAROLD, WE WERE THINKING IT WOULD BE COOL TO GET A LITTLE EXTRA FOR THE SHOW ON TUESDAY.
WE'RE PUTTING ARSES IN THE SEATS, SO IT'S ONLY FAIR, RIGHT?
YOU KNOW WHAT I'LL GRANT YOU, BRIAN, IN MY INFINITE MERCY?
marquee
CONCERT
LISTEN CAREFULLY...

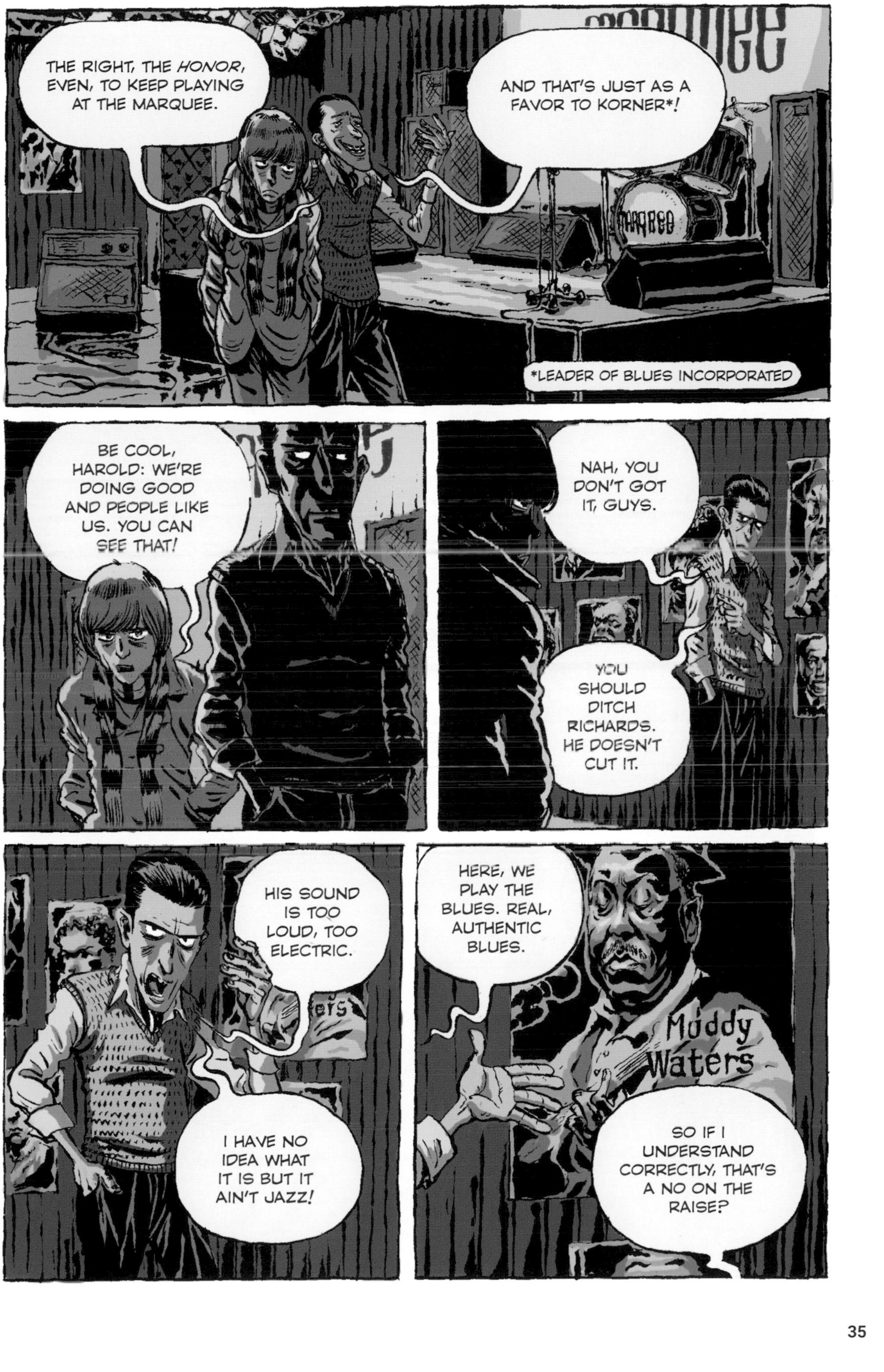
THE RIGHT, THE *HONOR*, EVEN, TO KEEP PLAYING AT THE MARQUEE.
AND THAT'S JUST AS A FAVOR TO KORNER*!
*LEADER OF BLUES INCORPORATED
BE COOL, HAROLD: WE'RE DOING GOOD AND PEOPLE LIKE US. YOU CAN SEE THAT!
NAH, YOU DON'T GOT IT, GUYS.
YOU SHOULD DITCH RICHARDS. HE DOESN'T CUT IT.
HIS SOUND IS TOO LOUD, TOO ELECTRIC.
I HAVE NO IDEA WHAT IT IS BUT IT AIN'T JAZZ!
HERE, WE PLAY THE BLUES. REAL, AUTHENTIC BLUES.
Muddy Waters
SO IF I UNDERSTAND CORRECTLY, THAT'S A NO ON THE RAISE?

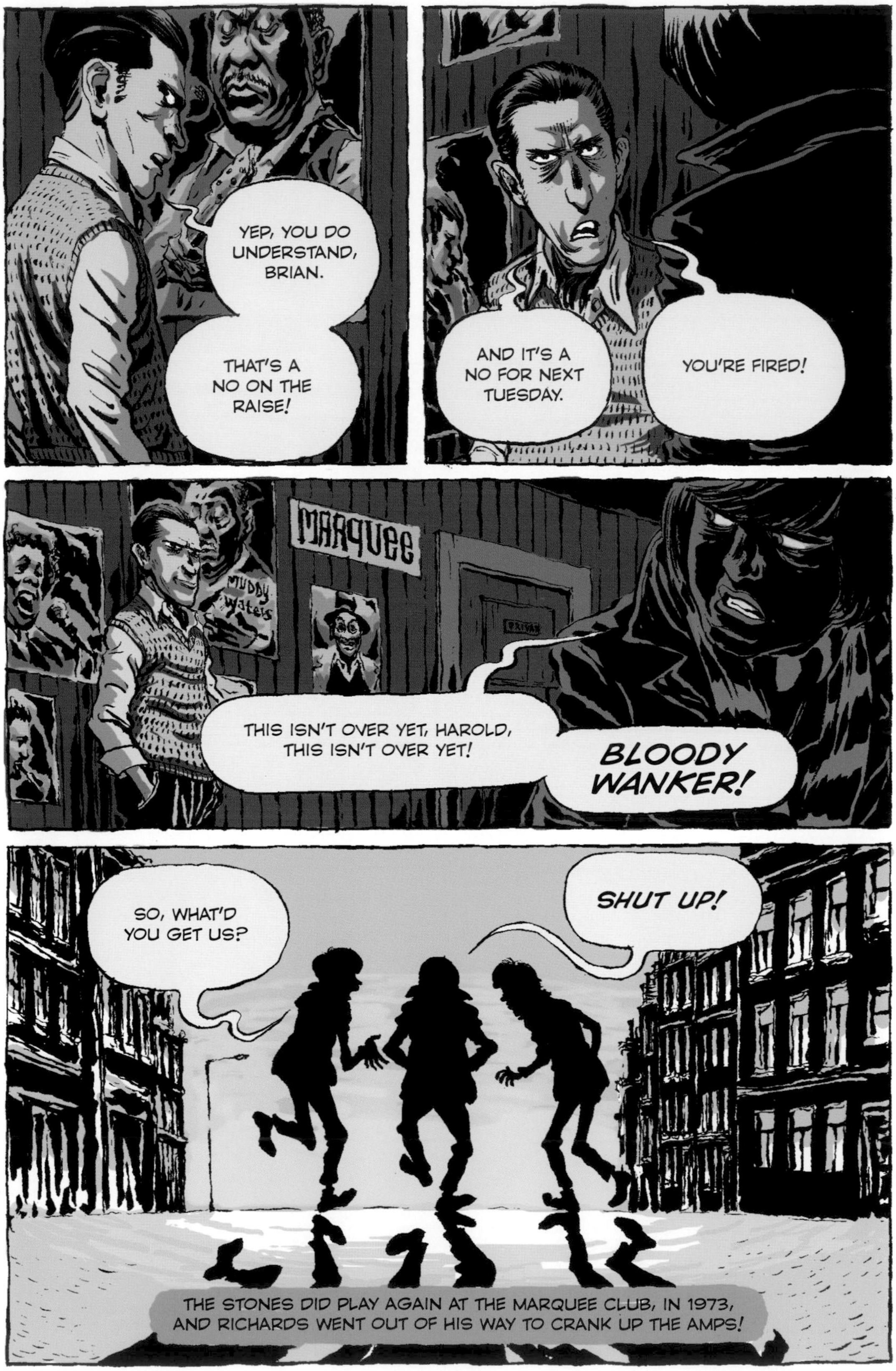
YEP, YOU DO UNDERSTAND, BRIAN.
THAT'S A NO ON THE RAISE!
AND IT'S A NO FOR NEXT TUESDAY.
YOU'RE FIRED!
MARQUEE
MUDDY Waters
THIS ISN'T OVER YET, HAROLD, THIS ISN'T OVER YET!
BLOODY WANKER!
SO, WHAT'D YOU GET US?
SHUT UP!
THE STONES DID PLAY AGAIN AT THE MARQUEE CLUB, IN 1973, AND RICHARDS WENT OUT OF HIS WAY TO CRANK UP THE AMPS!

The Man Who
Created the Stones

Andrew Loog Oldham ©The Telegraph

In April 1963, an article in the *Richmond and Twick-enham Times* stated that in just two months, the audience at the Crawdaddy Club had gone from 50 to 320 people thanks to the Rolling Stones. Something extraordinary was clearly happening. So much so, that the Beatles, who were already famous, came to see them play, as did a man by the name of Andrew Loog Oldham, who could smell a goose with golden eggs.

True fact! People in London were starting to talk about these rhythm & blues vagabonds, and that talk made it all the way to the ears of the Beatles, who came to see them play their regular gig at the Crawdaddy Club on April 14. The Beatles already had a few hits under their belts and were well on their way. Needless to say, the fact that they came to the show was a good sign for the Rolling Stones, as was the advice George Harrison gave to Dirk Rowe from Decca Records: sign them at once. But it was an ambitious man named Andrew Loog Oldham who made the first move. At the time, and in a rather troubling coincidence, he was doing P.R. work for Beatles manager Brian Epstein and was looking to make his own way. When he heard the Rolling Stones in concert, it was love at first sight, and he talked his way into being their manager. Three days later, they were signed!

The nineteen-year-old beginner with the dark glasses hardly looked the part. He was younger than all the Rolling Stones! And yet, thanks to great instincts and a natural feel for P.R., Oldham went on to "invent" the Stones by creating a fictitious rivalry between them and the Beatles, portraying the Stones as their antithesis. Using their anti-conformist tendencies and their natural talent for stirring things up, he made them a brand name, one that young people craving emancipation in dull, puritanical post-war England would go crazy for.

The Rolling Stones came from rhythm & blues, which came from urban black America. Perhaps that inspiration explained their naked contempt for the establishment and the guardians of proper behavior. They liked to shake things up around them and put on airs of insubordination. The Beatles were joyful troublemakers, but in a way that was acceptable for the majority of adults. Such was not the case with the Rolling Stones. As far as parents were concerned, their long hair and unkempt style made them inappropriate role models for children. Whereas the Beatles all wore the same stage outfit, the Rolling Stones soon started wearing the same clothes on stage and off. And don't expect a smile from them, even when they're being considerate and not standing with their backs to the audience. Outrageous!

Another major difference between the Beatles and the Rolling Stones was the way they expressed sexuality: sweetly romantic with the former and decidedly direct with the latter, with a little depravity occasionally thrown in. In 1964, the Stones did a cover of Slim Harpo's "I'm a King Bee," with the unambiguous lyrics "Well I can make honey baby, so let me come inside." In the inhibited English society of those days, that was downright unacceptable, as it was in the U.S., as well. When they appeared on the famous *Ed Sullivan Show* to sing their raunchy "Let's Spend the Night Together," they had to change the lyrics to "Let's Spend Some Time Together." The parents hated it but the kids gobbled it up!

The Rolling Stones didn't give a hoot, they loved being hated. "Why should we give up who we are just to please other people? People seem to think that if you don't behave like angels with the audience, you run the risk of losing it. But we'd rather keep being ourselves." And so, when the Beatles released "Let It Be", the Rolling Stones counter-attacked with "Let It Bleed" —something Andrew Loog Oldham could smile about!

"WHEN I HEARD THEM PLAY, I REALIZED THAT MY ENTIRE LIFE'S MEANING WAS RIGHT THERE, AND THAT THIS IS WHAT I HAD BEEN PREPARING FOR."

Andrew Loog Oldham

"IN A WAY, ANDREW BROUGHT OUT AND UNITED THE BAND'S INNATE TALENT. HE TURNED US INTO A GANG, INTO ACCOMPLICES. AND HE BROADENED OUR HORIZON. AT THE TIME, OUR CHIEF AMBITION WAS TO BE THE BEST BLUES BAND IN LONDON. THAT WOULD HAVE BEEN ENOUGH FOR US. BUT ANDREW SAID, "WHAT ARE WE TALKING ABOUT HERE? LISTEN, I JUST GOT DONE WORKING WITH THOSE FOUR HALFWITS FROM LIVERPOOL. YOU CAN DO IT NO SWEAT!"

Keith Richards

"YOU KNOW, PEOPLE USED TO SAY, AND IT'S A LITTLE TRUE, THAT THE BEATLES WERE HOODLUMS ACTING LIKE GENTLEMEN AND THE STONES WERE GENTLEMEN ACTING LIKE HOODLUMS."

Marianne Faithfull

"I'D NEVER SEEN SUCH A COMBINATION OF MUSIC AND SEX IN ANY OTHER BAND."

Andrew Loog Oldham

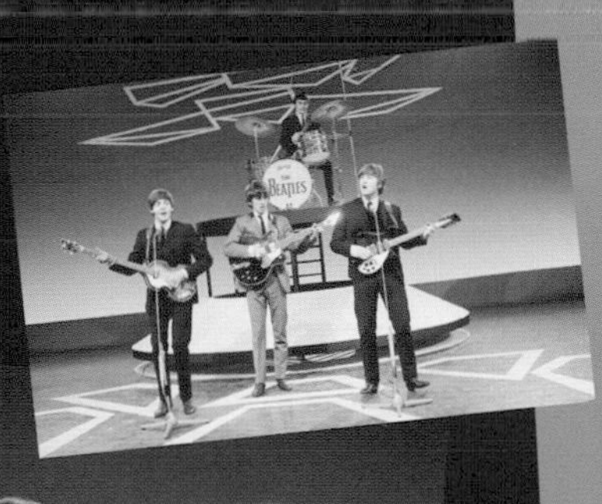

The Beatles in 1964 © Vara CC BY-SA 3.

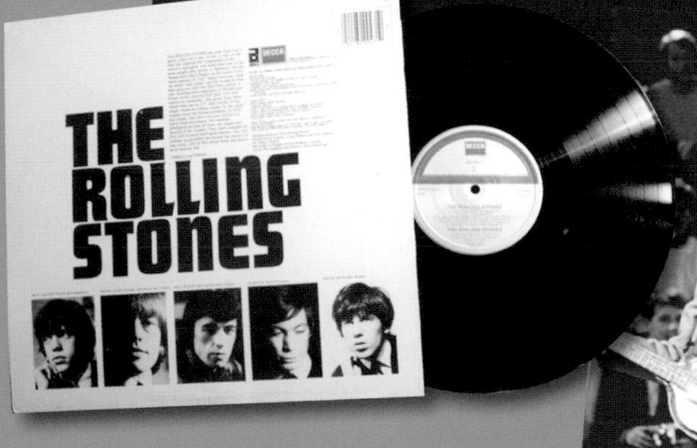
THE ROLLING STONES

Decca Records album ©Badgreeb records CC BY-SA 2

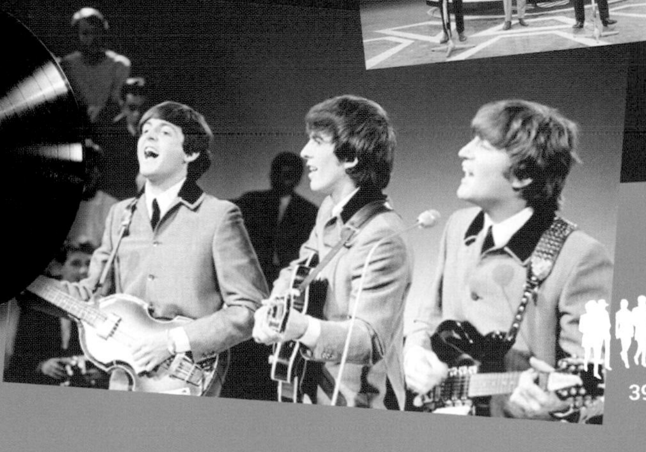

I Wanna Be Your Man

Artist: Domas

When Two Legendary Bands Meet.

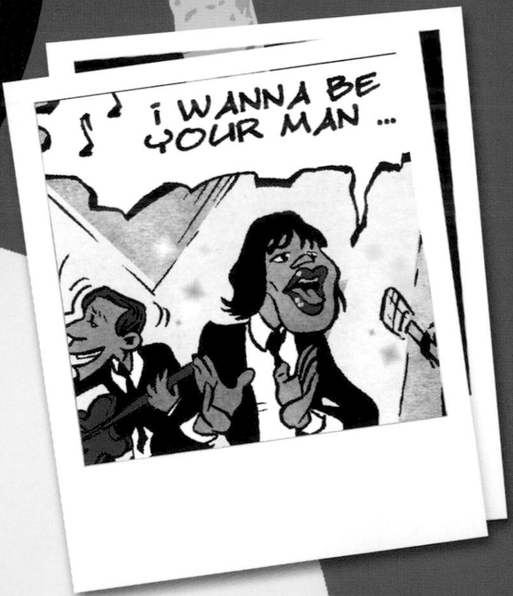
I WANNA BE YOUR MAN ...

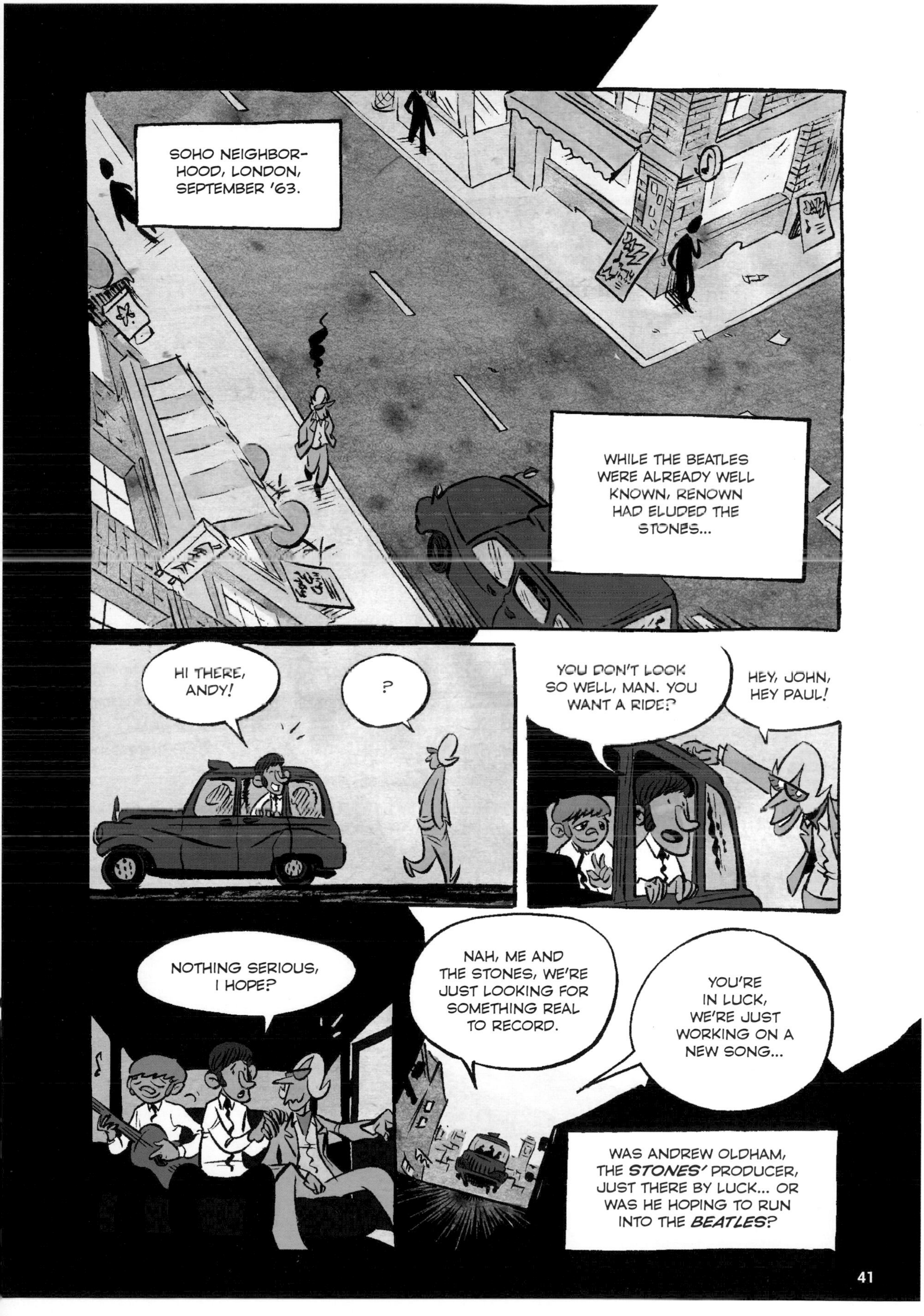
SOHO NEIGHBORHOOD, LONDON, SEPTEMBER '63.
WHILE THE BEATLES WERE ALREADY WELL KNOWN, RENOWN HAD ELUDED THE STONES...
HI THERE, ANDY!
?
YOU DON'T LOOK SO WELL, MAN. YOU WANT A RIDE?
HEY, JOHN, HEY PAUL!
NOTHING SERIOUS, I HOPE?
NAH, ME AND THE STONES, WE'RE JUST LOOKING FOR SOMETHING REAL TO RECORD.
YOU'RE IN LUCK, WE'RE JUST WORKING ON A NEW SONG...
WAS ANDREW OLDHAM, THE *STONES'* PRODUCER, JUST THERE BY LUCK... OR WAS HE HOPING TO RUN INTO THE *BEATLES*?

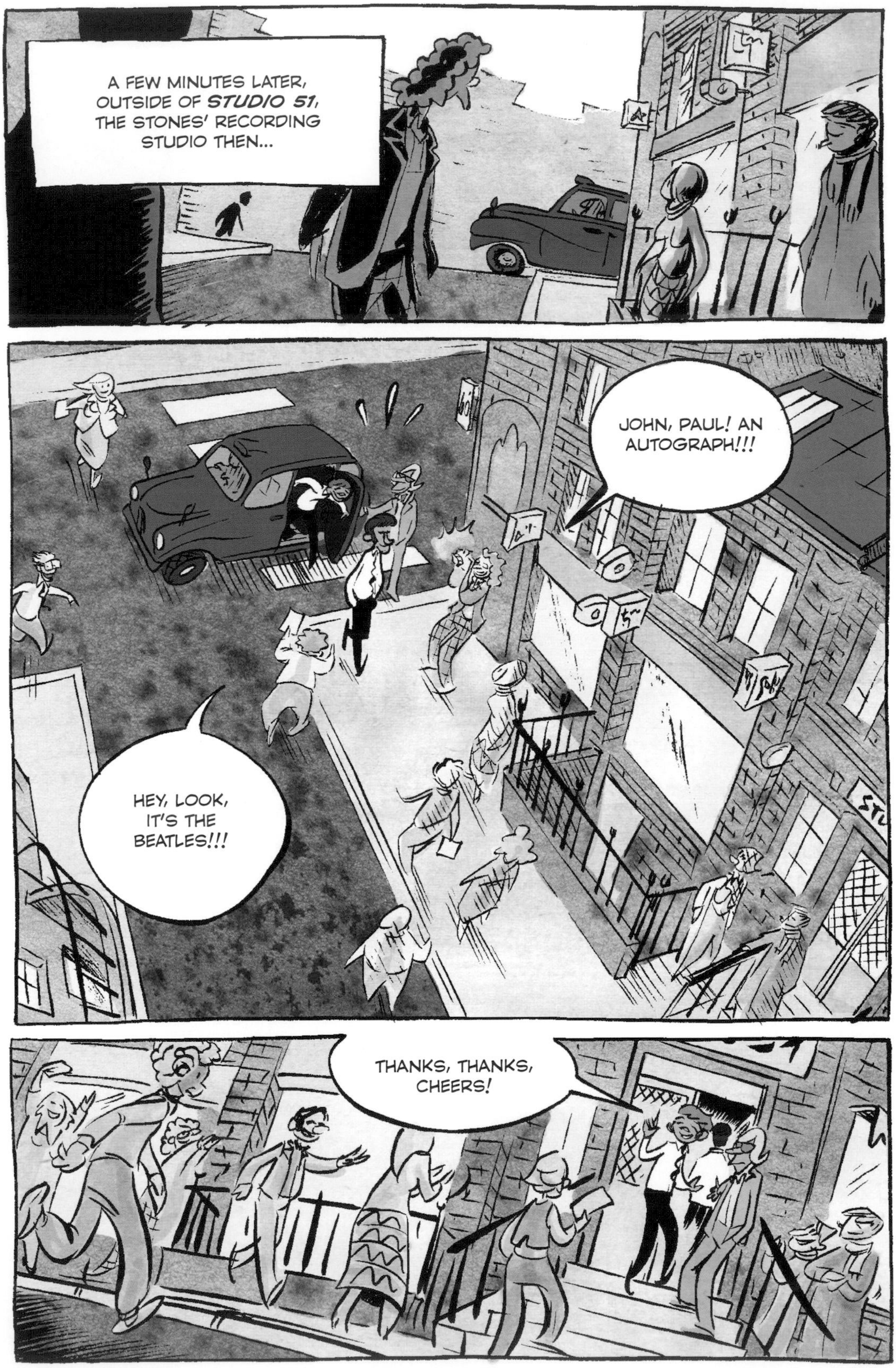
A FEW MINUTES LATER, OUTSIDE OF STUDIO 51, THE STONES' RECORDING STUDIO THEN...
JOHN, PAUL! AN AUTOGRAPH!!!
HEY, LOOK, IT'S THE BEATLES!!!
THANKS, THANKS, CHEERS!

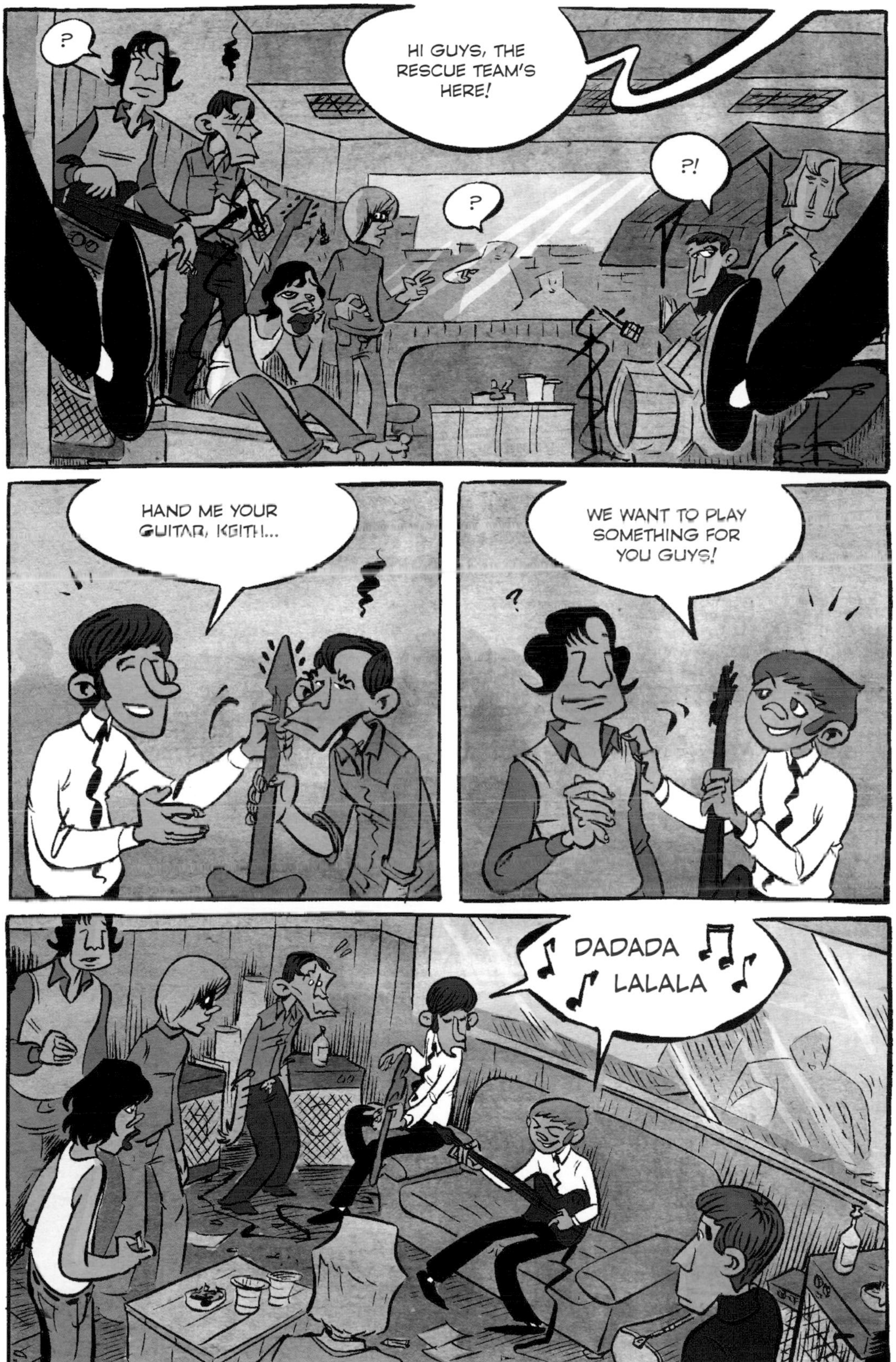
?
HI GUYS, THE RESCUE TEAM'S HERE!
?!
?
HAND ME YOUR GUITAR, KEITH...
WE WANT TO PLAY SOMETHING FOR YOU GUYS!
?
DADADA LALALA

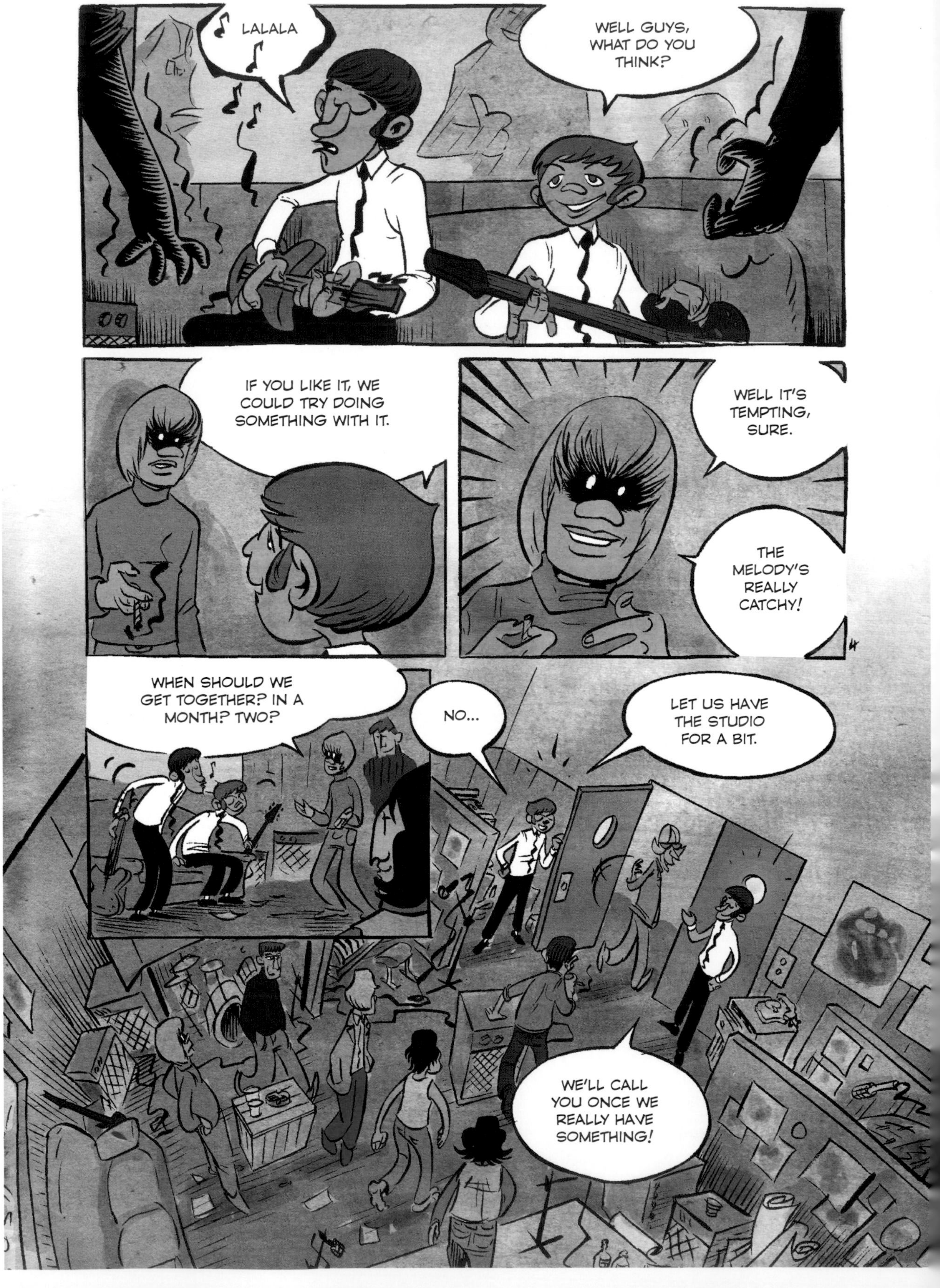
LALALA
WELL GUYS, WHAT DO YOU THINK?
IF YOU LIKE IT, WE COULD TRY DOING SOMETHING WITH IT.
WELL IT'S TEMPTING, SURE.
THE MELODY'S REALLY CATCHY!
WHEN SHOULD WE GET TOGETHER? IN A MONTH? TWO?
NO...
LET US HAVE THE STUDIO FOR A BIT.
WE'LL CALL YOU ONCE WE REALLY HAVE SOMETHING!

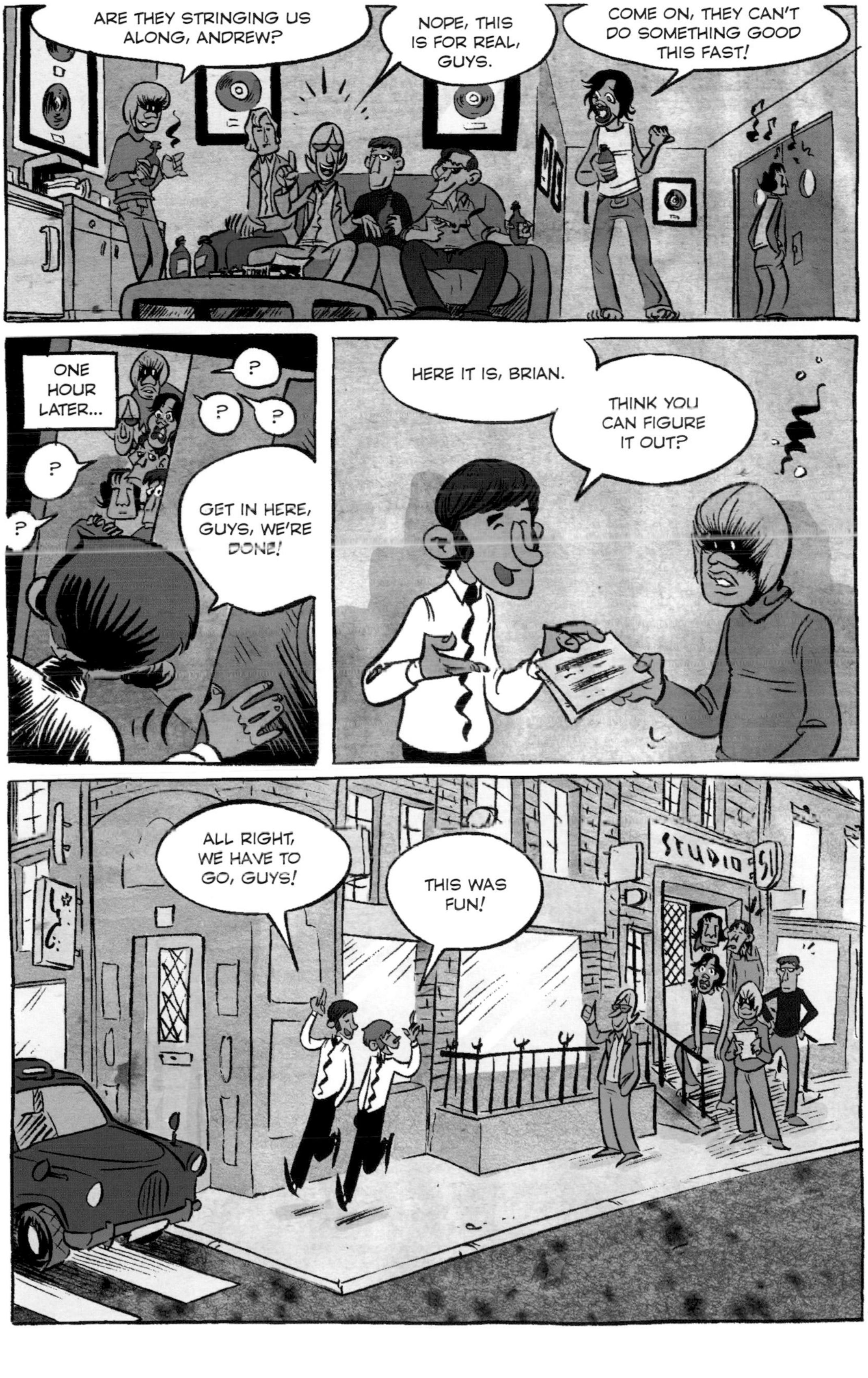
ARE THEY STRINGING US ALONG, ANDREW?
NOPE, THIS IS FOR REAL, GUYS.
COME ON, THEY CAN'T DO SOMETHING GOOD THIS FAST!
ONE HOUR LATER...
?
?
?
?
?
GET IN HERE, GUYS, WE'RE DONE!
HERE IT IS, BRIAN.
THINK YOU CAN FIGURE IT OUT?
ALL RIGHT, WE HAVE TO GO, GUYS!
THIS WAS FUN!
STUDIO 51

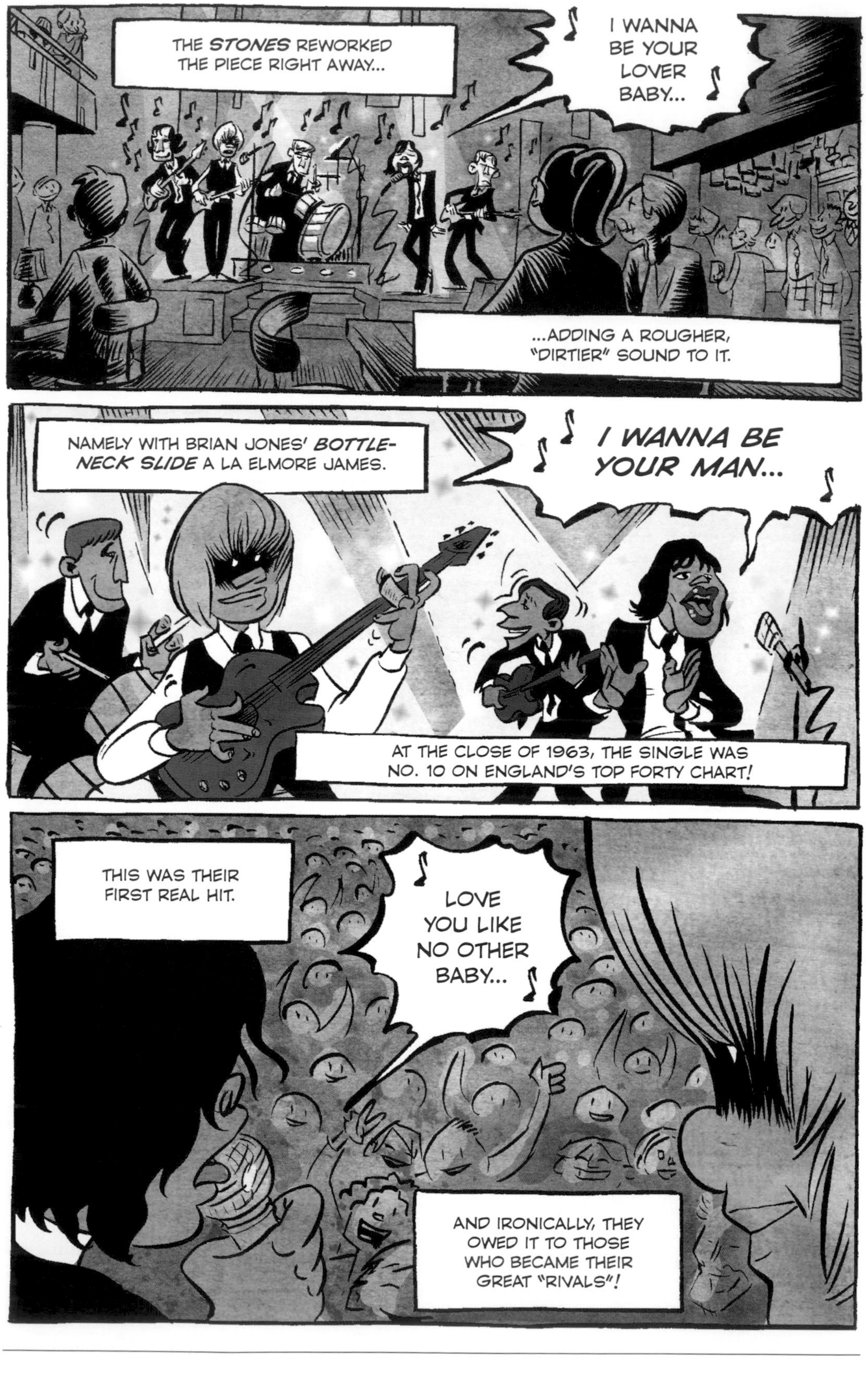
THE STONES REWORKED THE PIECE RIGHT AWAY...
I WANNA BE YOUR LOVER BABY...
...ADDING A ROUGHER, "DIRTIER" SOUND TO IT.
NAMELY WITH BRIAN JONES' BOTTLE-NECK SLIDE A LA ELMORE JAMES.
I WANNA BE YOUR MAN...
AT THE CLOSE OF 1963, THE SINGLE WAS NO. 10 ON ENGLAND'S TOP FORTY CHART!
THIS WAS THEIR FIRST REAL HIT.
LOVE YOU LIKE NO OTHER BABY...
AND IRONICALLY, THEY OWED IT TO THOSE WHO BECAME THEIR GREAT "RIVALS"!

Make Mine
Decca

© uderud - Riksarkivet (National Archives of Norway)

Andrew Loog Oldham quickly proved that he wasn't just a smooth
talker or a brainless dandy. As soon
as he became the Rolling Stones'
official manager, he put his address
book and his incredible self-assu-
rance to smart use. At breakneck
speed, he negotiated an amazing
contract with Decca Records; in
fact, the Rolling Stones got a better
deal than the Fab Four themselves.

With Eric Easton circa 1964

Unlike Crawdaddy Club owner Giorgio Gomelsky, who
had settled for a verbal contract with the Stones, Andrew Loog Oldham first signed a contract making him
their manager before he went looking for a record label.
It's what's called not putting the cart before the horse.
He was young, but he was clear-headed and demonstrated great psychological finesse. Nevertheless, he
overlooked a few details that could have ruined the
whole thing. First, he wasn't yet twenty-one, the legal
age for getting a license as a talent agent, and second,
he didn't have a penny to his name. So he joined forces
with Eric Easton, a well-respected agent with offices on
Regent Street, and they split the workload: Easton han-
dled the finances and the administrative issues, Oldham
focused on new ideas and the press.

Amsterdam, 1966 © Jac de Nijs CC BY SA 3.0

Another thorny problem to solve: the Rolling Stones had had the bright idea, while recording their second album with George Clewson, to sign an exclusive deal with his company, IBC. Brian Jones deftly managed to buy the rights back, claiming that the band was in the process of splitting up. He succeeded in having that contract ripped into pieces for a mere ninety-six pounds, and the Stones thus reclaimed total freedom. They could now go to Decca Records, where executive Dick Rowe had missed snagging the Beatles a few months earlier. Perhaps that explained the unbelievable terms the Rolling Stones managed to secure: the right to pick their recording studios and total artistic freedom. For a young band that still had everything to prove, that was an amazing advantage, though with it came the pressure to succeed.

"ACCORDING TO OLDHAM, STU DIDN'T FIT THE PART. AND SIX FACES ON A PICTURE WERE TOO MANY FOR FANS TO REMEMBER."

Keith Richards

At the contract signing, Decca asked the band to get rid of Mick Jagger, as they felt the vocalist was their weakest link. But the band's manager believed in his talent and fought tooth and nail to keep him. It was Brian Jones, as representative of the band, who signed the three-year contract alongside Easton and Oldham. Gomelsky was dumped at once and the big question was now whether or not to keep Ian Stewart, aka Stu...

"IN THE END, STU'S THE ONE WHO DECIDED TO STAY WITH US, WHICH WAS UNDERSTANDABLE. HE SAID, 'I'M STAYING AS LONG AS I CAN STILL PLAY PIANO. WE'LL BE TOGETHER AS A BAND, BUT NOT IN THE PHOTOS.'"

Keith Richards

Mick Jagger in 1976 ©Bert Verhoeff (ANEFO) CC BY-SA 2.0

The manager just did not like his look. He hardly came across as a rebel, what with his overly formal haircut, his protruding chin and his rugby player physique. And six bandmembers, well that was too orchestra-ish, especially since there were only four Beatles. What did his brothers in arms have to say about it? Nothing. He would be the one sacrificed at the altar of fame.

To his immense credit, he agreed to remain in the Rolling Stones' shadow, becoming their full-time road manager and their part-time piano player.

From that moment forward, the Rolling Stones became full-fledged musicians and Mick dropped out of school for good. Oldham didn't spare himself or his clients any of the hard work it took to climb up the ladder. They needed catchy songs and spent more and more time recording. That's how they discovered Studio Atlantic, which quickly became their favorite recording studio. However, though they had a number of early hits such as "Come On," "I Wanna Be Your Man," and "Not Fade Away," they hadn't yet reached their goal. **While they had found the Rolling Stones sound, along with that now well-established ruggedness, it was time to create their own songs.**

"AND THEN ANDREW GOT US SIGNED WITH DECCA RECORDS—QUICK AS LIGHTNING. THE THING THAT WAS WONDERFUL AND MARVELOUS WAS THAT DICK ROWE, AT DECCA, HAD TURNED DOWN THE BEATLES.
WAS HE GOING TO SAY "NO" TWICE? IN A WAY, WE KNEW WE HAD THEM BEFORE WE EVEN BEGAN NEGOTIATING, AND THAT'S THE REASON WE WERE ABLE TO GET WHAT WE WANTED."

Keith Richards

1975 ©Tony Morelli CC BY SA 2.0

Jagger and Wyman, Rotterdam, 1982 ©Marcel Antonisse CC BY SA

The Sixth Stone

Artist: Clément Baloup

Ian Stewart: Temporary Pianist,
Lifelong Friend.

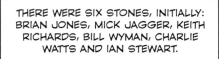

THERE WERE SIX STONES, INITIALLY: BRIAN JONES, MICK JAGGER, KEITH RICHARDS, BILL WYMAN, CHARLIE WATTS AND IAN STEWART.

SO WHY ARE THERE ONLY FIVE NOW?

LET'S FLASH BACK TO A PUB CALLED THE BRICKLAYER'S ARMS...

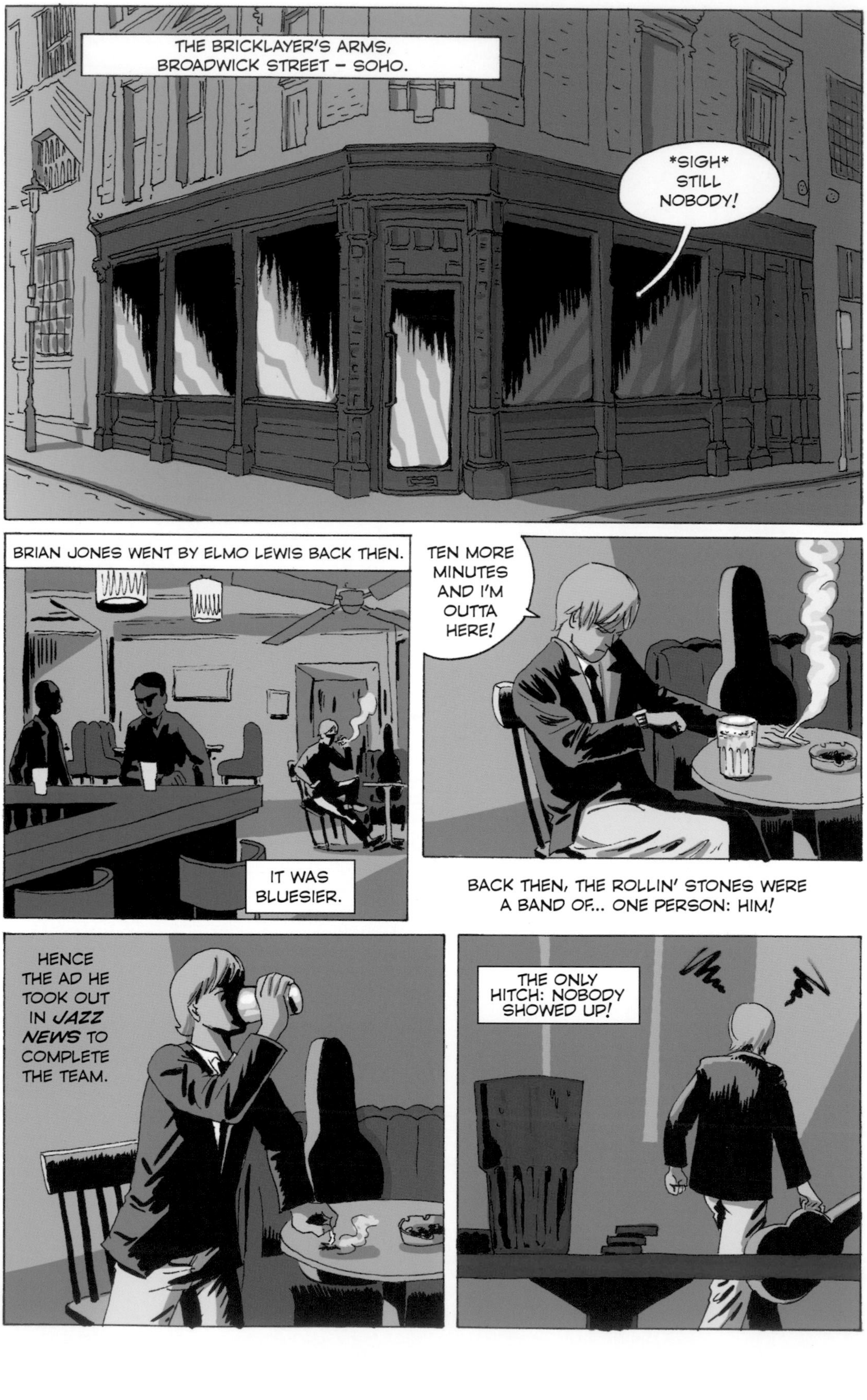
THE BRICKLAYER'S ARMS, BROADWICK STREET – SOHO.
SIGH STILL NOBODY!
BRIAN JONES WENT BY ELMO LEWIS BACK THEN.
IT WAS BLUESIER.
TEN MORE MINUTES AND I'M OUTTA HERE!
BACK THEN, THE ROLLIN' STONES WERE A BAND OF... ONE PERSON: HIM!
HENCE THE AD HE TOOK OUT IN *JAZZ NEWS* TO COMPLETE THE TEAM.
THE ONLY HITCH: NOBODY SHOWED UP!

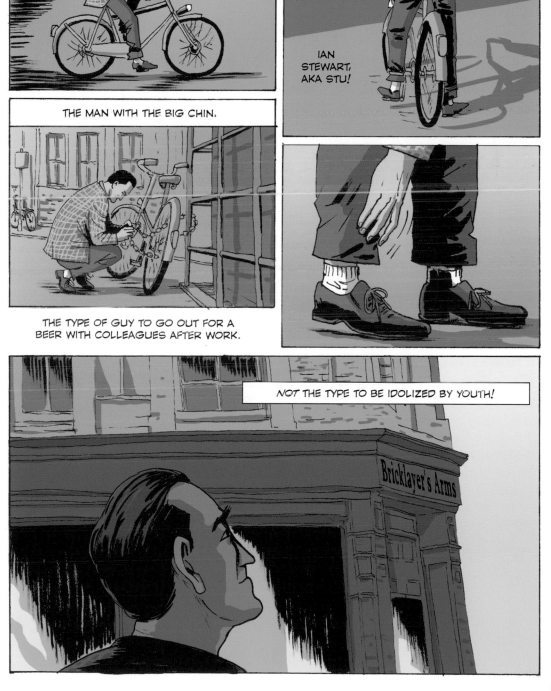

NOBODY EXCEPT FOR ONE ODD CHARACTER...

IAN STEWART, AKA STU!

THE MAN WITH THE BIG CHIN.

THE TYPE OF GUY TO GO OUT FOR A BEER WITH COLLEAGUES AFTER WORK.

NOT THE TYPE TO BE IDOLIZED BY YOUTH!

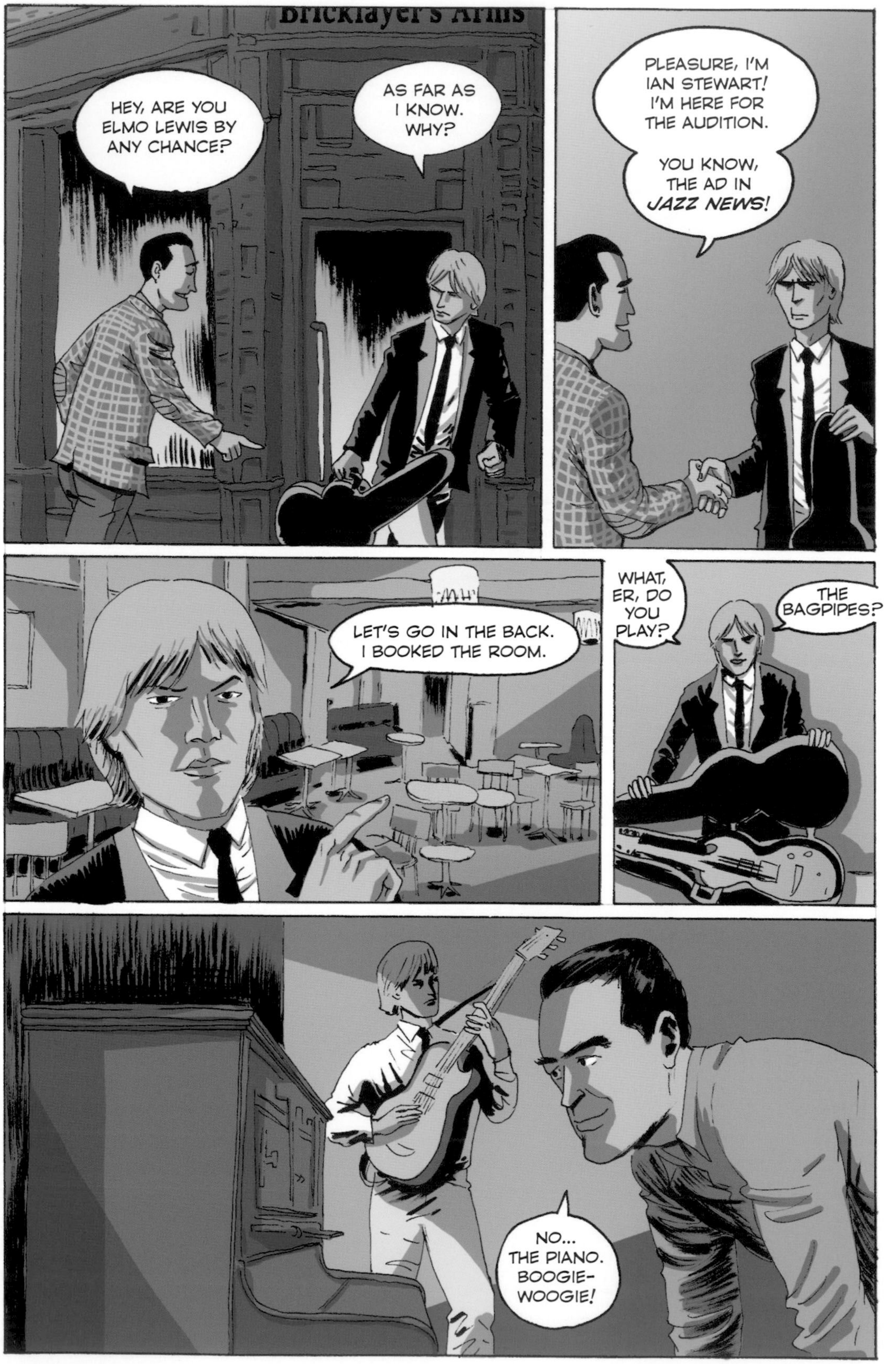
Bricklayer's Arms
HEY, ARE YOU ELMO LEWIS BY ANY CHANCE?
AS FAR AS I KNOW. WHY?
PLEASURE, I'M IAN STEWART! I'M HERE FOR THE AUDITION.
YOU KNOW, THE AD IN *JAZZ NEWS*!
LET'S GO IN THE BACK. I BOOKED THE ROOM.
WHAT, ER, DO YOU PLAY?
THE BAGPIPES?
NO... THE PIANO. BOOGIE-WOOGIE!

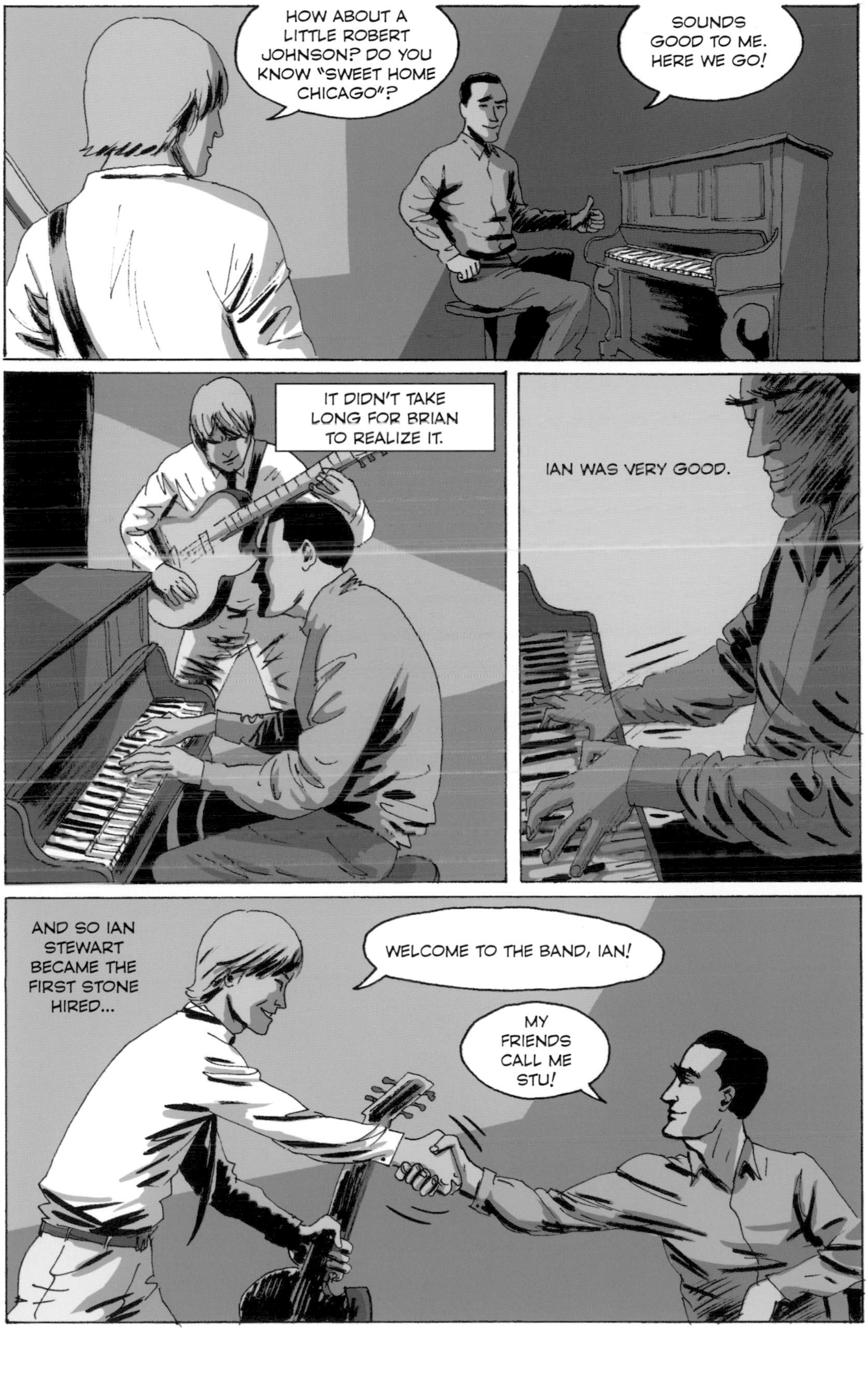
HOW ABOUT A LITTLE ROBERT JOHNSON? DO YOU KNOW "SWEET HOME CHICAGO"?
SOUNDS GOOD TO ME. HERE WE GO!
IT DIDN'T TAKE LONG FOR BRIAN TO REALIZE IT.
IAN WAS VERY GOOD.
AND SO IAN STEWART BECAME THE FIRST STONE HIRED...
WELCOME TO THE BAND, IAN!
MY FRIENDS CALL ME STU!

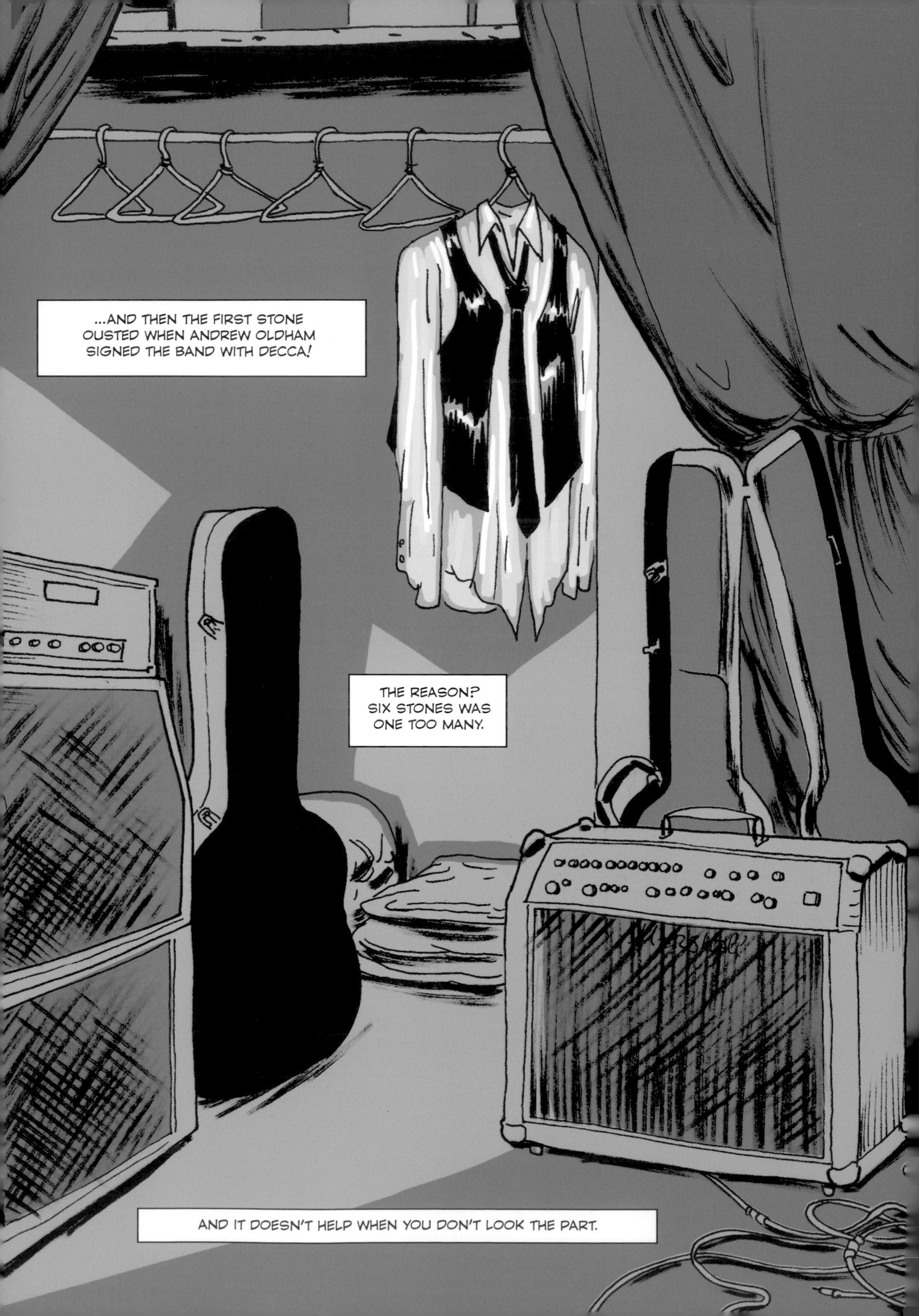
...AND THEN THE FIRST STONE OUSTED WHEN ANDREW OLDHAM SIGNED THE BAND WITH DECCA!
THE REASON? SIX STONES WAS ONE TOO MANY.
AND IT DOESN'T HELP WHEN YOU DON'T LOOK THE PART.

Singer, Songwriter

They viewed themselves as musicians first and foremost. They wanted to play R&B, end of story! But Andrew Loog Oldham understood that they needed to be doing their own material if they wanted to come across as a great band and be in it for the long haul. **If the Beatles could do it, so could they!**

For the time being, the Stones' entire repertory was R&B covers. Not so with the Beatles: Lennon and McCartney were natural-born songwriters and had been creating their own musical material for several years already. And as we saw, it was the Beatles who gave the Stones their first original track with "I Wanna Be Your Man." The song became their first big hit, but they owed that success to their "rivals." Oldham felt the time had come for the Stones to write their own songs if they didn't want to remain just a trendy little band... because the problem with trends is that they come and go!

> "I HAD A LITTLE TALENT FOR LYRICS, AND KEITH HAS ALWAYS HAD A LOT OF TALENT FOR MELODY, FROM DAY ONE. EVERYTHING, INCLUDING THE RIFFS, CAME FROM KEITH. BUT WE WORKED AT IT, WE WORKED AT IT REALLY HARD. WE DEVELOPED IT. YOU NEED TO APPLY YOURSELF. OUR FIRST SONGS WERE TERRIFIC."
>
> **Mick Jagger**

Gene Pitney in 1967

Plus, financially speaking, the royalties from their album sales didn't bring in nearly as much as the incredible sums generated by their songs playing on the airwaves. In other words, to really live the high life and buy a chateau in France, you had to make your own music! Once again, Oldham's instincts were right on track. So he turned to Keith Richards and Mick Jagger and told them they should write. But why them, when Brian Jones was the one who founded the Rolling Stones and was the best musician in the band, to boot? Was that intuition, or did that come from Oldham's hands-on collaboration with Keith and Mick in a house on Mapesbury Road? Whatever motivated it, his decision proved to be a lucid one.

The duo went at this new challenge half-heartedly, essentially forced to do it and basically thinking Oldham was a bit nuts. Asking them to write? What a goofy idea! One can just imagine how things unfolded... they struggled, feeling their way in the dark, drinking and smoking so as to better face the blank page. But then one morning a miracle happened: the manager turned on the Philips mono tape recorder and heard what became their very first original. The tape still exists to this day! The song was "It Should Be You." This was only their first composition, but it was a start! Now they understood the gist of it and they had put their duo to the test— in other words, the toughest part was over. All that remained to be seen was whether they would have what it takes to create some real gems.

We all know the answer to that. Wisely, Oldham decided that their first effort didn't really fit the Rolling Stones style, and he gave it to one of his other young clients, George Bean, to sing. Richards and Jagger went on to repeat the experience, writing more songs for other singers, including "That Girl Belongs To Yesterday," which took Gene Pitney to the Top 10 chart in the UK. There was also the famous "As Tears Go By," sung by a young woman fresh out of the convent: Marianne Faithfull. That sweet ballad proved to be the prelude to another, more tumultuous romance. It would take several more months for the Rolling Stones to finally write for themselves—part of the maturing process. But they were fast learners. Now, how were the others dealing with all this? Charlie Watts and Bill Wyman seemed to handle it very well, but not Brian Jones! It was clear that this passing of the torch was likely his first wound. He tried his hand at songwriting but seemed to struggle with it. He played multiple instruments but lacked confidence as a songwriter, Bill Wyman said: "Whenever he tried to write songs, he would get shot down, and not in a nice way... [...] they'd tell him: "You can't write." The status quo had changed; now Mick and Keith were the big shots—"The Glimmer Twins"—as they signed the compositions they wrote together.

"WHEN THE TWO OF US WORK ON THE MUSIC TOGETHER, SOMETHING ALWAYS HAPPENS. I'M NOT SURE HOW IT WORKS. LET'S JUST CALL IT THE MYSTERIES OF ALCHEMY."

Keith Richards

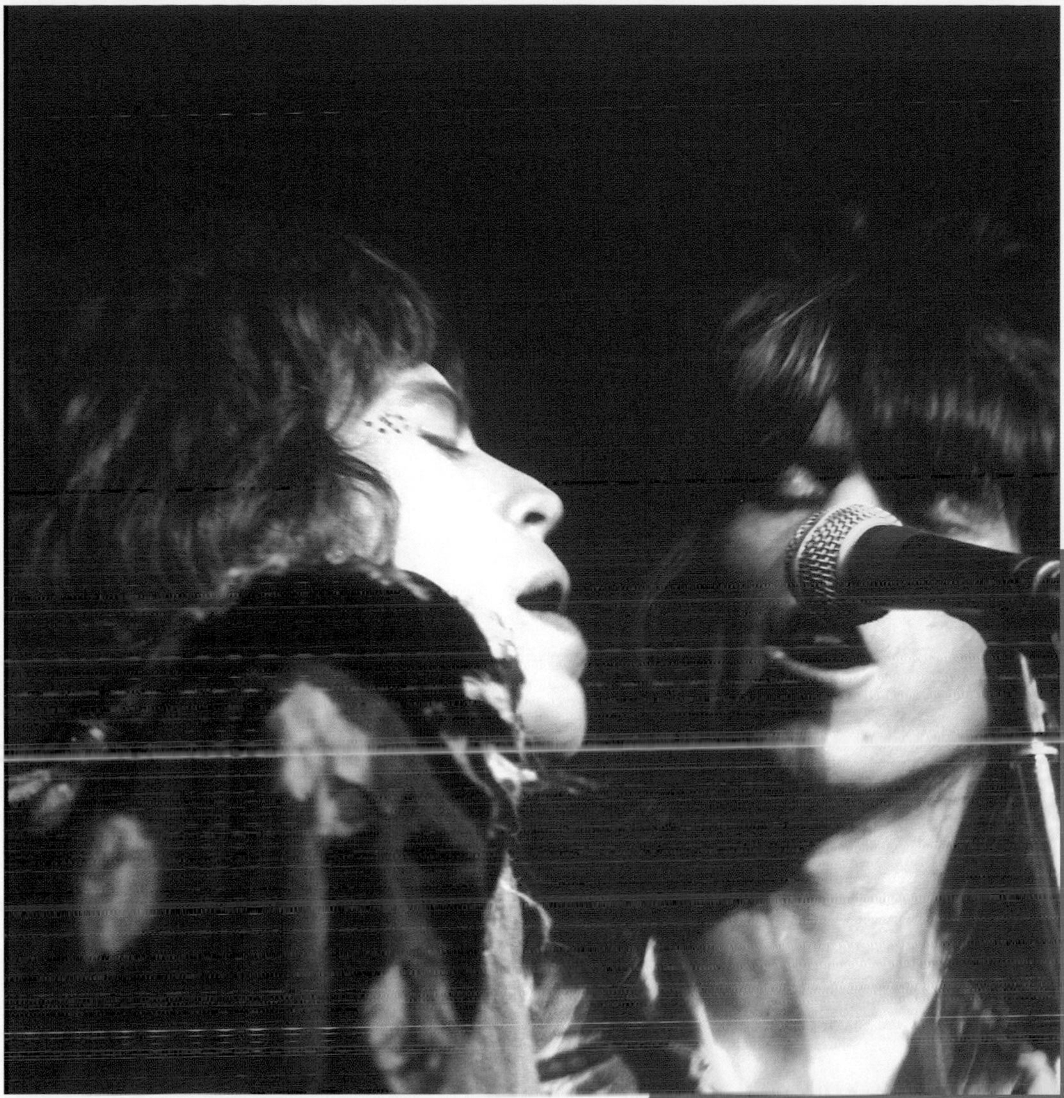

Mick Jagger and Keith Richards in concert in San Francisco in 1972 ©Larry Rogers CC BY SA 2

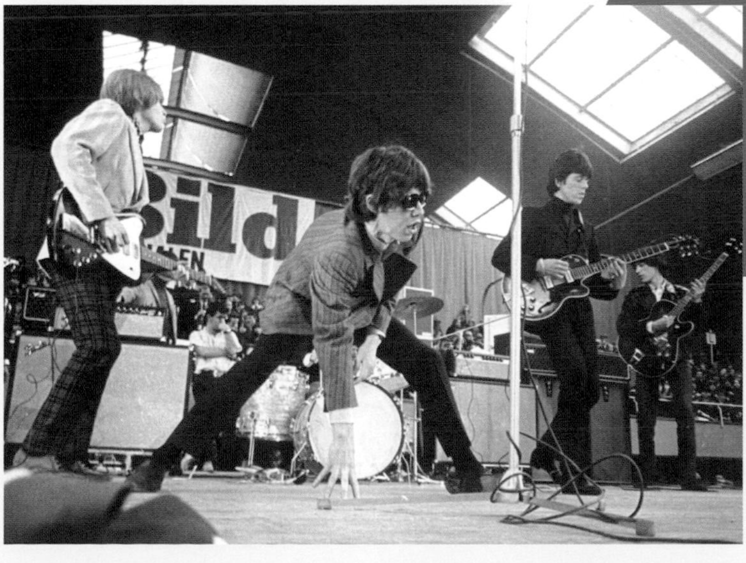

Concert in San Francisco in 1972 ©Larry Rogers CC BY SA 2.0

The Glimmer Twins

Artist: Dominique Hennebaut

Doing Covers Is Great...
Writing Your Own Songs Is Better!

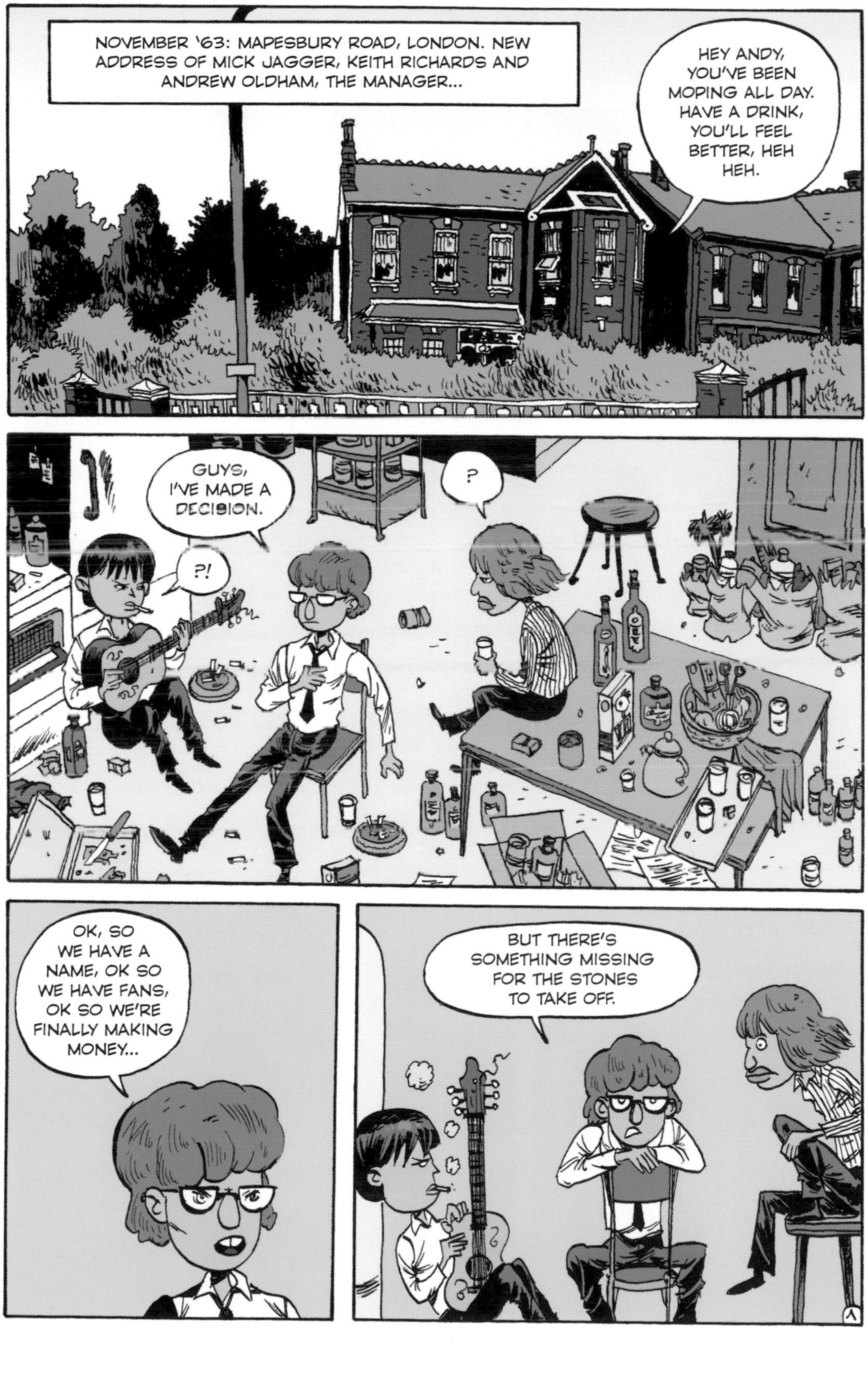
NOVEMBER '63: MAPESBURY ROAD, LONDON. NEW ADDRESS OF MICK JAGGER, KEITH RICHARDS AND ANDREW OLDHAM, THE MANAGER...
HEY ANDY, YOU'VE BEEN MOPING ALL DAY. HAVE A DRINK, YOU'LL FEEL BETTER, HEH HEH.
GUYS, I'VE MADE A DECISION.
?
?!
OK, SO WE HAVE A NAME, OK SO WE HAVE FANS, OK SO WE'RE FINALLY MAKING MONEY...
BUT THERE'S SOMETHING MISSING FOR THE STONES TO TAKE OFF.

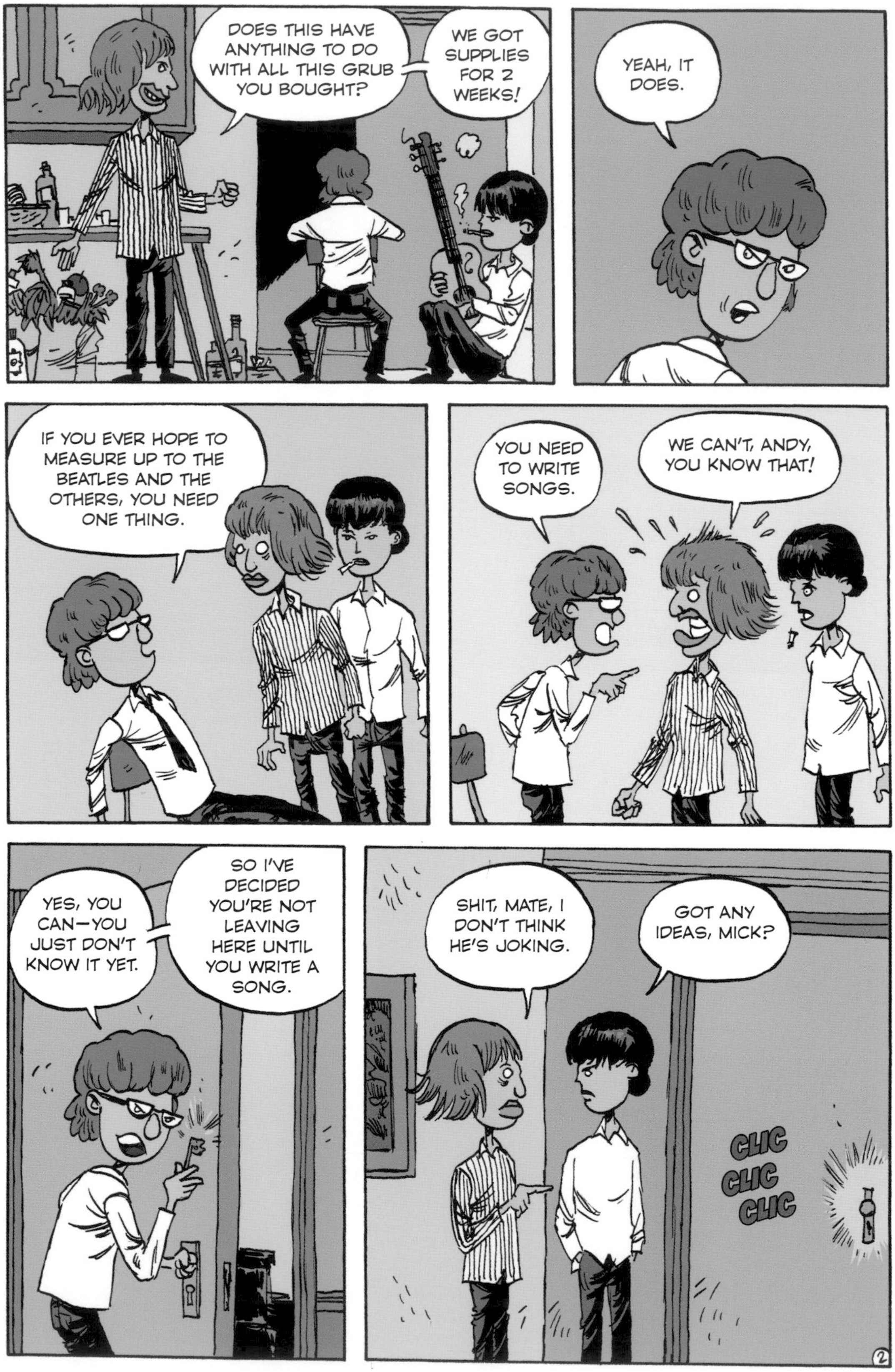

DOES THIS HAVE ANYTHING TO DO WITH ALL THIS GRUB YOU BOUGHT?
WE GOT SUPPLIES FOR 2 WEEKS!
YEAH, IT DOES.
IF YOU EVER HOPE TO MEASURE UP TO THE BEATLES AND THE OTHERS, YOU NEED ONE THING.
YOU NEED TO WRITE SONGS.
WE CAN'T, ANDY, YOU KNOW THAT!
YES, YOU CAN—YOU JUST DON'T KNOW IT YET.
SO I'VE DECIDED YOU'RE NOT LEAVING HERE UNTIL YOU WRITE A SONG.
SHIT, MATE, I DON'T THINK HE'S JOKING.
GOT ANY IDEAS, MICK?
CLIC
CLIC
CLIC

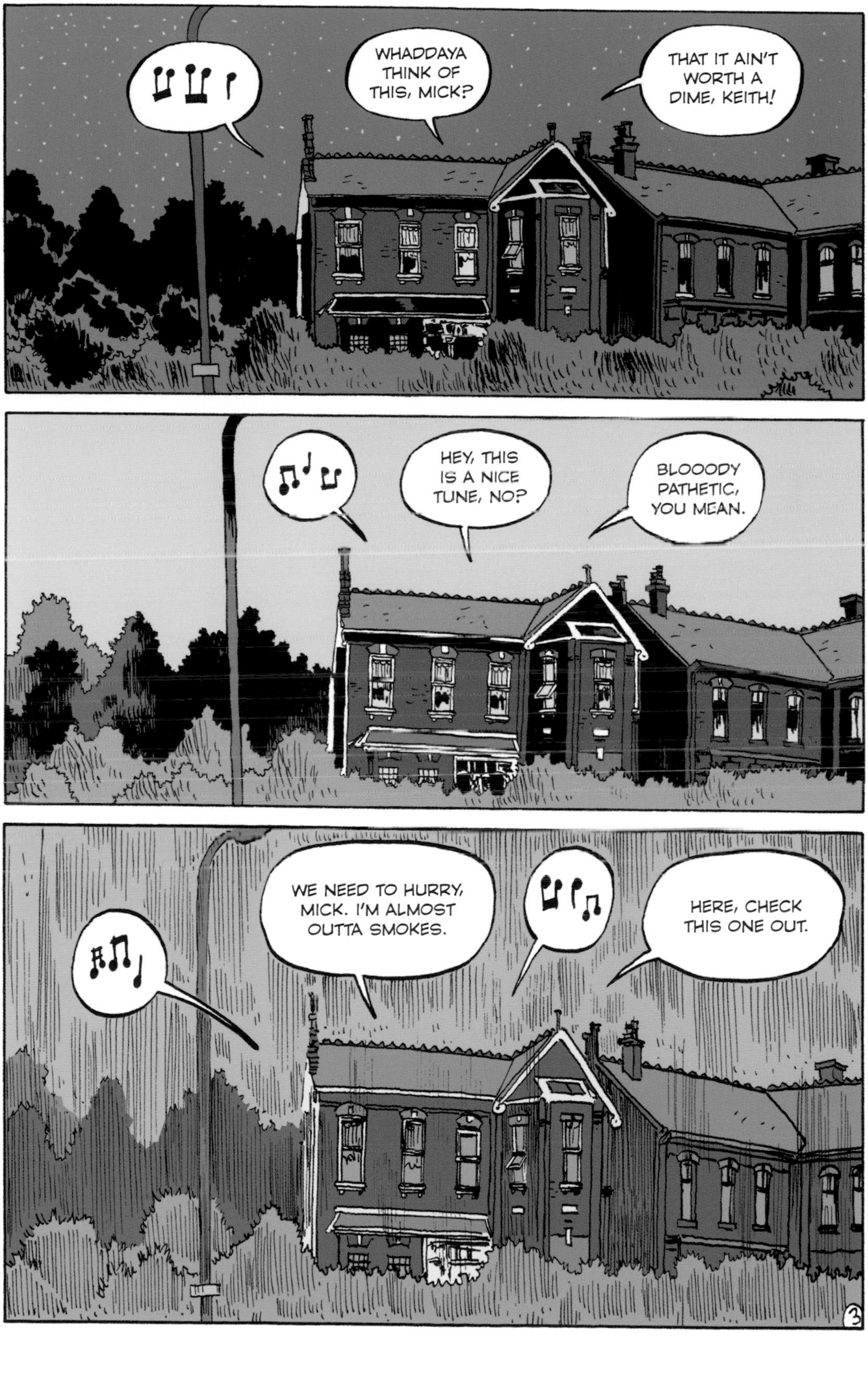
WHADDAYA THINK OF THIS, MICK?
THAT IT AIN'T WORTH A DIME, KEITH!
HEY, THIS IS A NICE TUNE, NO?
BLOOODY PATHETIC, YOU MEAN.
WE NEED TO HURRY, MICK. I'M ALMOST OUTTA SMOKES.
HERE, CHECK THIS ONE OUT.
3

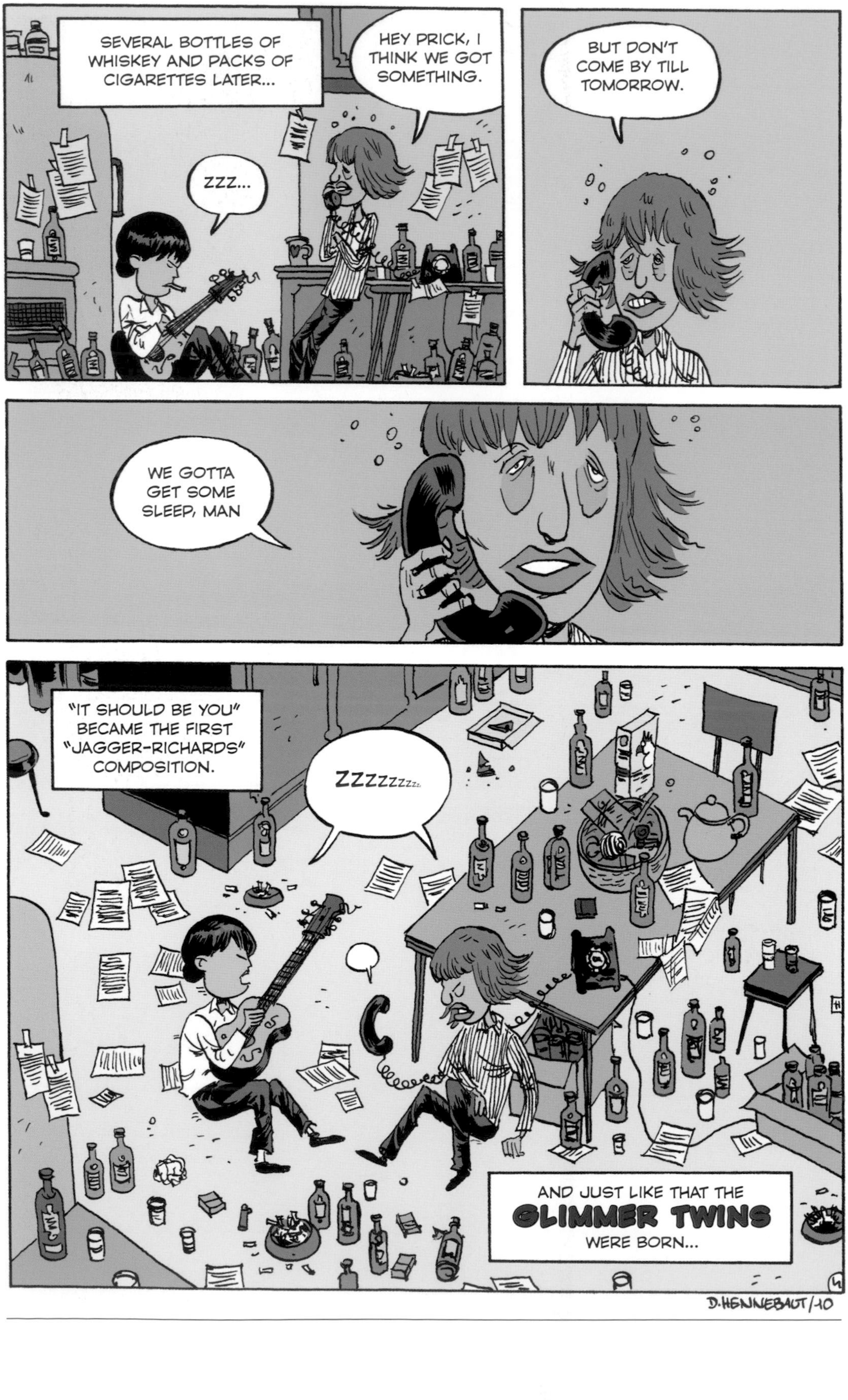
SEVERAL BOTTLES OF WHISKEY AND PACKS OF CIGARETTES LATER...
HEY PRICK, I THINK WE GOT SOMETHING.
ZZZ...
BUT DON'T COME BY TILL TOMORROW.
WE GOTTA GET SOME SLEEP, MAN
"IT SHOULD BE YOU" BECAME THE FIRST "JAGGER-RICHARDS" COMPOSITION.
ZZZzzzzz
AND JUST LIKE THAT THE
GLIMMER TWINS
WERE BORN...
D.HENNEBAUT/10

Drug City

Mick Jagger in 1967 ©Jac. de Nijs CC BY-SA

Drugs were a key component of the Rolling Stones universe, just like absinthe was for artists in the 19th century. At first, it was a symbol of their transgressive, anti-conformist attitude; later it became a way to fight against exhaustion and stress; later still, a way to expand their imagination. And after that? Brushes with the law and stints in rehab…

Even before the Rolling Stones were officially formed, some of the bandmembers had dabbled in illicit substances. Their friend Dick Taylor, for instance, once said that as early as 1961, "Keith and I were on a pretty steady diet of pep pills, which not only kept us awake but gave us a lift. We took all kinds of things... inhalers like Nostrilene and other stuff. Later, Mick, Keith and Brian developed the habit of taking pills before their shows, so they could make it through the whole thing and maintain the required level of energy. **It's important to note that while drugs were closely linked to the Rolling Stones' image, they meant different things to different bandmembers.**

Keith Richards in Finland in 1965 ©Olavi Kaskisuo

"THE STRANGEST THING
I'VE EVER SNORTED?
MY FATHER. I SNORTED
MY FATHER."

Keith Richards

65

> "ACCORDING TO KEITH RICHARDS,
> A BIG PART OF THAT EXPLOSION
> OF CREATIVITY CAN BE
> DIRECTLY ATTRIBUTED TO
> THE INGESTION OF VARIOUS
> PSYCHOACTIVE SUBSTANCES
> THAT WERE COMMONPLACE
> IN THOSE DAYS."
>
> **Rob Bowman**

It wasn't until they met Robert Fraser, the scandalous art dealer, and Christopher Gibbs, an antique dealer, that they graduated to more dangerous drugs, namely cocaine. Those two men took Brian Jones and Anita Pallenberg to Morocco for the first time, where they tasted forbidden pleasures in luxury hotels. A variety of happy combinations followed: alcohol to set the mood, drugs to trip on, uppers for concert energy, and sleeping pills and downers to compensate. It's not too hard to imagine why those cocktails caused so much damage. That psychedelic counter-culture had the authorities worried. Swinging London was increasingly hard for them to grasp. The Rolling Stones as the symbol of a generation, why not... as long as it wasn't the "cocaine generation"!

> "THERE WERE A LOT OF
> DRUGS CIRCULATING BACK THEN,
> BUT IT WAS VERY MUCH IN VOGUE.
> IT WASN'T UNUSUAL FOR MUSICIANS
> TO DROP LSD BEFORE WALKING
> ON STAGE WITH A BOTTLE
> OF JACK DANIELS."
>
> **Charlie Watts**

Police in the UK figured it was time for a big coup, and what a better way to make a statement than with a trial! What followed became known as the Redlands Affair. Redlands was where Keith Richards had bought a nice home close to the sea. On February 12, 1967, police officers who were likely tipped off raided the place in the middle of the night, confiscating a lot of illegal substances. **This was an absolute disaster for the Rolling Stones.**

With artists like The Who, newspapers like the *Times*, and hundreds of thousands of fans protesting and voicing their support, the band got away with just conditional release for Mick Jagger. But law enforcement was after them now and the next one to be arrested on similar charges was Brian Jones, which would prove to be the beginning of the end for him. He pleaded guilty, which meant he couldn't get a visa for the United States. That was more than a little problematic for the band, as they were planning another cross-Atlantic tour. Even so, the Rolling Stones weren't done with drugs just yet. The game of cat and mouse would go on for years. They would come up with crazy schemes and achieve great feats of imagination to escape snoops the world over. For instance, they would purchase—directly from the New York mafia, mind you—shaving cream cans with a double, unscrewable bottom in which to hide their coke. They'd go to Morocco and Jamaica to snort coke to their heart's content, using mules and other police-evading tactics to avoid unpleasant surprises. It worked, and they successfully managed to get high in peace! Keith Richards told the magazine *New Musical Express* that he once snorted his father's ashes mixed with a little coke. He took that confession back shortly afterwards. **Another "high" the Stones were used to: high-tailing it out of a situation to avoid being searched!**

"WE REALIZED THAT WHILE THE AUTHORITIES THAT WERE SPYING ON US HAD ENOUGH POWER TO MAKE SUCH A BIG CASE OUT OF THAT AND TO WIELD THAT AXE, THEY HAD ALSO MADE US INTO SOMETHING MUCH MORE IMPORTANT THAN WE WERE BEFORE."

Keith Richards

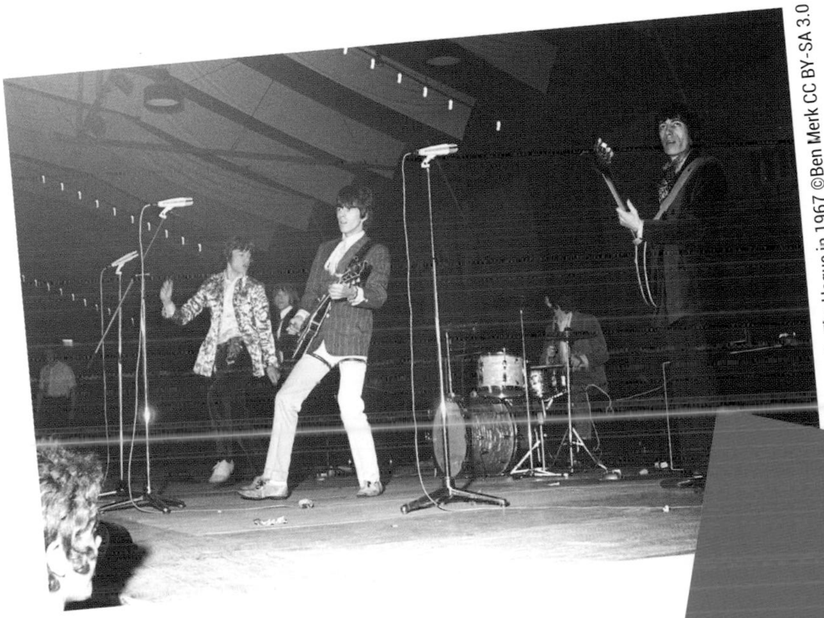

Concert in The Hague in 1967 ©Ben Merk CC BY-SA 3.0

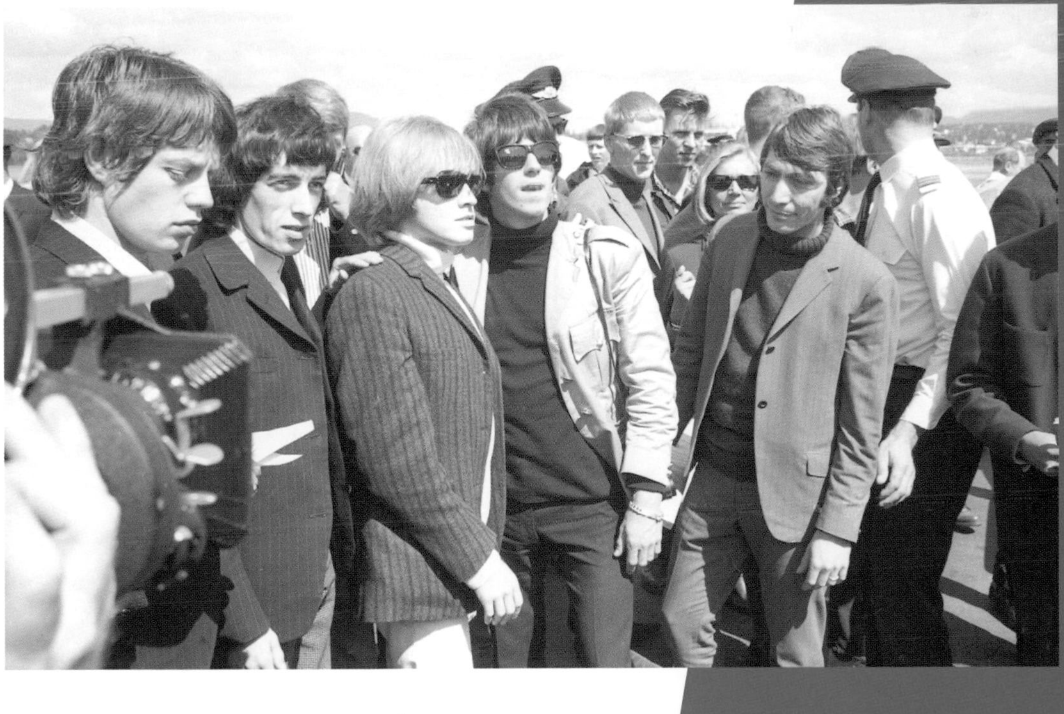

Mick Jagger, Bill Wyman, Brian Jones, Keith Richards and Charlie Watts, Oslo 1965 © National Archives of Norway.

The Redlands Affair

Artist: Amandine Puntous

The Rolling Stones' Brushes
With the Law.

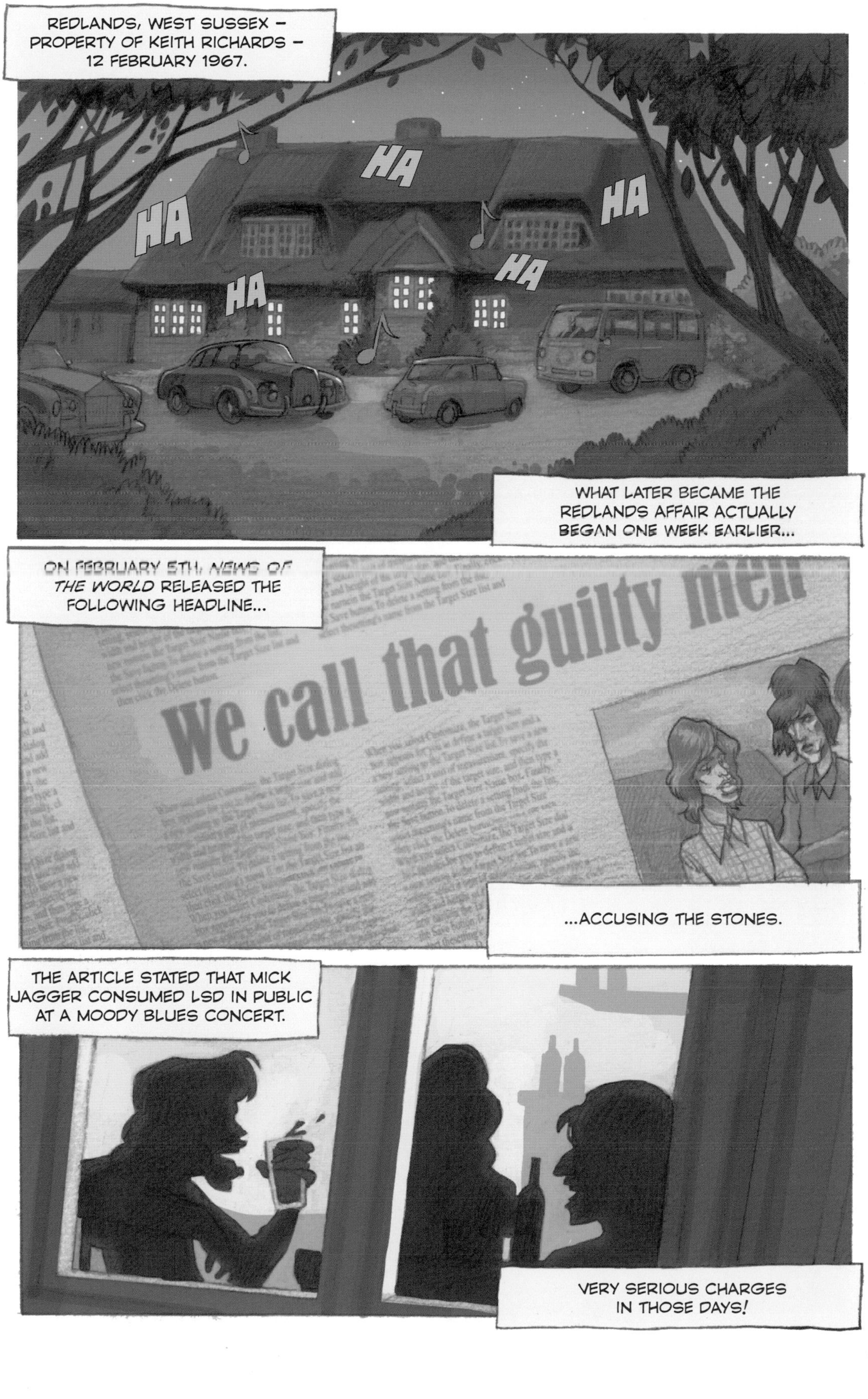
REDLANDS, WEST SUSSEX – PROPERTY OF KEITH RICHARDS – 12 FEBRUARY 1967.
HA
HA
HA
HA
HA
WHAT LATER BECAME THE REDLANDS AFFAIR ACTUALLY BEGAN ONE WEEK EARLIER...
ON FEBRUARY 5TH, *NEWS OF THE WORLD* RELEASED THE FOLLOWING HEADLINE...
We call that guilty men
...ACCUSING THE STONES.
THE ARTICLE STATED THAT MICK JAGGER CONSUMED LSD IN PUBLIC AT A MOODY BLUES CONCERT.
VERY SERIOUS CHARGES IN THOSE DAYS!

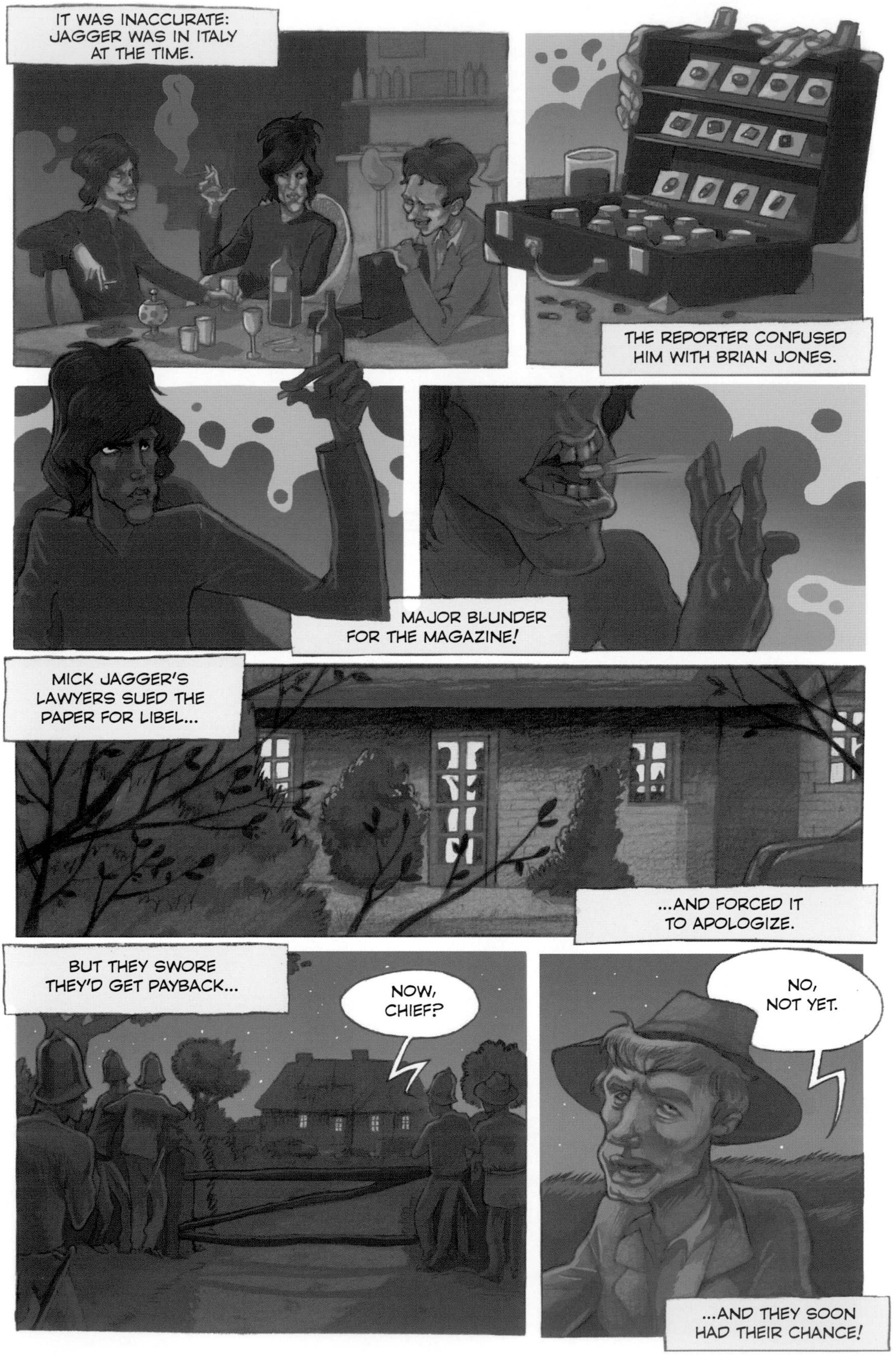
IT WAS INACCURATE: JAGGER WAS IN ITALY AT THE TIME.
THE REPORTER CONFUSED HIM WITH BRIAN JONES.
MAJOR BLUNDER FOR THE MAGAZINE!
MICK JAGGER'S LAWYERS SUED THE PAPER FOR LIBEL...
...AND FORCED IT TO APOLOGIZE.
BUT THEY SWORE THEY'D GET PAYBACK...
NOW, CHIEF?
NO, NOT YET.
...AND THEY SOON HAD THEIR CHANCE!

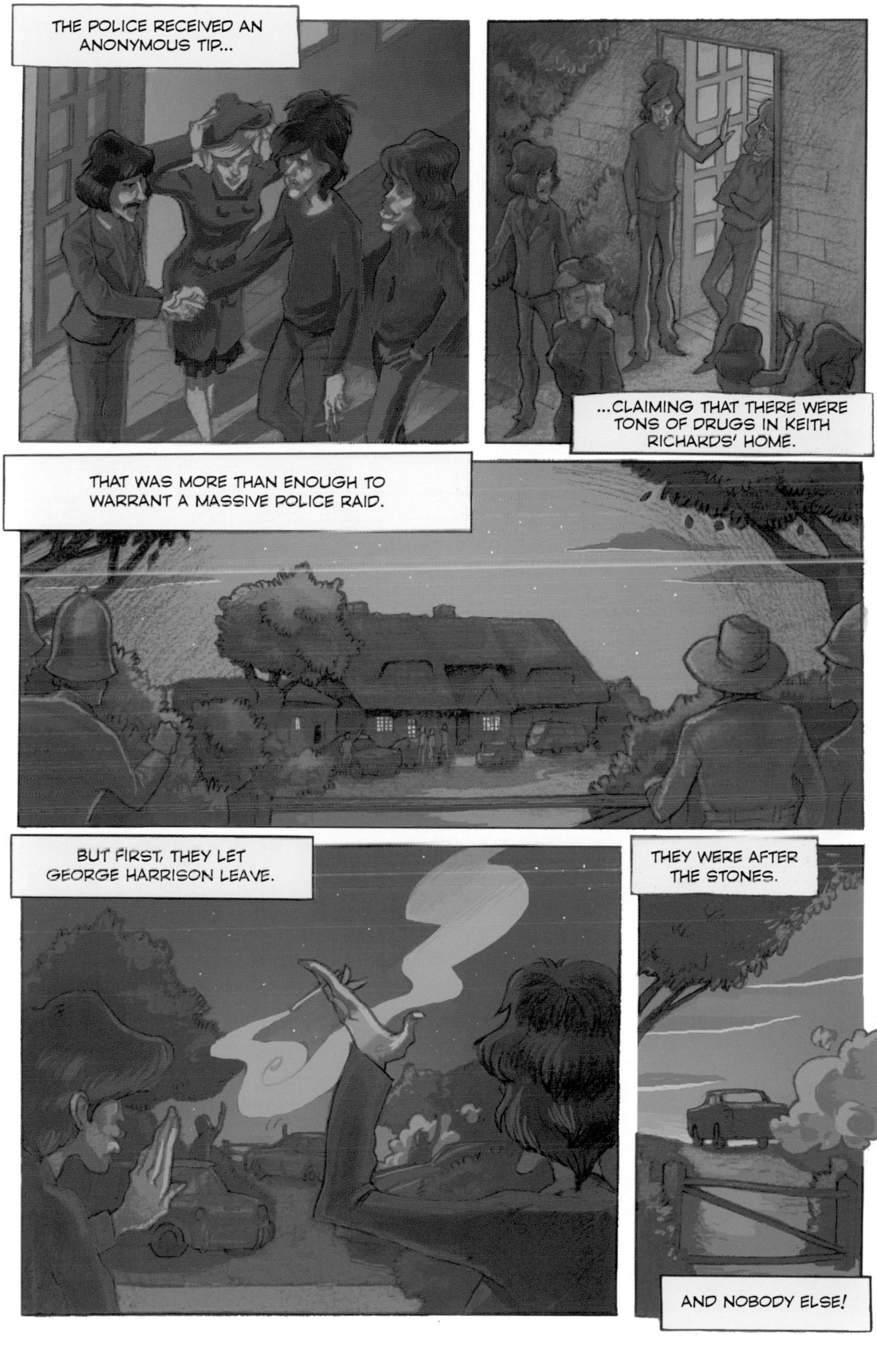
THE POLICE RECEIVED AN ANONYMOUS TIP...
...CLAIMING THAT THERE WERE TONS OF DRUGS IN KEITH RICHARDS' HOME.
THAT WAS MORE THAN ENOUGH TO WARRANT A MASSIVE POLICE RAID.
BUT FIRST, THEY LET GEORGE HARRISON LEAVE.
THEY WERE AFTER THE STONES.
AND NOBODY ELSE!

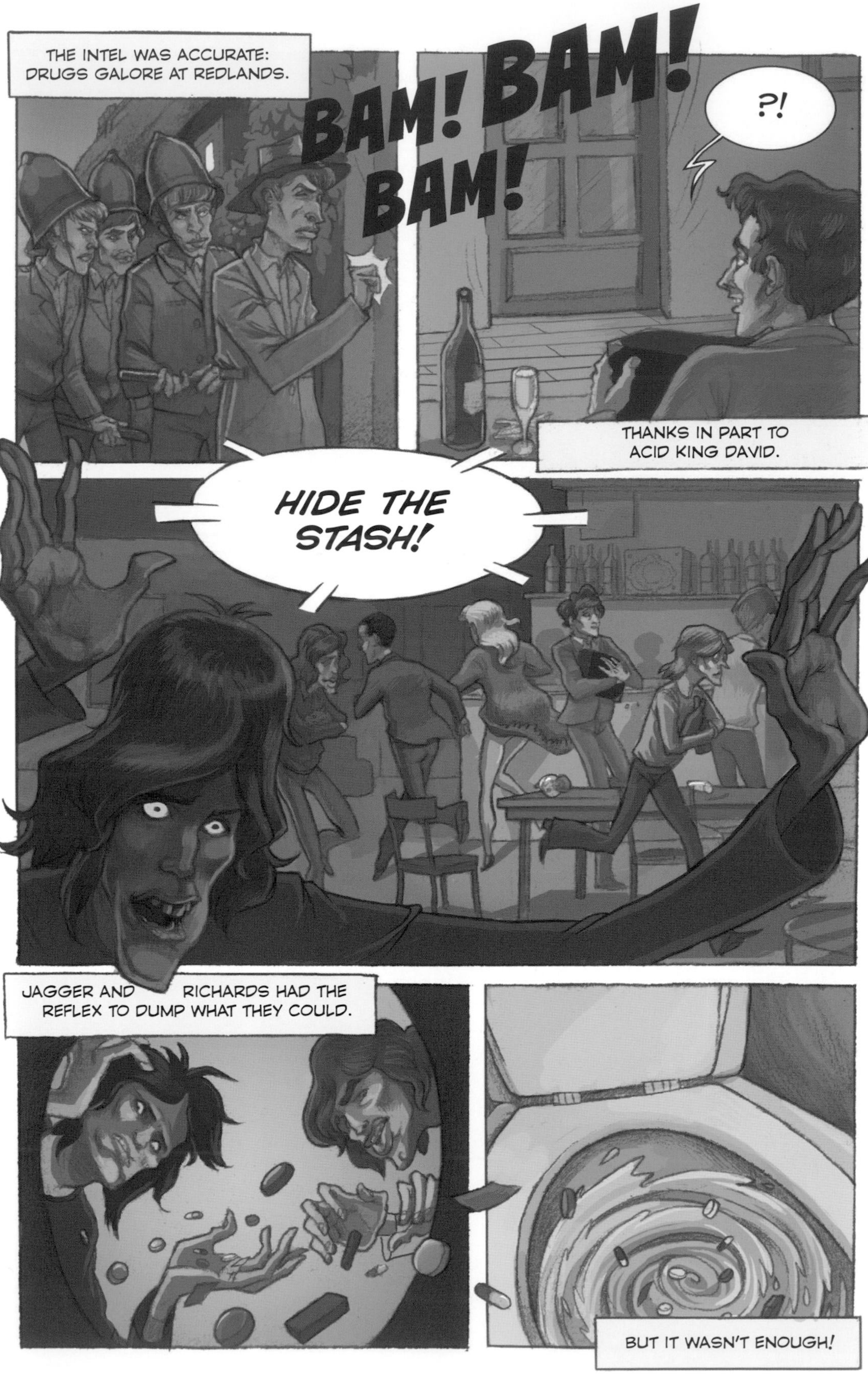
THE INTEL WAS ACCURATE: DRUGS GALORE AT REDLANDS.
BAM! BAM! BAM!
?!
THANKS IN PART TO ACID KING DAVID.
HIDE THE STASH!
JAGGER AND RICHARDS HAD THE REFLEX TO DUMP WHAT THEY COULD.
BUT IT WASN'T ENOUGH!

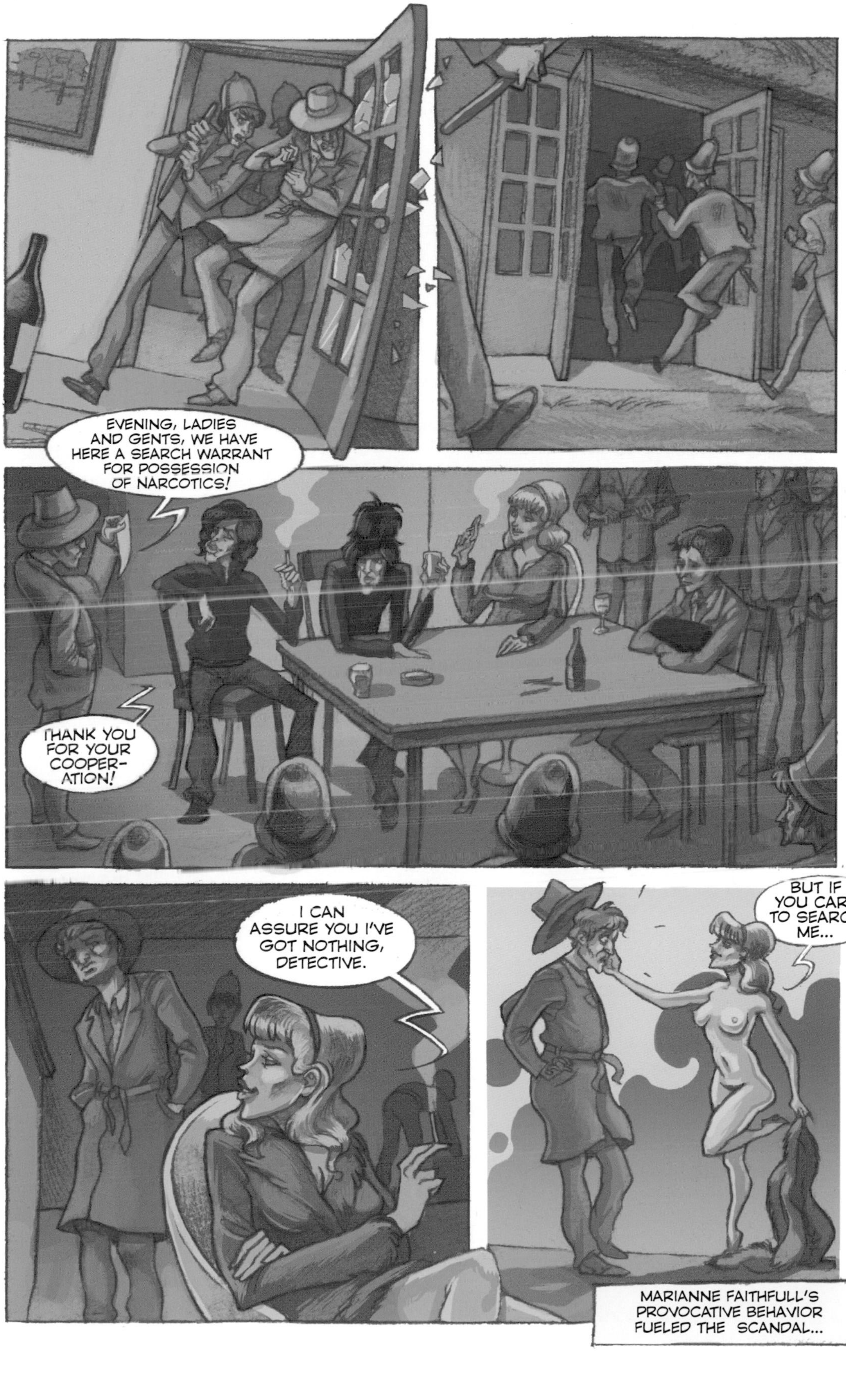
EVENING, LADIES AND GENTS, WE HAVE HERE A SEARCH WARRANT FOR POSSESSION OF NARCOTICS!
THANK YOU FOR YOUR COOPER-ATION!
I CAN ASSURE YOU I'VE GOT NOTHING, DETECTIVE.
BUT IF YOU CARE TO SEARCH ME...
MARIANNE FAITHFULL'S PROVOCATIVE BEHAVIOR FUELED THE SCANDAL...

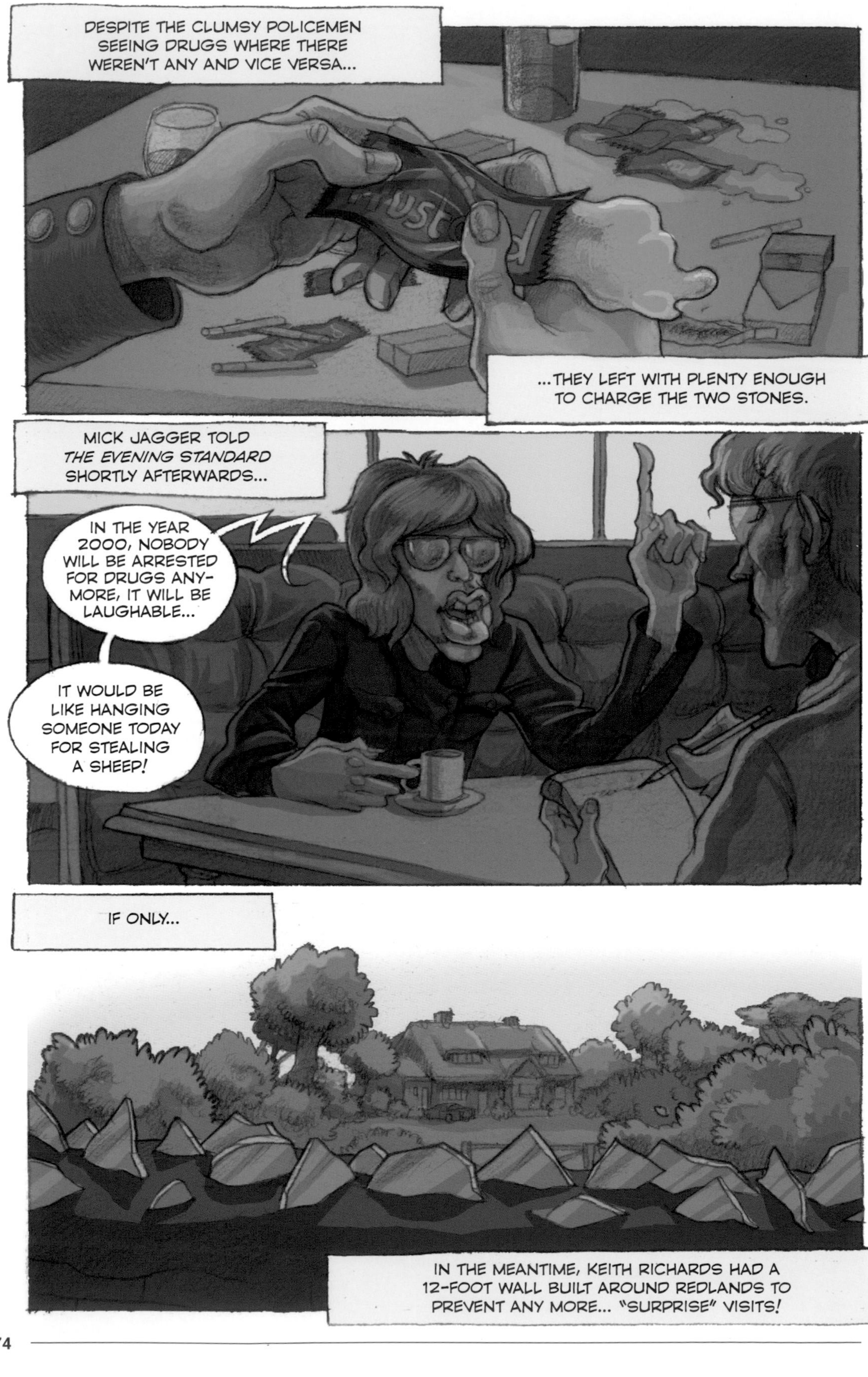
DESPITE THE CLUMSY POLICEMEN SEEING DRUGS WHERE THERE WEREN'T ANY AND VICE VERSA...
...THEY LEFT WITH PLENTY ENOUGH TO CHARGE THE TWO STONES.
MICK JAGGER TOLD *THE EVENING STANDARD* SHORTLY AFTERWARDS...
IN THE YEAR 2000, NOBODY WILL BE ARRESTED FOR DRUGS ANY-MORE, IT WILL BE LAUGHABLE...
IT WOULD BE LIKE HANGING SOMEONE TODAY FOR STEALING A SHEEP!
IF ONLY...
IN THE MEANTIME, KEITH RICHARDS HAD A 12-FOOT WALL BUILT AROUND REDLANDS TO PREVENT ANY MORE... "SURPRISE" VISITS!

Rock and Role?

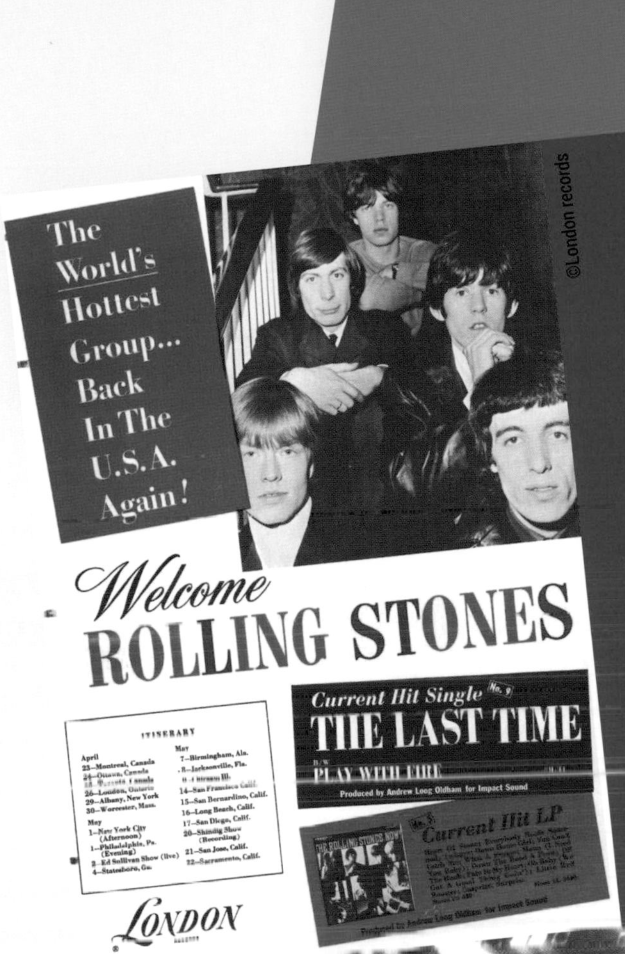

The World's Hottest Group... Back In The U.S.A. Again!
Welcome
ROLLING STONES
Current Hit Single No. 9
THE LAST TIME
b/w
PLAY WITH FIRE
Produced by Andrew Loog Oldham for Impact Sound
Current Hit LP
LONDON

With their rugged music, crass lyrics, insolent attitude, subversive speak and wild outfits, the Rolling Stones embodied the counter-culture movement. They symbolized young people's desire for social, intellectual and sexual emancipation. Yet underneath that rebel exterior there lurked the souls of socialites...

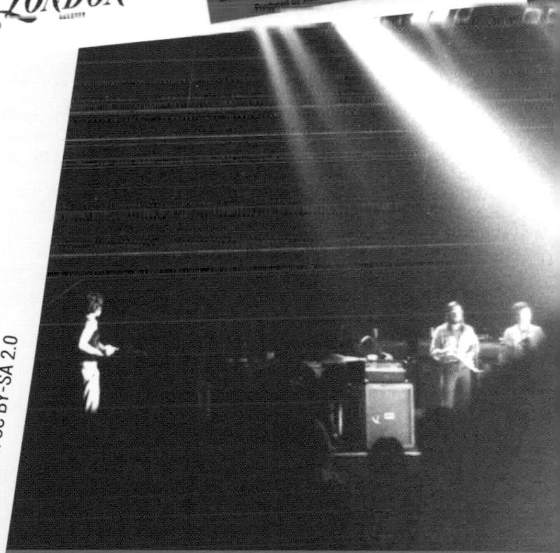

Up until June 1963, the Stones played essentially at home, i.e. at their regular venues in the greater London area. But with the "package tours" devised by Eason and Oldham, from 1963 to 1966 they were almost constantly on stage. Picture this: between July 13 and September 28, 1963, they performed in concert seventy-eight times, in the space of... seventy-six days. They appeared on four TV shows and they did two recording sessions and three photo shoots. When did they ever rest? Never! Which explains why they started popping pills to help fight the urge to sleep. And if that wasn't enough, Andrew was there to supply them with quaaludes, Demerol and other miracle "cures." This was only the beginning. Package tours were collective tours where the order of appearance on the poster reflected the various levels of fame. The Rolling Stones started out at the bottom of the poster.

Just being part of these tours was a significant step up for them, as they were lucky to rub shoulders with some of the top performers of the day, including the Everly Brothers, Bo Diddley, their idol, and Little Richard. Thanks to their musical prowess, the Stones went on to become the headliners after just a few months, finally acquiring notoriety at the national level, even though magazines were still very skeptical about their outlandish style. This was when the first public scandals broke out...

No doubt about it: the Rolling Stones were anti-establishment. As for the frustrations and privations of the post-war period, enough! They wanted to take a huge bite out of life and suck the marrow from all angles. "Under the paved streets there lay rage," according to the French expression of the uprising of May 1968. The rage of freedom. However, while they were the standard-bearers of this movement of change, they didn't have a true political message like artists such as Bob Dylan or The Who did. Nevertheless, it was the Rolling Stones that Jean-Luc Godard called on to carry on the struggle of May 1968 via other means. At the time they worked together on *One Plus One*, the band had already integrated the Jet Set scene of Swinging London, even though they kept on portraying themselves as bad boys on stage.

But how did they actually feel about the revolution? They did release "Street Fighting Man," which was deeply inspired by the uprising in May 1968 in France. Mick Jagger did take part in a demonstration, and for a while he let the rumor circulate that he wanted to run for Parliament as MP with the Labour Party. Naturally, they were all for the decriminalization of drugs. Naturally, they fought for sexual liberation, never hesitating to give of their bodies. Free love? Sure they were in favor of freely loving who they

wanted... more out of a sense of entitlement than out of devotion to a cause, though. **They may have been rebels in spirit, but they became socialites in real life.** Bad boys perhaps, but dandies first and foremost. When Mick Jagger ordered a Chateau Mouton Rothschild 1939 one day in an upscale restaurant, Keith Richards grabbed it and drank it straight from the bottle. **The Rolling Stones never wanted to change the world. Only to free it.**

"MICK SEES HIMSELF AS THE LEADER OF SOME SORT OF WORKING CLASS REVOLUTION. BUT HOW COULD HE BE, WHEN HE LIVES IN A 40-ROOM MANSION AND DRIVES A ROLLS-ROYCE."

John Peel, DJ

Mick Jagger and Ron Wood in concert in Turin in 1982 ©Gorup de Besanez CC BY SA 3.0

"ROCK HAS BECOME THE VEHICLE FOR A KIND OF SECULAR EVANGELIZATION
IN WHICH THE GOSPEL OF THE FULFILLMENT OF FREE LOVE HAS
TAKEN PRECEDENCE OVER THE PROHIBITIONS OF THE DECALOGUE."

Prince Rupert Loewenstein

Knebworth Fair, 1976 ©Richard Humphrey CC BY-SA 2.0

Rebel in a Bentley

Artist: Lapuss

Mick Jagger,
the Richest Hippie in England.

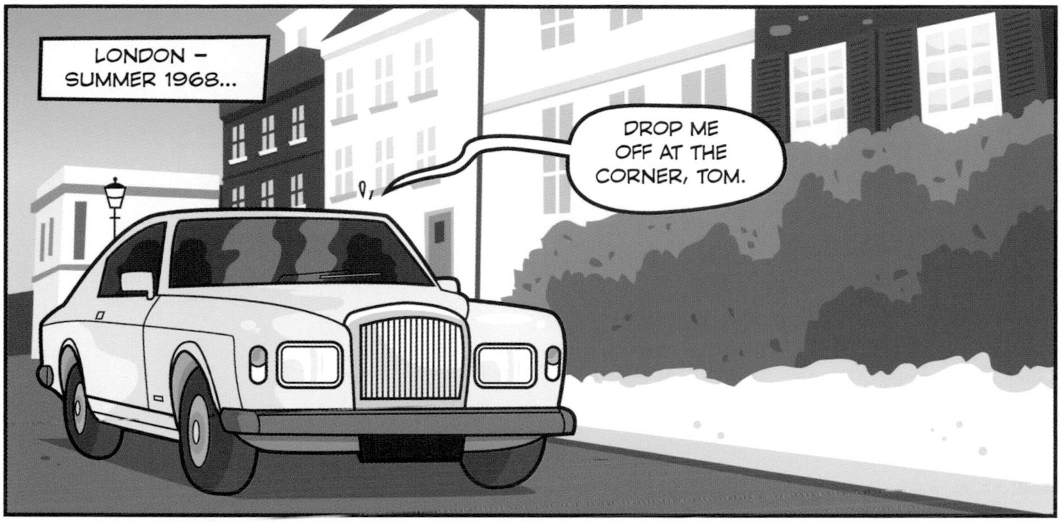
LONDON – SUMMER 1968...
DROP ME OFF AT THE CORNER, TOM.

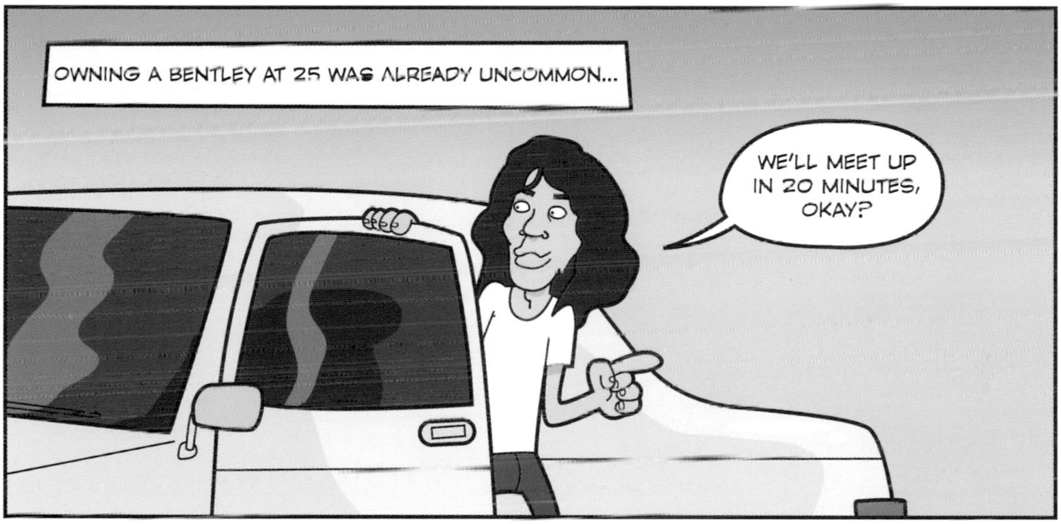
OWNING A BENTLEY AT 25 WAS ALREADY UNCOMMON...
WE'LL MEET UP IN 20 MINUTES, OKAY?

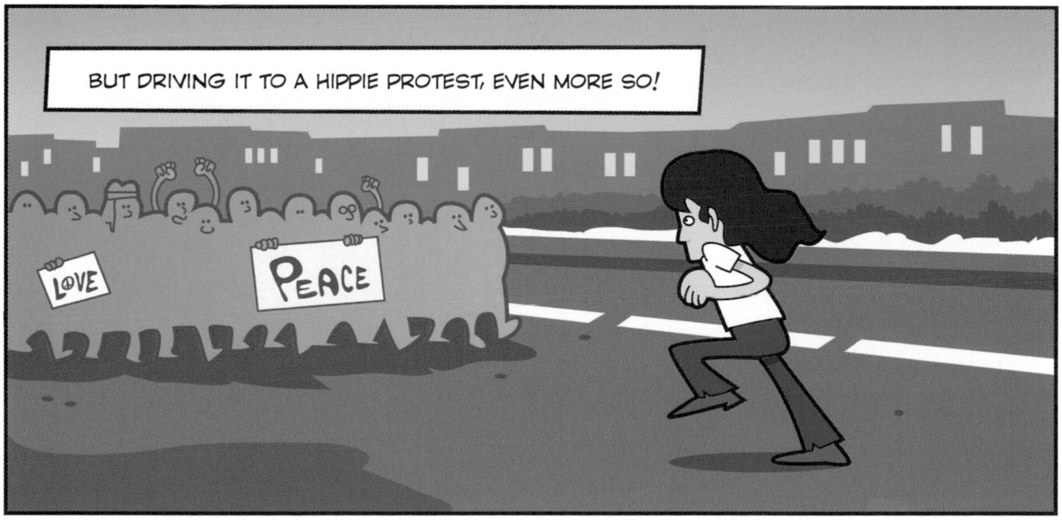
BUT DRIVING IT TO A HIPPIE PROTEST, EVEN MORE SO!
LOVE
PEACE

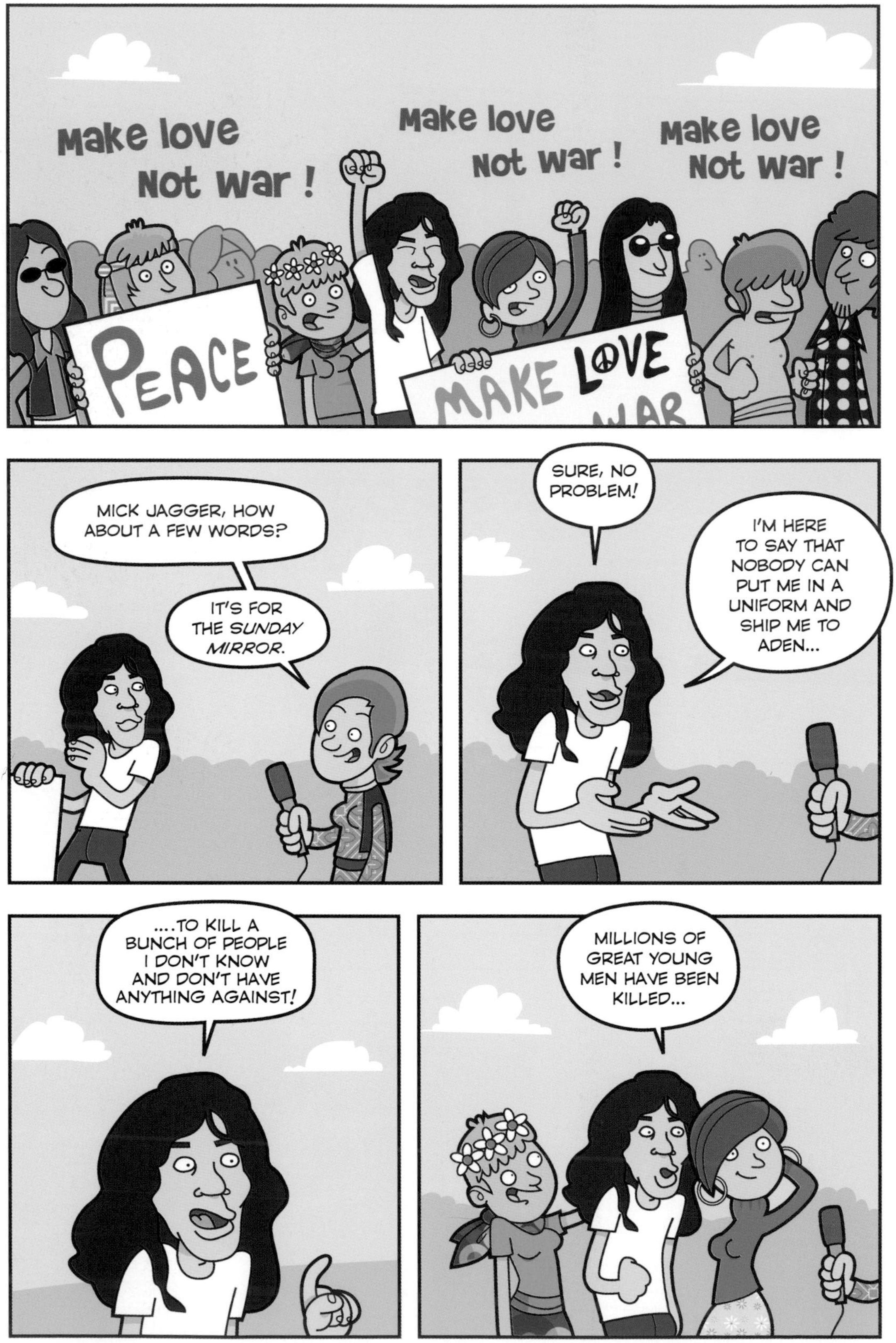

Make love Not war !
Make love Not war !
Make love Not war !
PEACE
MAKE LOVE
MICK JAGGER, HOW ABOUT A FEW WORDS?
IT'S FOR THE *SUNDAY MIRROR*.
SURE, NO PROBLEM!
I'M HERE TO SAY THAT NOBODY CAN PUT ME IN A UNIFORM AND SHIP ME TO ADEN...
....TO KILL A BUNCH OF PEOPLE I DON'T KNOW AND DON'T HAVE ANYTHING AGAINST!
MILLIONS OF GREAT YOUNG MEN HAVE BEEN KILLED...

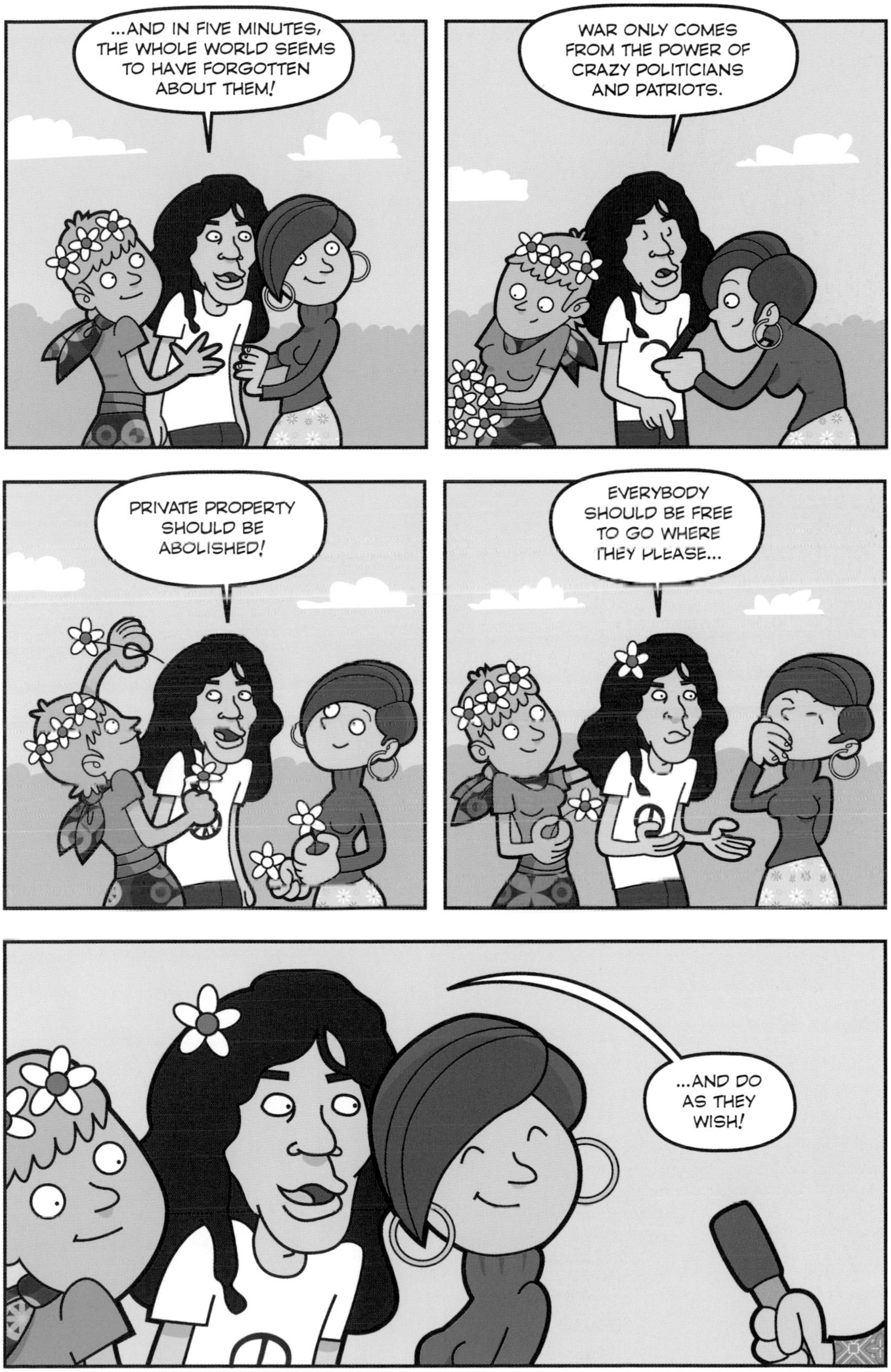
...AND IN FIVE MINUTES, THE WHOLE WORLD SEEMS TO HAVE FORGOTTEN ABOUT THEM!
WAR ONLY COMES FROM THE POWER OF CRAZY POLITICIANS AND PATRIOTS.
PRIVATE PROPERTY SHOULD BE ABOLISHED!
EVERYBODY SHOULD BE FREE TO GO WHERE THEY PLEASE...
...AND DO AS THEY WISH!

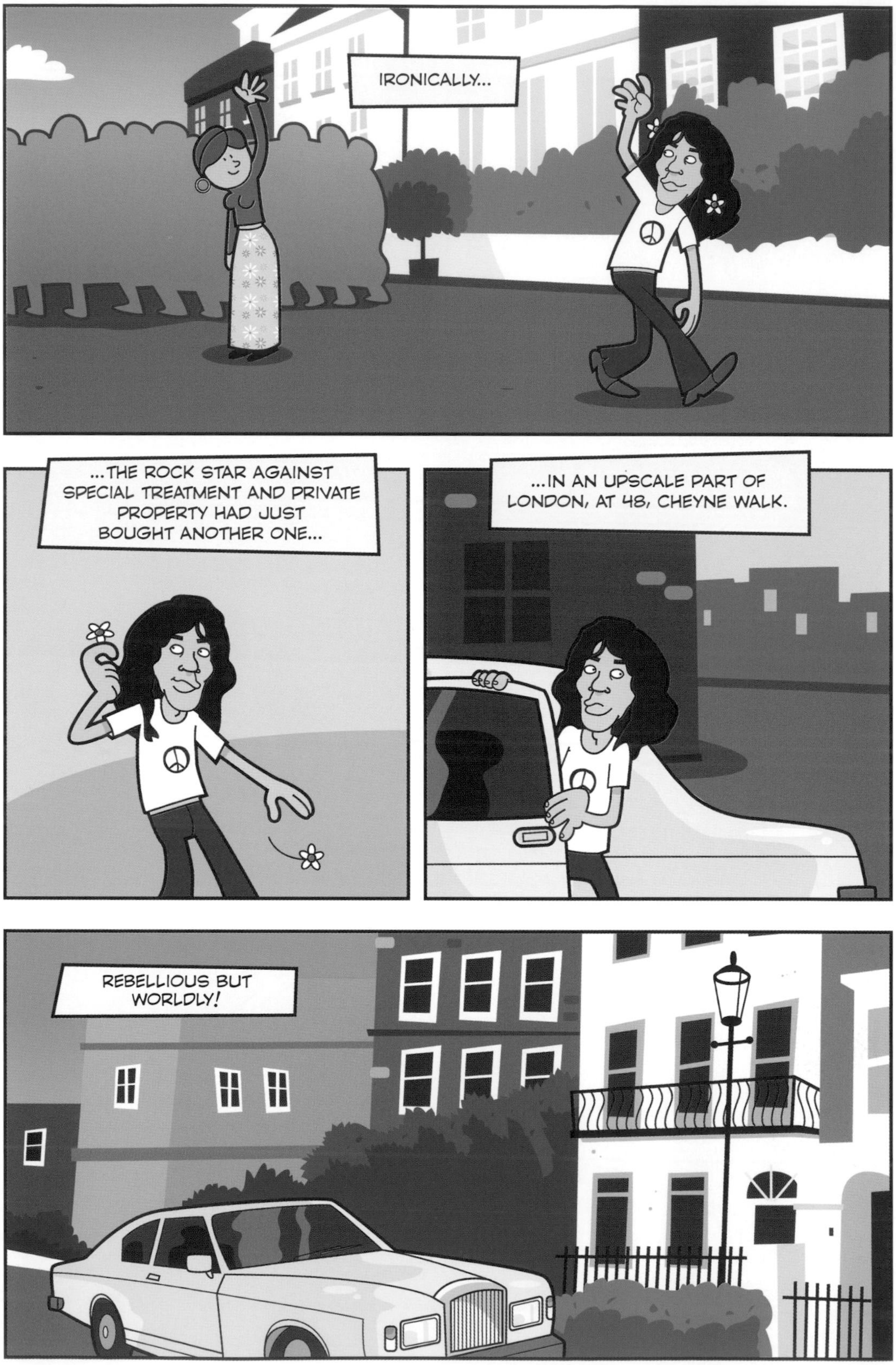
IRONICALLY...
...THE ROCK STAR AGAINST SPECIAL TREATMENT AND PRIVATE PROPERTY HAD JUST BOUGHT ANOTHER ONE...
...IN AN UPSCALE PART OF LONDON, AT 48, CHEYNE WALK.
REBELLIOUS BUT WORLDLY!

Light Hair
and Dark Thoughts

As *Rolling Stone* magazine aptly put it after the death of Brian Jones: "If Keith and Mick were the body and spirit of the Stones, Brian, assuredly, was its soul." The whole idea of the band was his; then it became an obsession followed by a source of frustration and, ultimately, a mortal wound. As Bill Wyman would say, "While we all got roughed up, one way or another, by the Rolling Stones, Brian was the only one who didn't make it out alive."

Brian Jones in 1967 ©Ber Merk (ANEFO) CC BY-SA 3.0

On July 3, 1969, the news hit like a ton of bricks: Brian Jones was found dead, having drowned in the pool at his house in Hartfield, Sussex. What happened that night of July 2? Why had he felt the urge to take a dip? Did he have an asthma attack or a dizzy spell? Or was he murdered, as some rumors would have it? Why wasn't anyone able to rescue him in time? Questions that will likely remain forever unanswered. **The official cause of death following an inquest was death by drowning, ingestion of narcotics and liver degeneration.**

> "BRIAN WASN'T COMFORTABLE IN HIS OWN SKIN, AND THAT CAUSED HIM SUFFERING; HE WANTED ALL EYES ON HIM, BUT THAT WASN'T THE CASE. ONE OF THE THINGS HE SUFFERED FROM THE MOST, AND WHICH LEAD TO HIS DOWNFALL, WAS THAT HE WANTED TO BE THE LEADER BUT DIDN'T HAVE THE TALENT FOR IT."

Charlie Watts

But how did he get to that point, to a death that was virtually predictable? In several stages... **Even though he was the Stones' first leader, the one who signed the contract with Decca, Brian Jones was quickly relegated to second fiddle.** When Oldham decided that the band needed to start writing its own songs, he chose the Richards—Jagger duo over Jones. He felt that Brian was an excellent musician but not a songwriter. He wasn't the only one. Others hinted at it too— or said it right to his face! That's when Mister Shampoo, as his partners used to ironically call him, started abusing alcohol and then drugs to greater and greater extremes.

It was a tragic downward spiral: he showed up less and less for band practice, sometimes disappearing for days at a time with nobody knowing where he was. He would sometimes, sporadically, contribute his own personal touch to some of the songs with his exotic instrumentation. As Mick Jagger once said about him, "Brian had the knack for capturing new sounds. That didn't work in his favor, in the end, but he was good at fiddling around with stuff." Keith Richards stabbed Brian Jones in the back when he took his latest girlfriend, Anita Pallenberg, for himself. Everything Jones cared about was slowly slipping through his fingers... At the same time, the police had finally managed to catch the blond angel on drug charges: he was sentenced to prison but after appealing the de-cision he was put on probation for three years. He was free on the condition that he went into psychiatric treatment. Shortly after that, he was arrested again on suspicion of marijuana possession. This time, there was no doubt about it: he would not be able to get a visa for the Stones' U.S. tour. In other words, he basically signed his own death sentence, at least with respect to the band. The legal harassment seemed to destroy him. Just looking at the recording sessions for "Sympathy for the Devil," in Godard's film *One Plus One*, you can tell that already, he was nothing more than a tragic version of his former self.

> "BRIAN WAS INCAPABLE OF WRITING SONGS. EVERYTHING WAS WORKING AGAINST HIM: HIS INNER TURMOIL, HIS SADNESS, HIS LACK OF SELF-CONFIDENCE. IT WAS TRAGIC BECAUSE WHAT HE WANTED MOST OF ALL WAS TO BE A SONGWRITER. I SAW HIM STRUGGLE WITH IT PAINFULLY. HE WOULD MUTTER A FEW WORDS TO A TUNE AND THEN THROW DOWN HIS GUITAR OUT OF FRUSTRATION."

Marianne Faithfull

The Rolling Stones decided to part ways with him on June 8, 1969. Mick, Keith and Charlie went to his house to tell him the news. Charlie Watts would later describe that as "the worst thing I had ever had to do up until then." The official reason for the split was "artistic differences," an expression coined for the occasion. But his replacement was already lurking in the shadows. Brian Jones really did go off the deep end, and this time, he wasn't coming back up...

"THERE IS A DEMON IN ME, BUT JUST ONE. BRIAN
PROBABLY HAD ABOUT FORTY-FIVE OF THEM."

Keith Richards

Anita Pallenberg ©Vikki Blondie

"BRIAN AND I BOTH KNEW HE WOULDN'T LIVE LONG. I REMEMBER
TELLING HIM: 'YOU'LL NEVER MAKE IT TO THIRTY, MATE.'
AND HE SAID: 'I KNOW!'"

Keith Richards

Fallen Angel

Artist: Bast

1969: Brian Jones' Death by Drowning
Marks a Turning Point in the Life of the Stones.

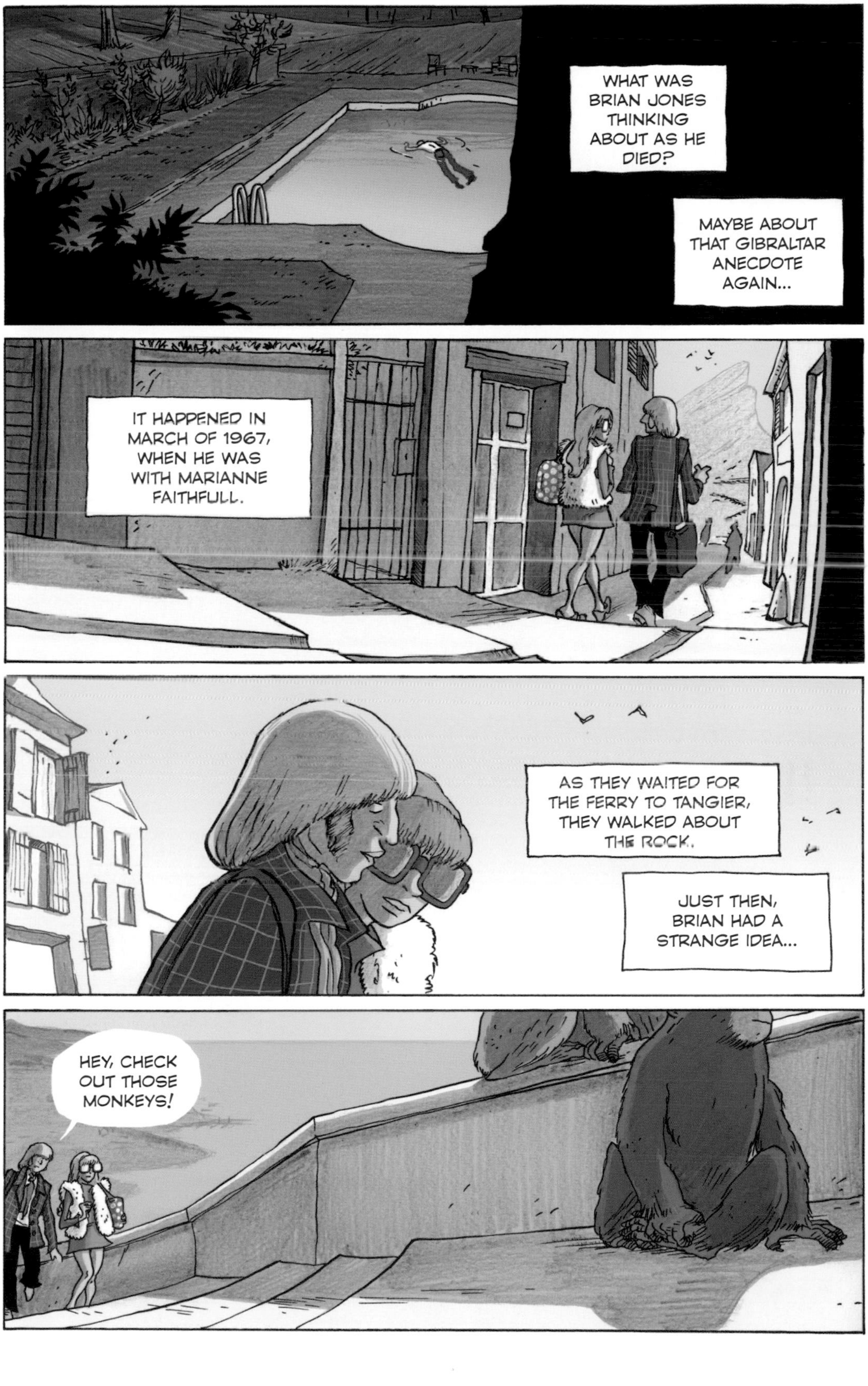
WHAT WAS BRIAN JONES THINKING ABOUT AS HE DIED?
MAYBE ABOUT THAT GIBRALTAR ANECDOTE AGAIN...
IT HAPPENED IN MARCH OF 1967, WHEN HE WAS WITH MARIANNE FAITHFULL.
AS THEY WAITED FOR THE FERRY TO TANGIER, THEY WALKED ABOUT THE ROCK.
JUST THEN, BRIAN HAD A STRANGE IDEA...
HEY, CHECK OUT THOSE MONKEYS!

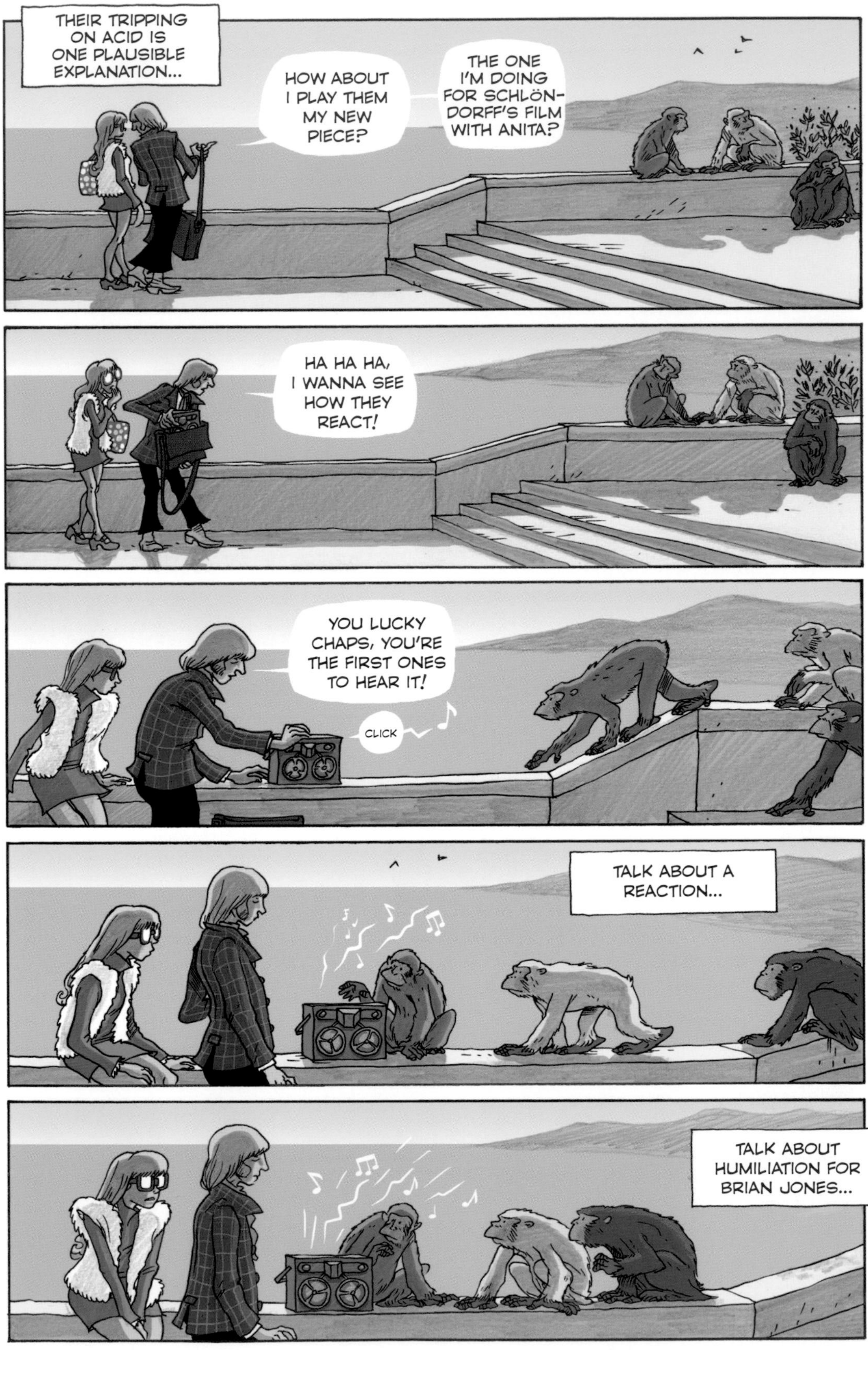

THEIR TRIPPING ON ACID IS ONE PLAUSIBLE EXPLANATION...
HOW ABOUT I PLAY THEM MY NEW PIECE?
THE ONE I'M DOING FOR SCHLÖNDORFF'S FILM WITH ANITA?
HA HA HA, I WANNA SEE HOW THEY REACT!
YOU LUCKY CHAPS, YOU'RE THE FIRST ONES TO HEAR IT!
CLICK
TALK ABOUT A REACTION...
TALK ABOUT HUMILIATION FOR BRIAN JONES...

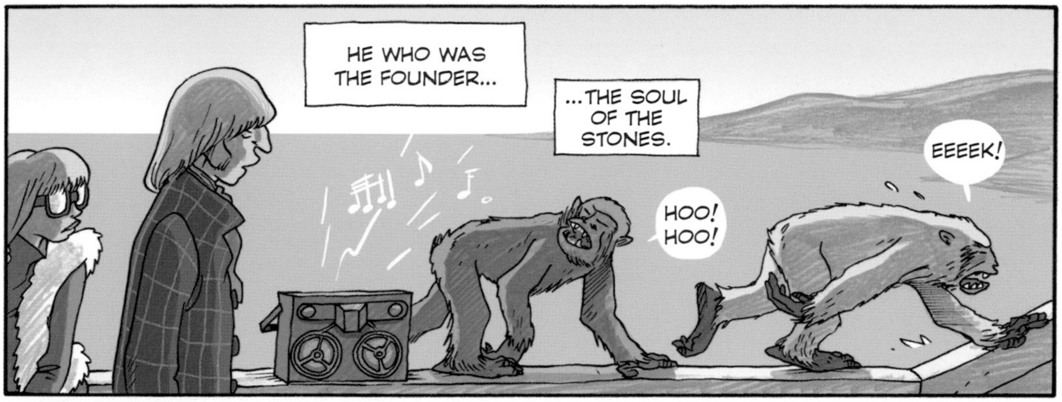
HE WHO WAS THE FOUNDER...
...THE SOUL OF THE STONES.
HOO! HOO!
EEEEK!

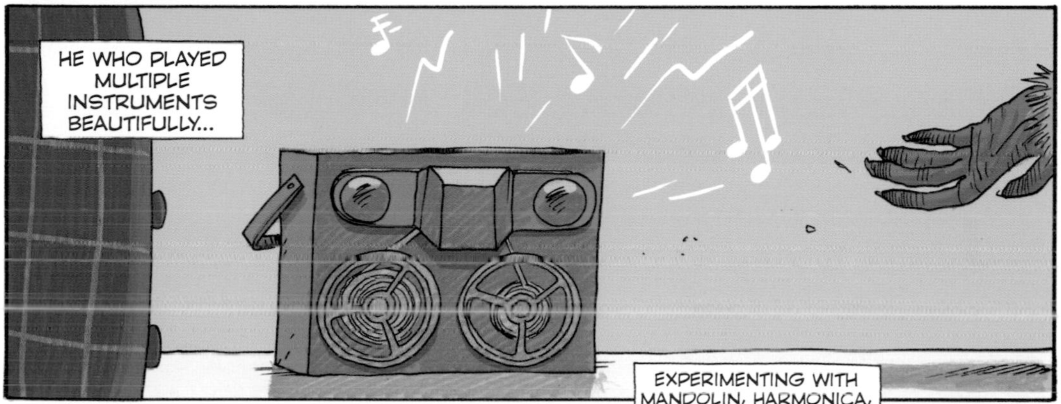
HE WHO PLAYED MULTIPLE INSTRUMENTS BEAUTIFULLY...
EXPERIMENTING WITH MANDOLIN, HARMONICA, SITAR, MELLOTRON, HARPSICHORD...

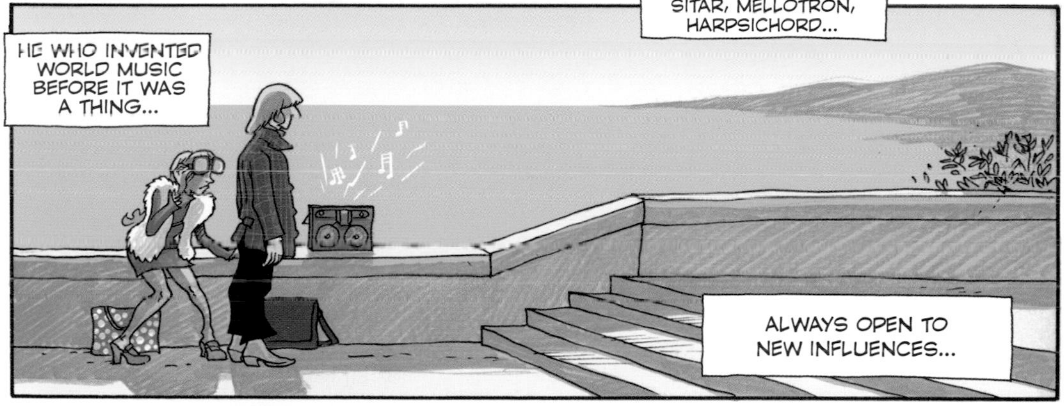
HE WHO INVENTED WORLD MUSIC BEFORE IT WAS A THING...
ALWAYS OPEN TO NEW INFLUENCES...

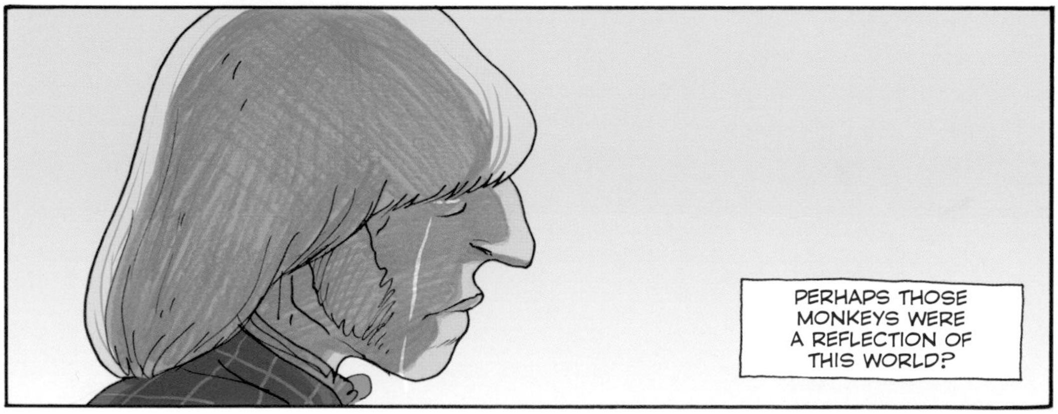
PERHAPS THOSE MONKEYS WERE A REFLECTION OF THIS WORLD?

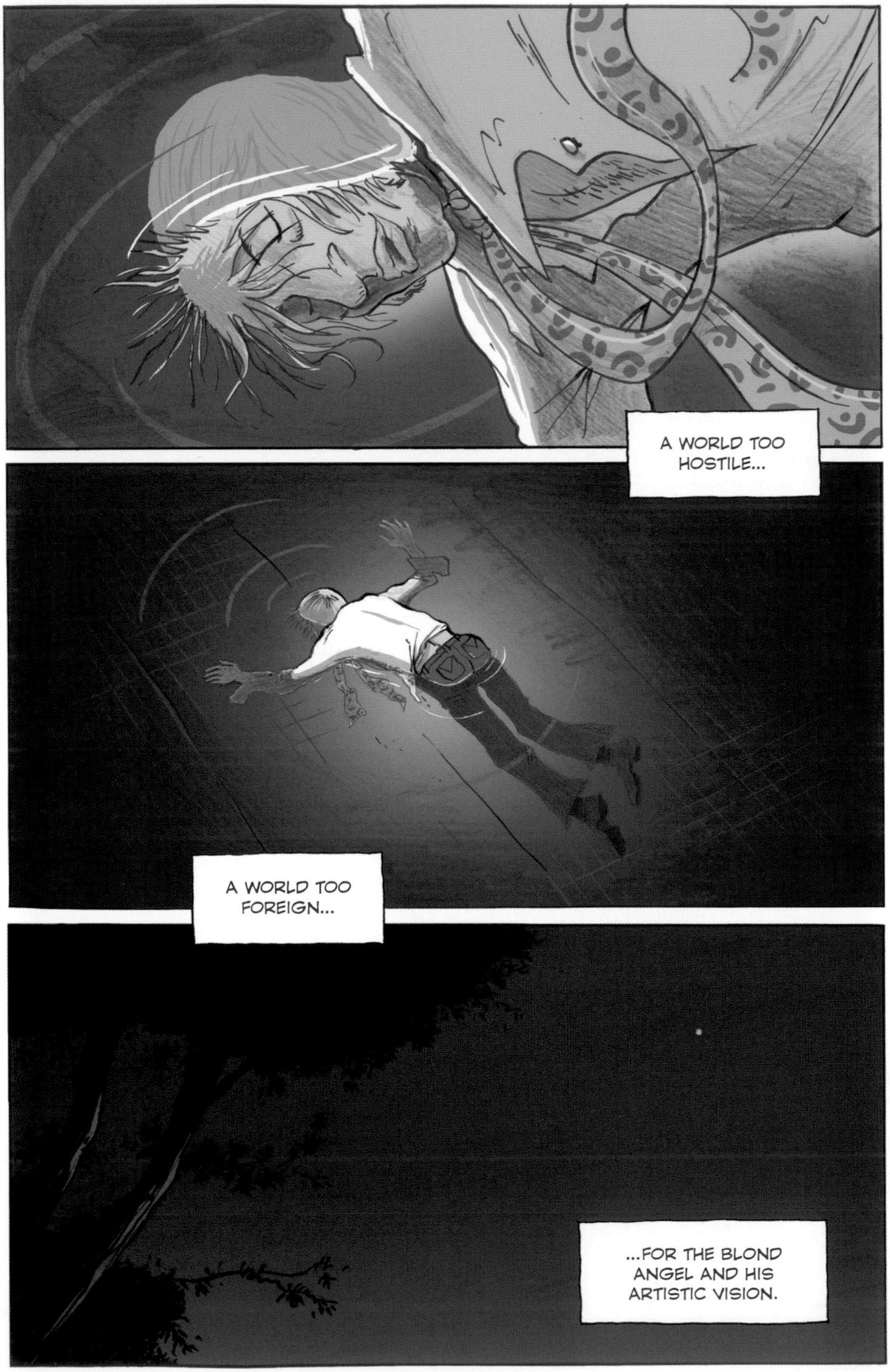
A WORLD TOO HOSTILE...
A WORLD TOO FOREIGN...
...FOR THE BLOND ANGEL AND HIS ARTISTIC VISION.

Back to the Future

Brian's death was the catalyst for rebooting a band in the throes of self-doubt. The future, of course, meant the arrival of young virtuoso Mick Taylor, who replaced Brian on guitar. It also meant touring again, which fans had been eagerly waiting for. "Back" meant a return to the blues for Keith Richards, who began using the open tuning approach, i.e. open chords. **The band was breaking a new sound barrier.**

The Rolling Stones had planned on doing a free London concert in Hyde Park. With Brian Jones' sudden passing, they weren't sure whether to cancel or not. They decided not to, in honor of their former partner. And so, on July 5, 1969, they walked on stage before a crowd of about 300,000 people. Mick started off by reading a poem by Percy Shelley titled "Adonais" in memory of Brian, as clouds of white butterflies were released into the air. The band hadn't toured in a while and so the Hyde Park concert didn't go down in history as a milestone event, but it was the perfect time to introduce the new Stone: Mick Taylor.

Bill Wyman in 1975 ©Jim Summaria CC BY-SA 3.0.jpg

"THEY MET WITH STAGGERING SUCCESS BY PREACHING MACHISMO, SEX, FREEDOM, AND VIOLENT REVOLUTION."

New York Daily News

Mick Taylor ®Dina Regine CC BY SA 2.0

"MICK TAYLOR SHOWED UP AND
PLAYED LIKE AN ANGEL. I WASN'T
ABOUT TO SAY NO."

Keith Richards

"Who's that guitar player? Born on January 17, 1949, in Welwyn Garden City, he was only twenty when he joined the Stones. In other words, he was a baby compared to the other bandmembers. There was a half-generation age gap between him and Bill Wyman! Case in point: **they quickly nicknamed him The Kid.** That difference in both age and personality with Wyman partly explains why things had never really gelled before in the band. Creative frustrations and drugs account for the rest. Despite his young age, Mick Taylor already had a reputation as a virtuoso lead guitarist, having started out with John Mayalle and the Bluesbreakers, like Eric Clapton and Peter Green before him.

For the Rolling Stones, this meant a new start with a fresh sound.

In fact, during that transition period from 1967 to 1969, Keith Richards went back to music lessons and studied the secrets of open tuning with Ry Cooder. That way of playing the guitar with open chords comes from the blues. It involves de-tuning a guitar for easier positioning of the fingers to make a chord. With that kind of tuning, you can get a more or less full chord with a simple barred chord. The first and memorable song played using the open tuning method was "Jumpin' Jack Flash." Bill Wyman actually composed the original riff, but didn't receive credit for it.

Many more followed, including "Honky Tonk Women," "Brown Sugar," and "Start Me Up." To play with open chords, Keith Richards' instrument of choice was a Fender Telecaster Custom.

Now that the band was fully assembled, they could get to work. The Rolling Stones were dying to get back on stage again and went on an exhilarating four-week tour in the U.S. Tickets for all twenty-three concerts sold out in a few hours and additional shows had to be added in New York and L.A. **That tour broke all previous attendance records, including the one held by the Beatles for their concert at the Forum in L.A.**

"IT WAS LIKE A PHOENIX RISING
FROM THE ASHES FOR THE BAND.
THE 1969 U.S. TOUR WAS OUR
FIRST RESURRECTION."

Keith Richards

Rarely was the band so in tune with their fans as they were then, thanks to Mick Jagger's electric stage presence as he matured into a charismatic performer and to lyrics to songs such as "You Can't Always Get What You Want" and

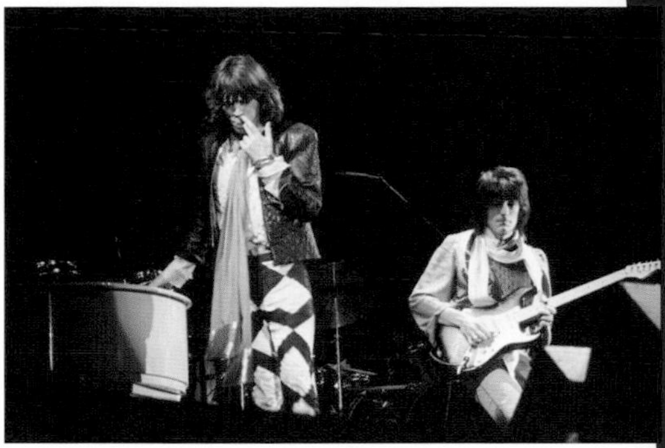

The Hague, 1976 ©Ben Verhoeff CC BY SA 3.0

"Sympathy For The Devil," which young people then really connected with. The media were now on track and referring to the Rolling Stones as the greatest rock-and-roll band in the world. When one reporter asked Mick Jagger: "'Satisfaction' is one of your biggest hits. Have you yourself found that satisfaction in the meantime?" Without missing a beat, he shot back: **"Sexually, yes. Financially, no. Philosophically, I'm still trying."**

"THOSE NEW WAYS OF TUNING FORCED KEITH TO LEARN NEW GUITAR CHORDS AND EVENTUALLY LED TO A NEW WAY OF COMPOSING. GOING BACK TO RIFFS AGAIN FOR MANY OF THEIR NEW SONGS, RICHARDS AND THE STONES DEVELOPED A NEW STYLE THAT HELPED PROPEL ROCK MUSIC INTO THE MODERN ERA."

Rob Bowman

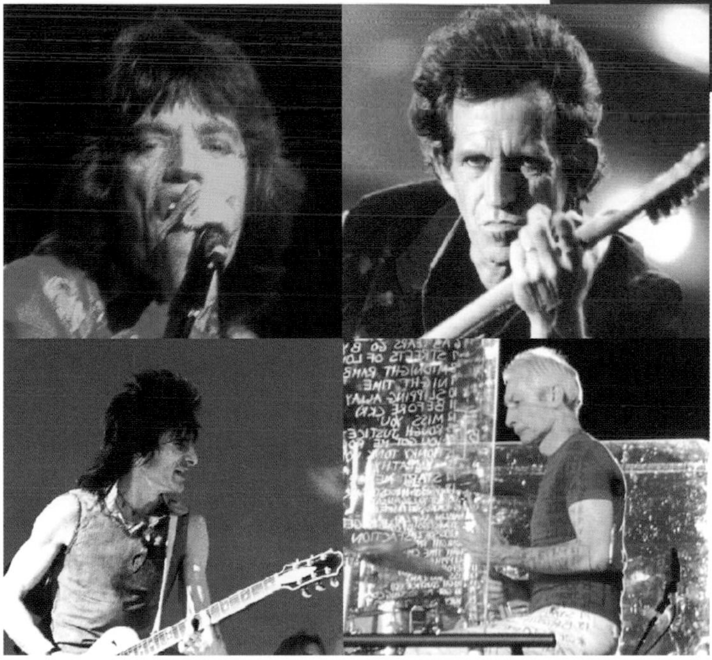

Mick Jagger, Keith Richards, Ron Wood and Charlie Watts ©Larry Rogers CC BY 3

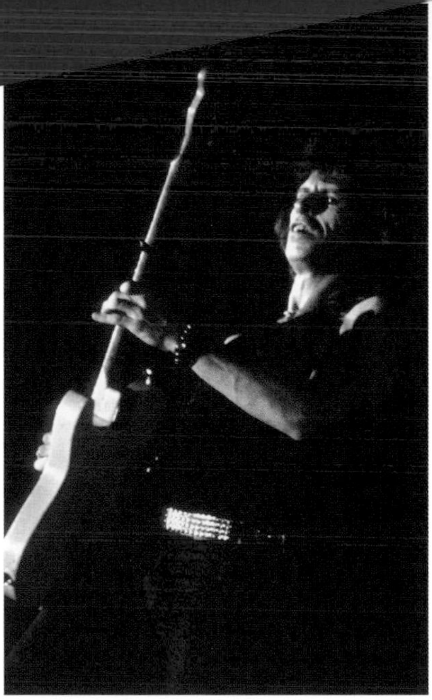

Open Tuning

Artist: Patès

A Pro Explains the Open Chord Technique,
Keith Richards' Trademark.

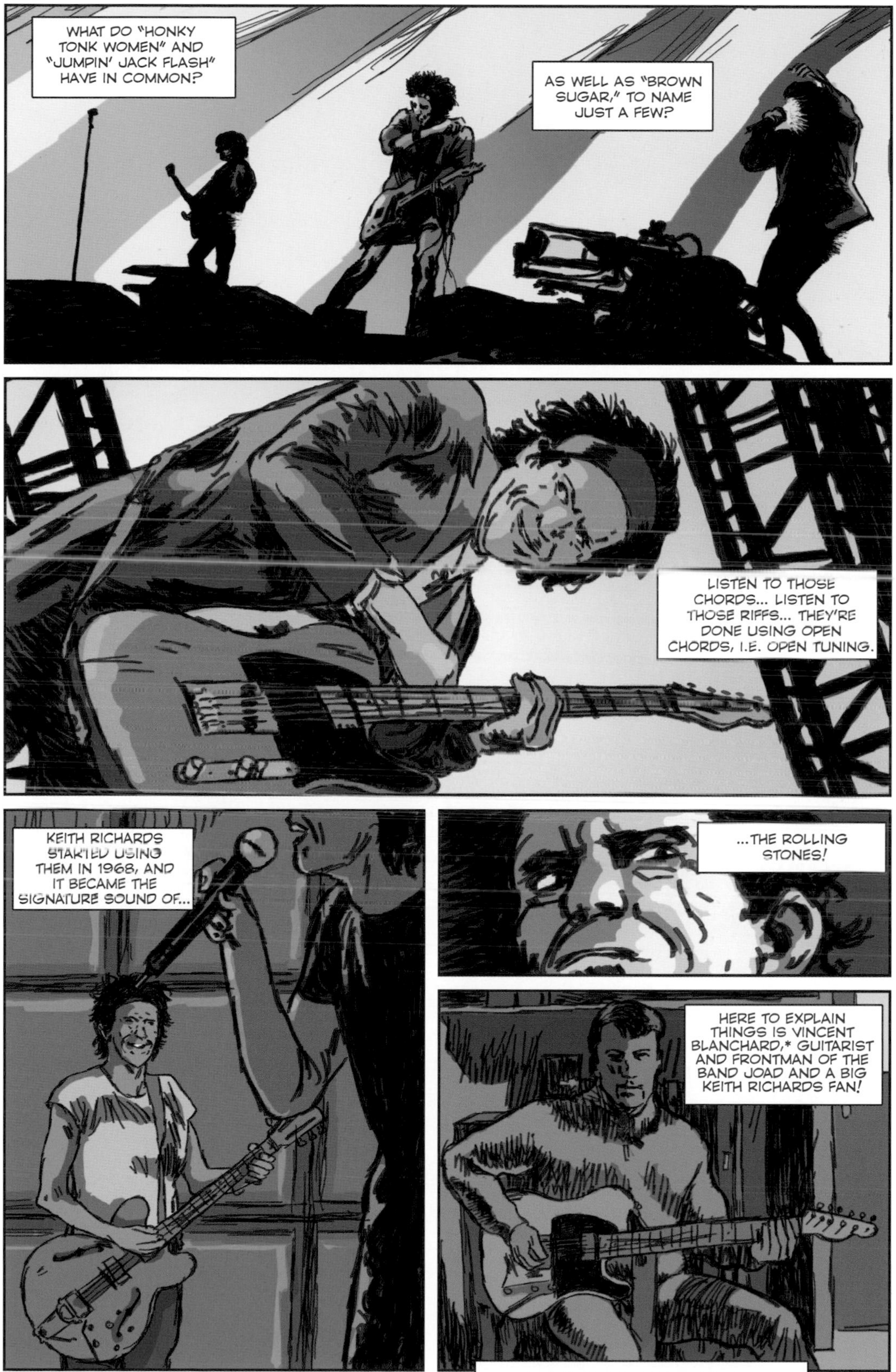
WHAT DO "HONKY TONK WOMEN" AND "JUMPIN' JACK FLASH" HAVE IN COMMON?
AS WELL AS "BROWN SUGAR," TO NAME JUST A FEW?
LISTEN TO THOSE CHORDS... LISTEN TO THOSE RIFFS... THEY'RE DONE USING OPEN CHORDS, I.E. OPEN TUNING.
KEITH RICHARDS STARTED USING THEM IN 1968, AND IT BECAME THE SIGNATURE SOUND OF...
...THE ROLLING STONES!
HERE TO EXPLAIN THINGS IS VINCENT BLANCHARD,* GUITARIST AND FRONTMAN OF THE BAND JOAD AND A BIG KEITH RICHARDS FAN!
*MORE INFO AT: WWW.JOAD.FR

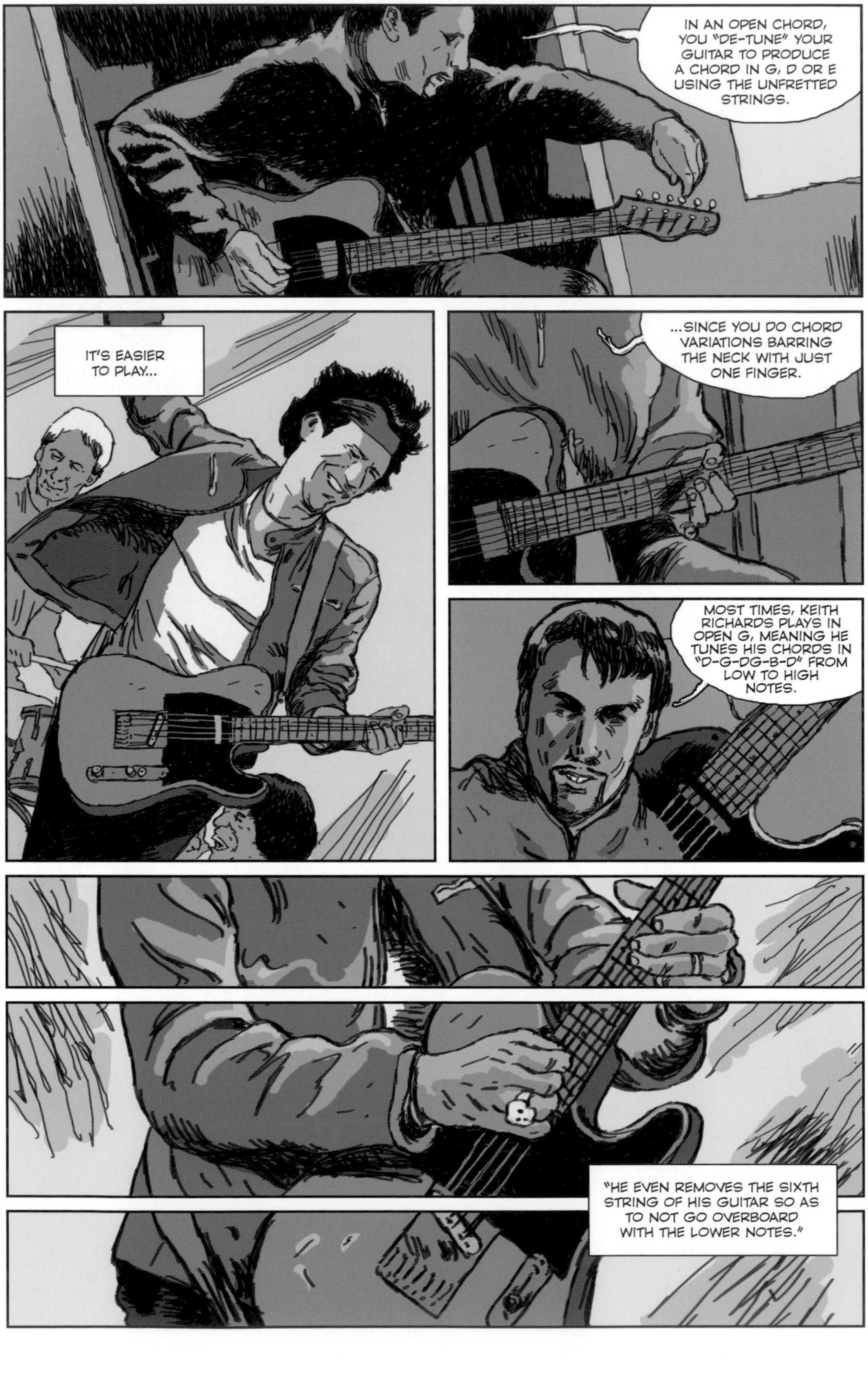
IN AN OPEN CHORD, YOU "DE-TUNE" YOUR GUITAR TO PRODUCE A CHORD IN G, D OR E USING THE UNFRETTED STRINGS.
IT'S EASIER TO PLAY...
...SINCE YOU DO CHORD VARIATIONS BARRING THE NECK WITH JUST ONE FINGER.
MOST TIMES, KEITH RICHARDS PLAYS IN OPEN G, MEANING HE TUNES HIS CHORDS IN "D-G-DG-B-D" FROM LOW TO HIGH NOTES.
"HE EVEN REMOVES THE SIXTH STRING OF HIS GUITAR SO AS TO NOT GO OVERBOARD WITH THE LOWER NOTES."

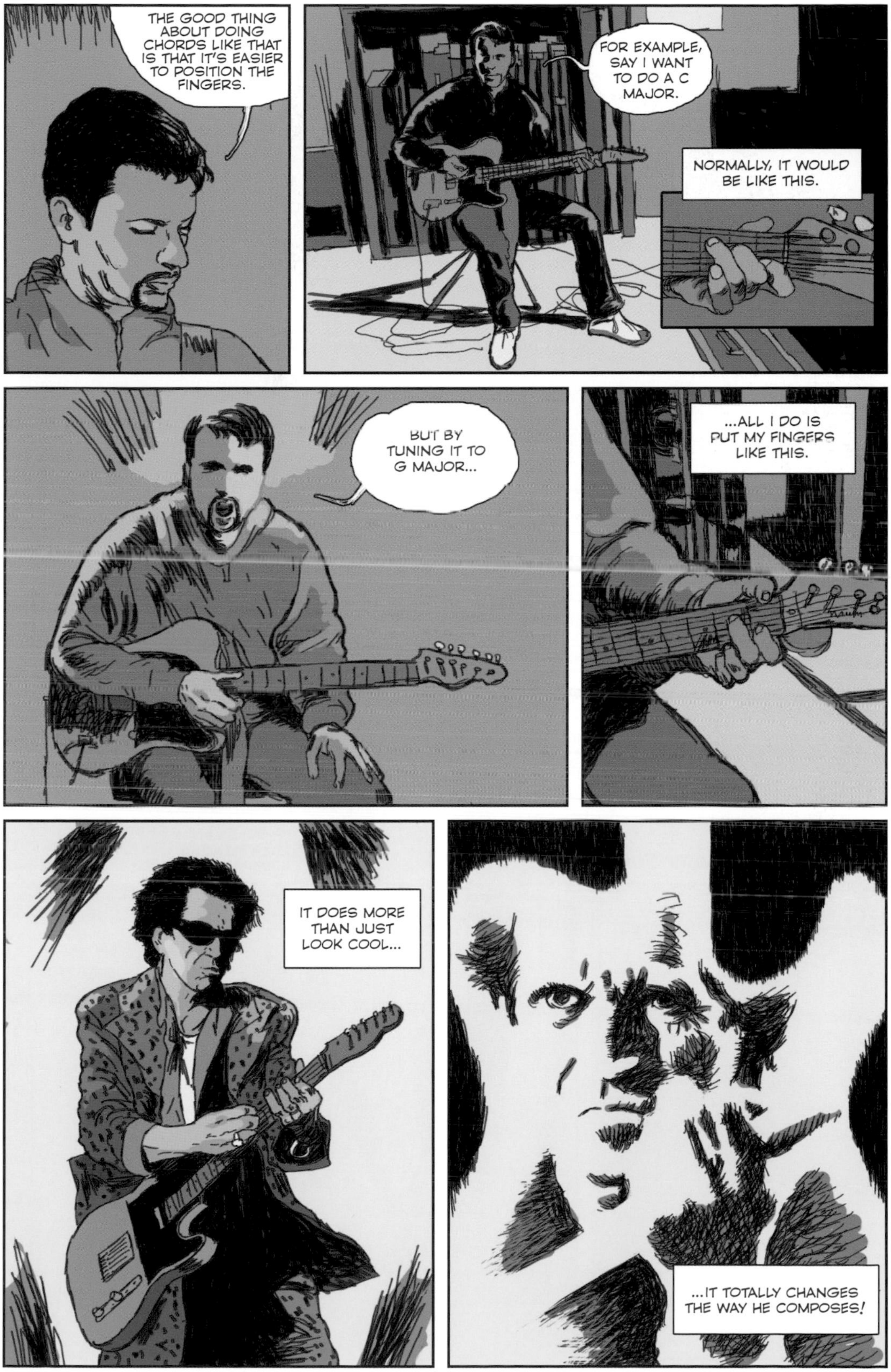
THE GOOD THING ABOUT DOING CHORDS LIKE THAT IS THAT IT'S EASIER TO POSITION THE FINGERS.
FOR EXAMPLE, SAY I WANT TO DO A C MAJOR.
NORMALLY, IT WOULD BE LIKE THIS.
BUT BY TUNING IT TO G MAJOR...
...ALL I DO IS PUT MY FINGERS LIKE THIS.
IT DOES MORE THAN JUST LOOK COOL...
...IT TOTALLY CHANGES THE WAY HE COMPOSES!

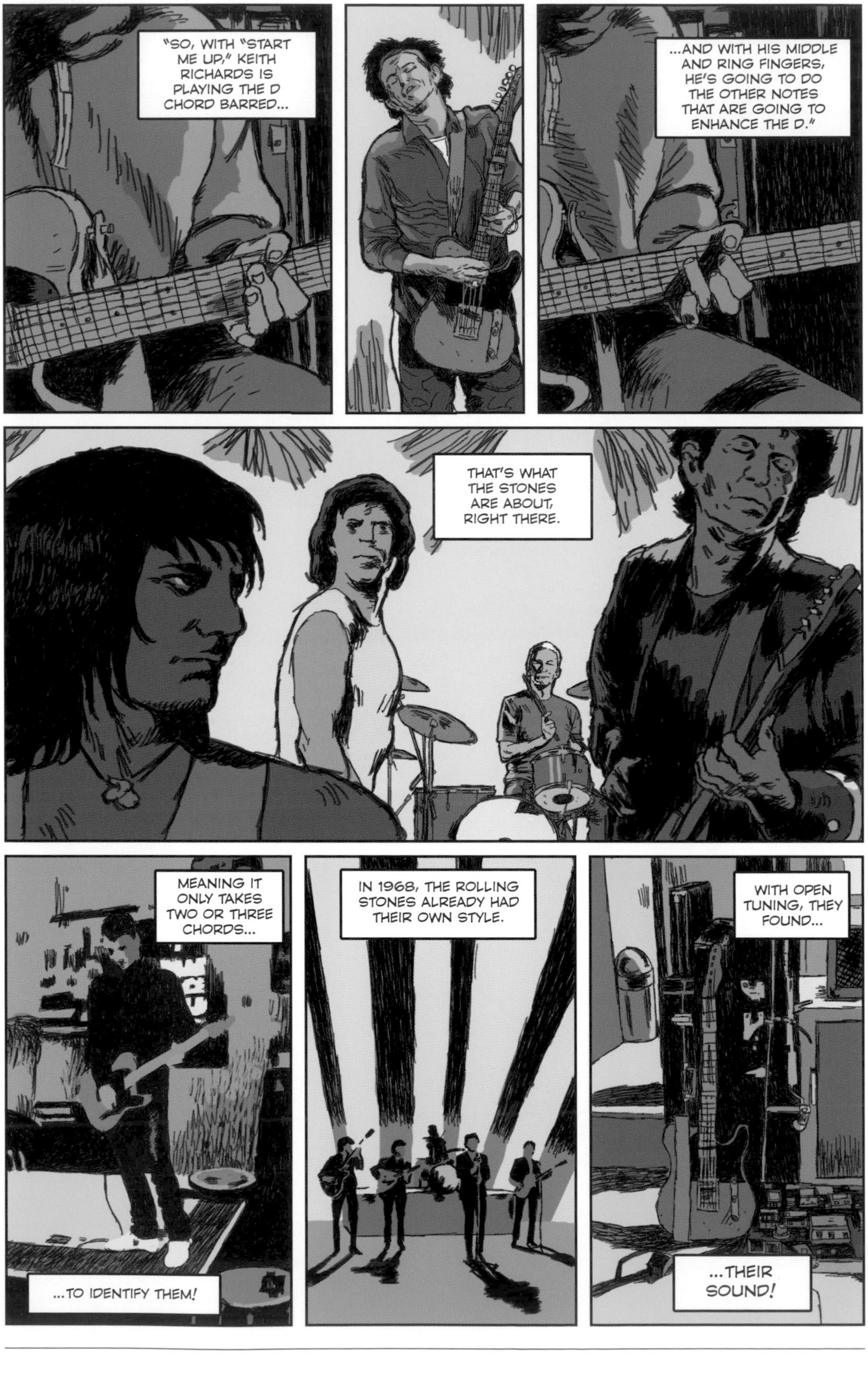
"SO, WITH "START ME UP," KEITH RICHARDS IS PLAYING THE D CHORD BARRED...
...AND WITH HIS MIDDLE AND RING FINGERS, HE'S GOING TO DO THE OTHER NOTES THAT ARE GOING TO ENHANCE THE D."
THAT'S WHAT THE STONES ARE ABOUT, RIGHT THERE.
MEANING IT ONLY TAKES TWO OR THREE CHORDS...
...TO IDENTIFY THEM!
IN 1968, THE ROLLING STONES ALREADY HAD THEIR OWN STYLE.
WITH OPEN TUNING, THEY FOUND...
...THEIR SOUND!

The End of the Sixties

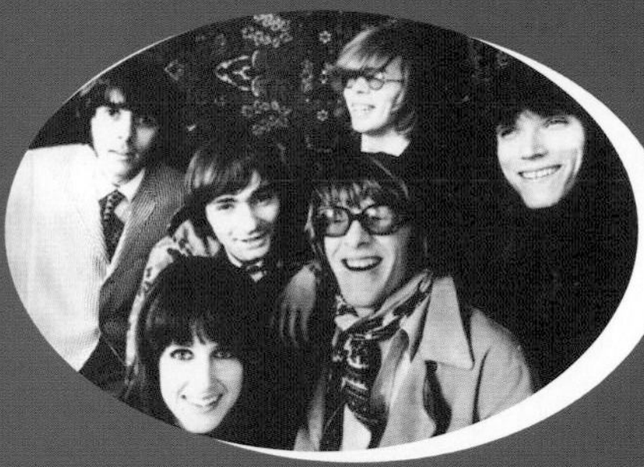

Jefferson Airplane in 1967 ©RCA Records

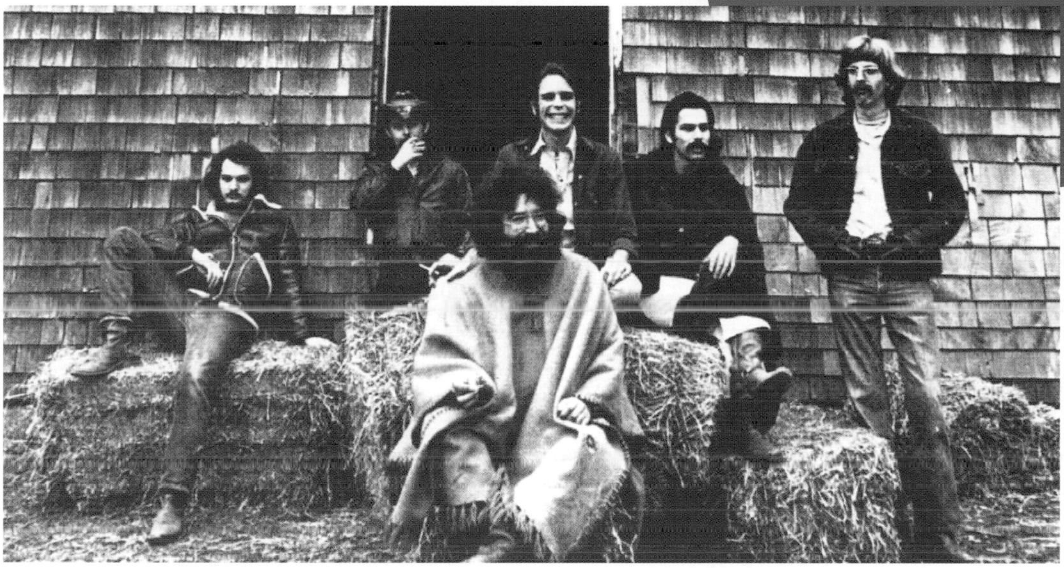

Grateful Dead (1970) ©Warner Bros. Records

The Rolling Stones were criticized by the press for the high cost of tickets on their U.S. tour. "Can the Rolling Stones actually need all that money?" a reporter was quoted as saying in a ***Rolling Stone*** magazine article titled "The Stones Tour: Is That a Lot?"
Odd, really, since ticket prices were relatively close to what they were for other concerts. Be that as it may, to show their appreciation, the Stones decided to finish the tour with a huge free concert in Altamont. This grand finale would end in tragedy and mark the end of the sixties, as well...

"ALTAMONT WAS AN UTTER DISASTER. IN HINDSIGHT, ALL I CAN SAY IS THAT IT WAS NAIVETÉ THAT GOT US INTO THAT MESS, AND IT WAS LUCK THAT GOT US OUT OF IT."

Bill Wyman

"SISTERS. BROTHERS AND SISTERS. BROTHERS AND SISTERS. COME ON, NOW. THAT MEANS EVERYBODY JUST COOL OUT!"

Mick Jagger

David Crosby, 1974 ℗ Mark Estabrook CC BY 2.0

In the sixties, huge gatherings were in vogue. They started in San Francisco in 1965, with "happenings" and "love-ins." They were new places to voice protest against the Vietnam War and fight for equal rights for women, blacks and gays. In 1967, Brian Jones had attended the first big festival of the kind, in Monterey. **The Rolling Stones didn't perform at Woodstock, in August 1969, or at the Isle of Wight Festival, with its all-star lineup that included Bob Dylan.** So for the band, Altamont was their way of getting with the times, even though they had already organized their own big free concert in Hyde Park. Woodstock took place on the East Coast; they would do Altamont on the West Coast. Woodstock was summer; Altamont would be winter. Woodstock was a huge success; Altamont, just the opposite.

To organize this huge event, they called on Chip Monck, the man who had planned the setup at Woodstock. But everything fell to pieces due to lack of time. They thought of Golden State Park as a possible location, but the City said no. Then they found a racetrack, Sears Point Raceway, but that venue slipped through their fingers the day before the concert and they had to find an emergency backup venue. Chip Monck set everything up in just 24 hours. **A herculean task!** But the stage wasn't high

enough and the place wasn't equipped to accommodate 300,000 people. To top it all off: the Hells Angels were hired for security. They asked to be paid in beer. LSD on one side, beer on another... things were bound to explode, and not just musically...

From the moment the concert began, the tension was palpable. Carlos Santana was the first one on stage. Standing before the spectacle of Hells Angels pushing fans back with their feet, baseball bats or pool sticks, he called it quits after just a few pieces. Jefferson Airplane was up next. Marty Balin and then his fellow bandmembers were assaulted by Hells Angels. In the end, only Grace Slick emerged unscathed from their set! The next lambs to the slaughter: Crosby, Stills, Nash and Young, who played in a deafening brouhaha. Next came Ike and Tina Turner, who were lucky to play during a lull in the chaos. As for the Grateful Dead, they decided to leave without playing.

After much hesitation, the Rolling Stones strutted out on stage as the final act. The atmosphere was increasingly explosive, with a veritable battlefield taking shape below the stage, between groupies trying to jump onto a stage that was built way too low and Hells Angels beating everybody up. It was while they performed "Under

Carlos Santana, Hamburg 1973
© Heinrich Klaffs CC BY-SA

"THERE WERE BAD VIBES FROM THE START. FIGHTS BROKE OUT BECAUSE THE HELLS ANGELS WERE SPREADING PANIC. THERE WAS NO PROVOCATION FROM THE AUDIENCE, THE HELLS ANGELS STARTED IT."

Carlos Santana

Hells Angels

The Altamont Festival

"IT WAS AT THE END OF THAT TOUR THAT THE ALTAMONT CONCERT TOOK PLACE. WE ARRIVED AT THE SITE BY HELICOPTER AND WE SAW THAT TOTALLY OUT OF CONTROL SEA OF PEOPLE, BOYS THAT WERE HIGH AS KITES, HALF-NAKED GIRLS.

IT WAS LIKE ANOTHER WOODSTOCK, THE KIND OF THING THAT WAS POPULAR BACK THEN—BUT IT WAS A FAD THAT WAS FADING. IF WOODSTOCK STARTED IT, THAT DAY ENDED IT."

Charlie Watts

My Thumb" that the tragedy occurred: a young black man, Meredith Hunter, was stabbed by a Hells Angel while holding a gun and then beaten to death. The toll of that bloody night: four dead and hundreds wounded, not to mention 400,000 dollars worth of damages. A meager consolation: two births. December 1969 ushered in the end of the sixties and of the Love Generation. **Sadly, reality caught up with fantasy at Altamont.**

101

Altamont

Artist: Filippo Néri
Colorist: Piero Ruggeri

How the Altamont Festival
Turned to Tragedy.

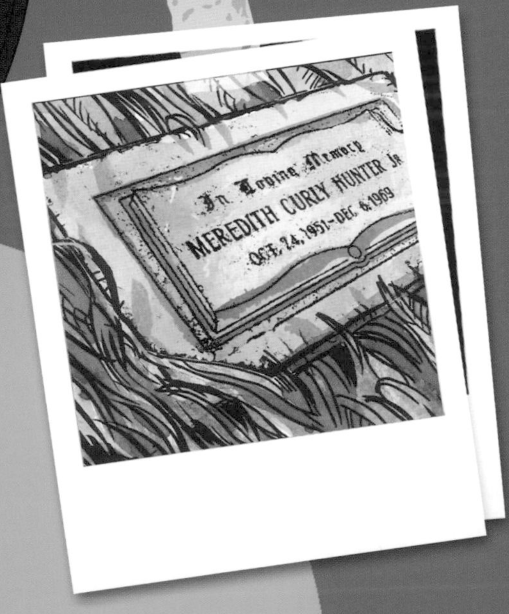
In Loving Memory
MEREDITH CURLY HUNTER JR
OCT. 24, 1951 - DEC. 6, 1969

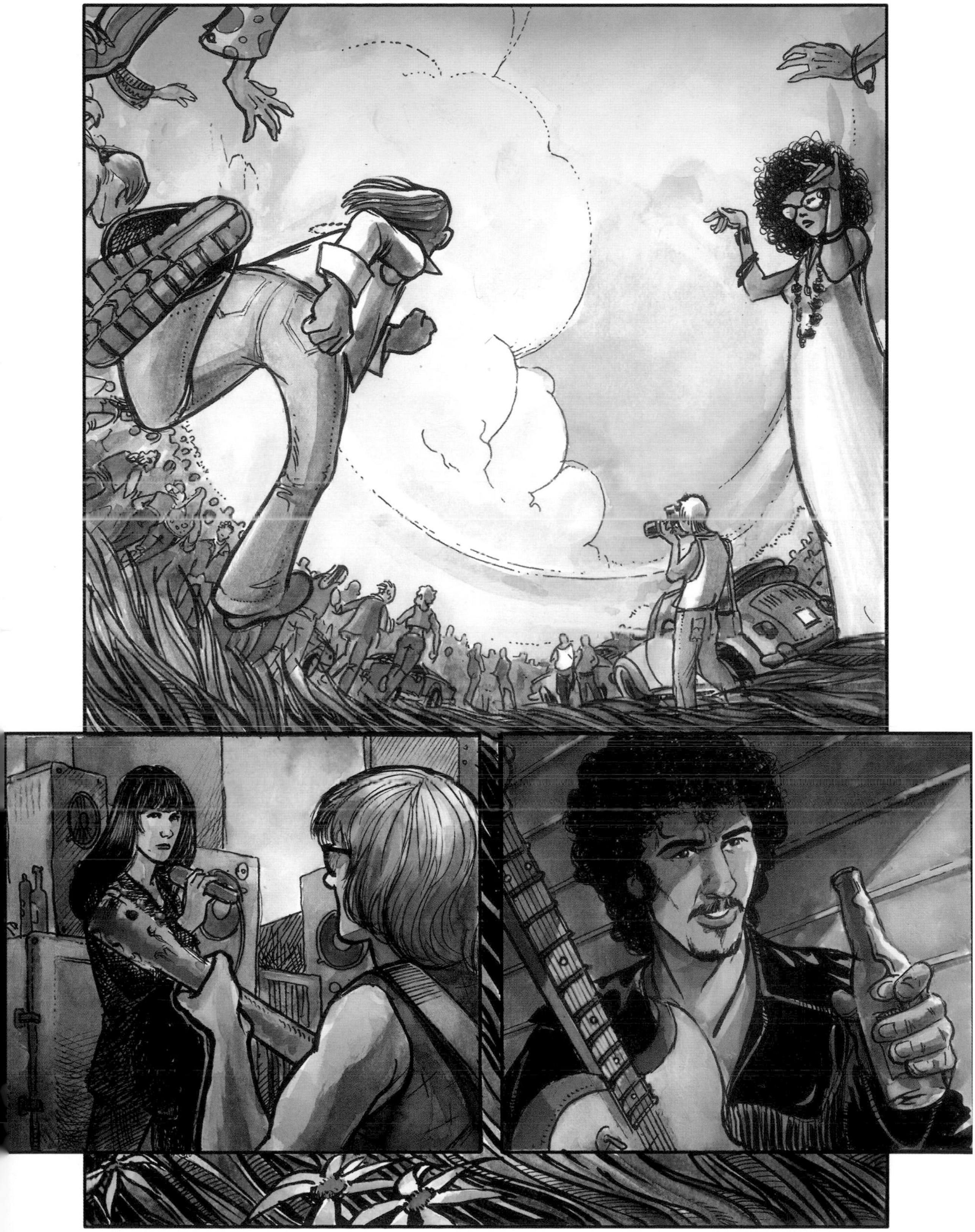

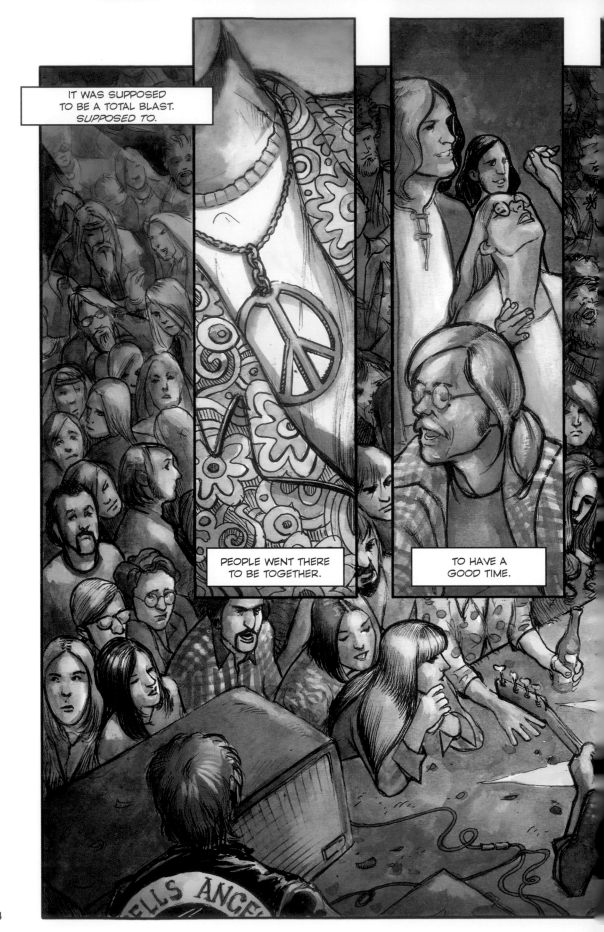

IT WAS SUPPOSED
TO BE A TOTAL BLAST.
SUPPOSED TO.

PEOPLE WENT THERE
TO BE TOGETHER.

TO HAVE A
GOOD TIME.

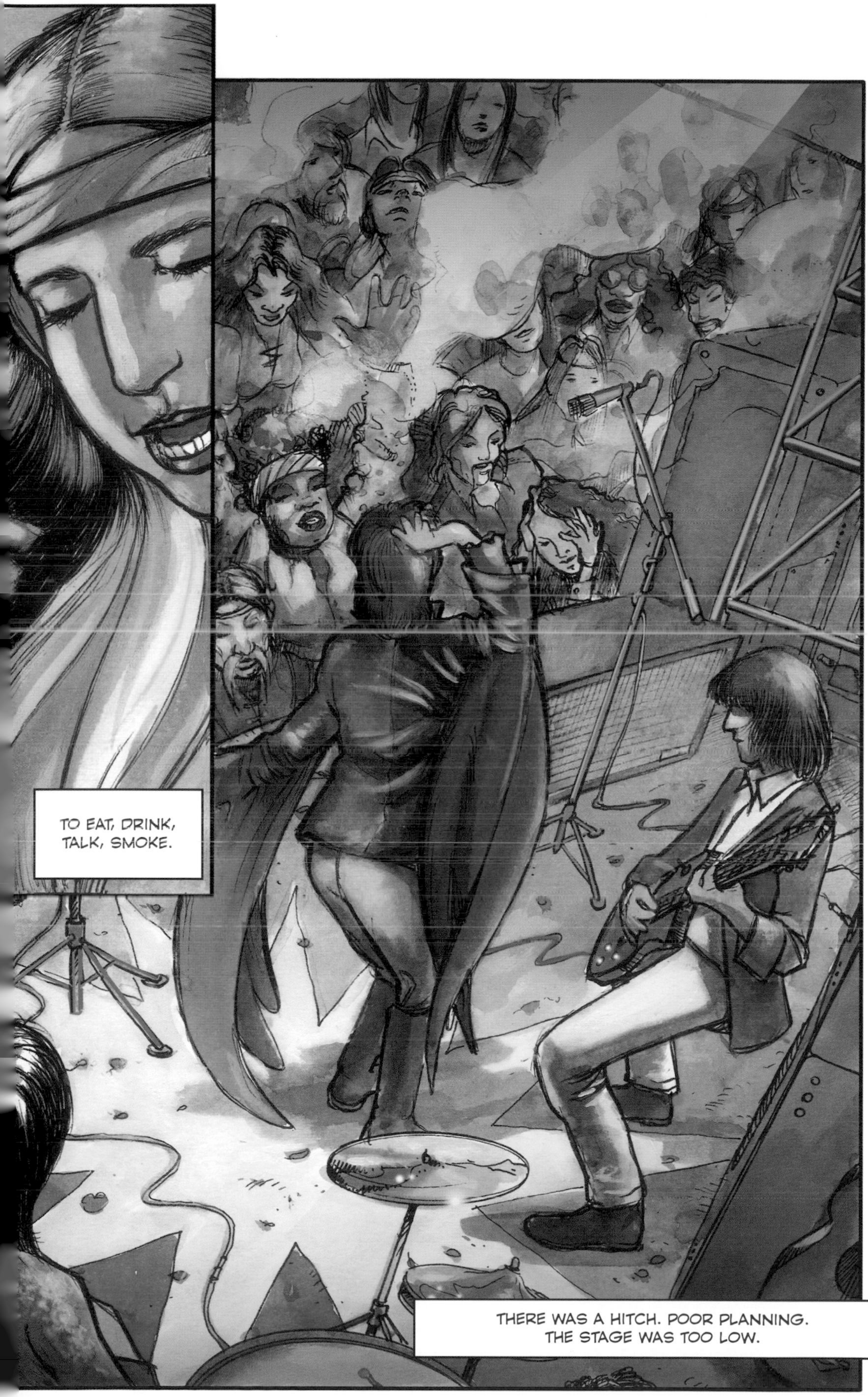
TO EAT, DRINK, TALK, SMOKE.
THERE WAS A HITCH. POOR PLANNING. THE STAGE WAS TOO LOW.

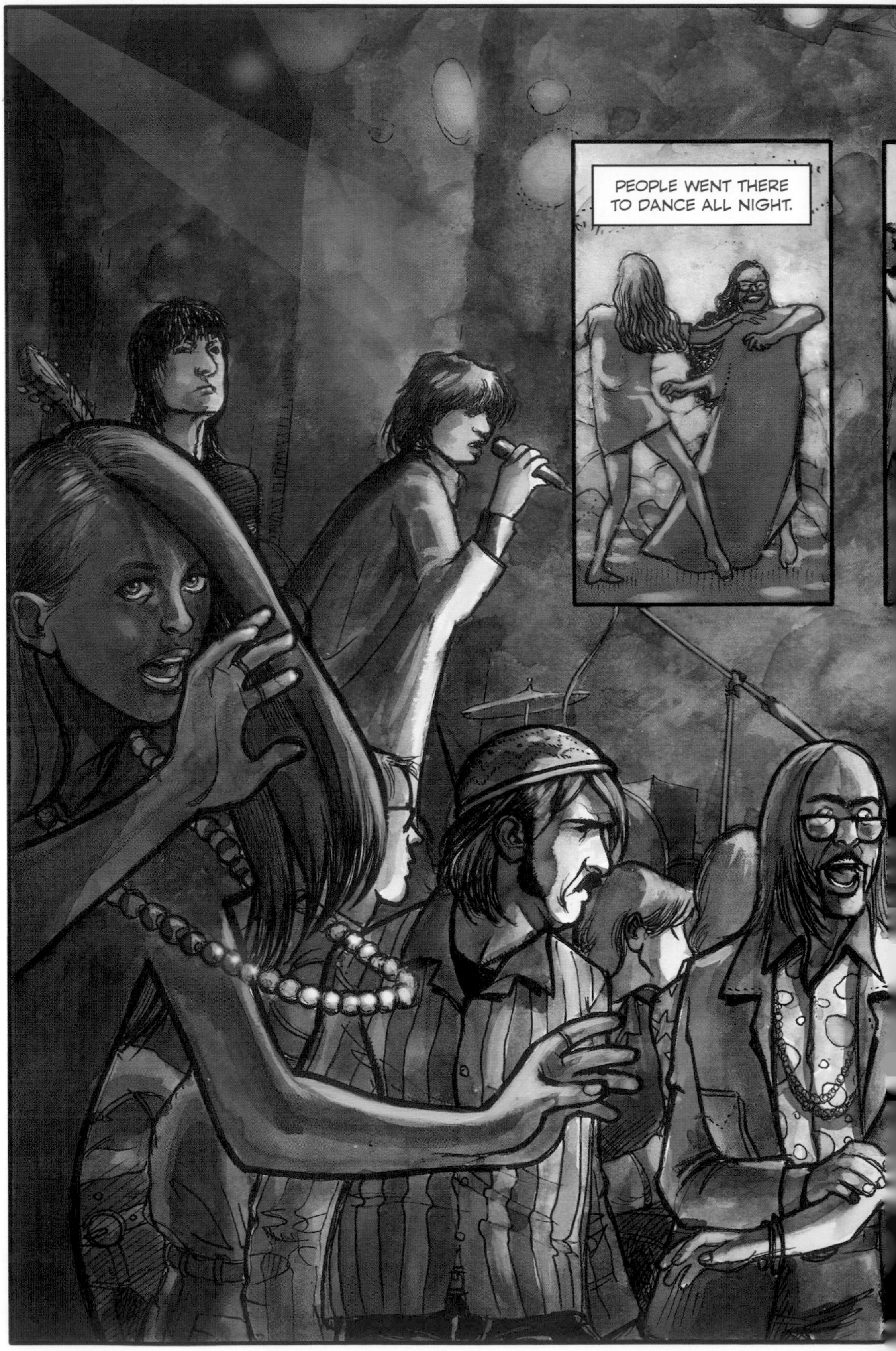
PEOPLE WENT THERE TO DANCE ALL NIGHT.

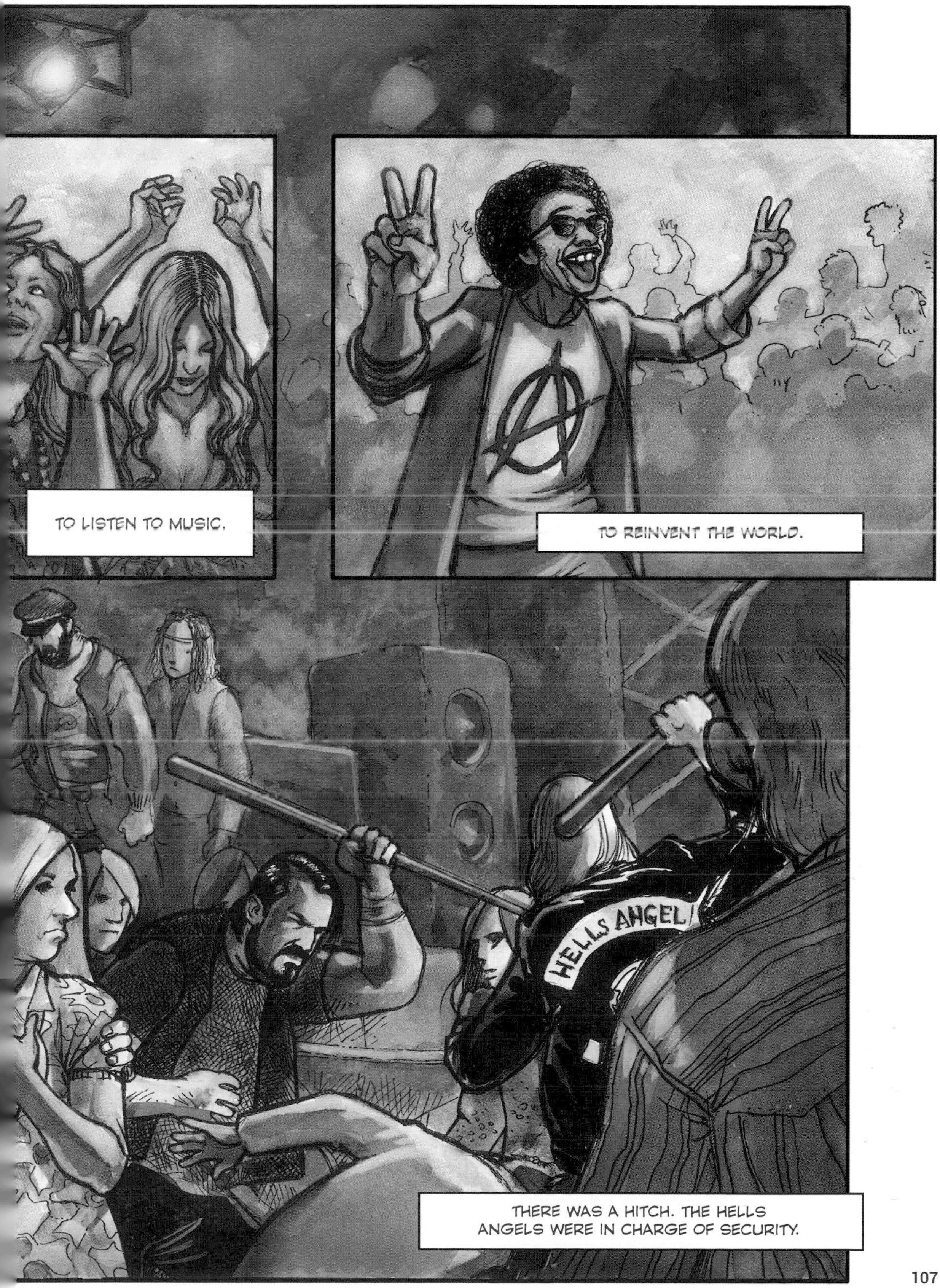
TO LISTEN TO MUSIC.
TO REINVENT THE WORLD.
HELLS ANGEL
THERE WAS A HITCH. THE HELLS ANGELS WERE IN CHARGE OF SECURITY.

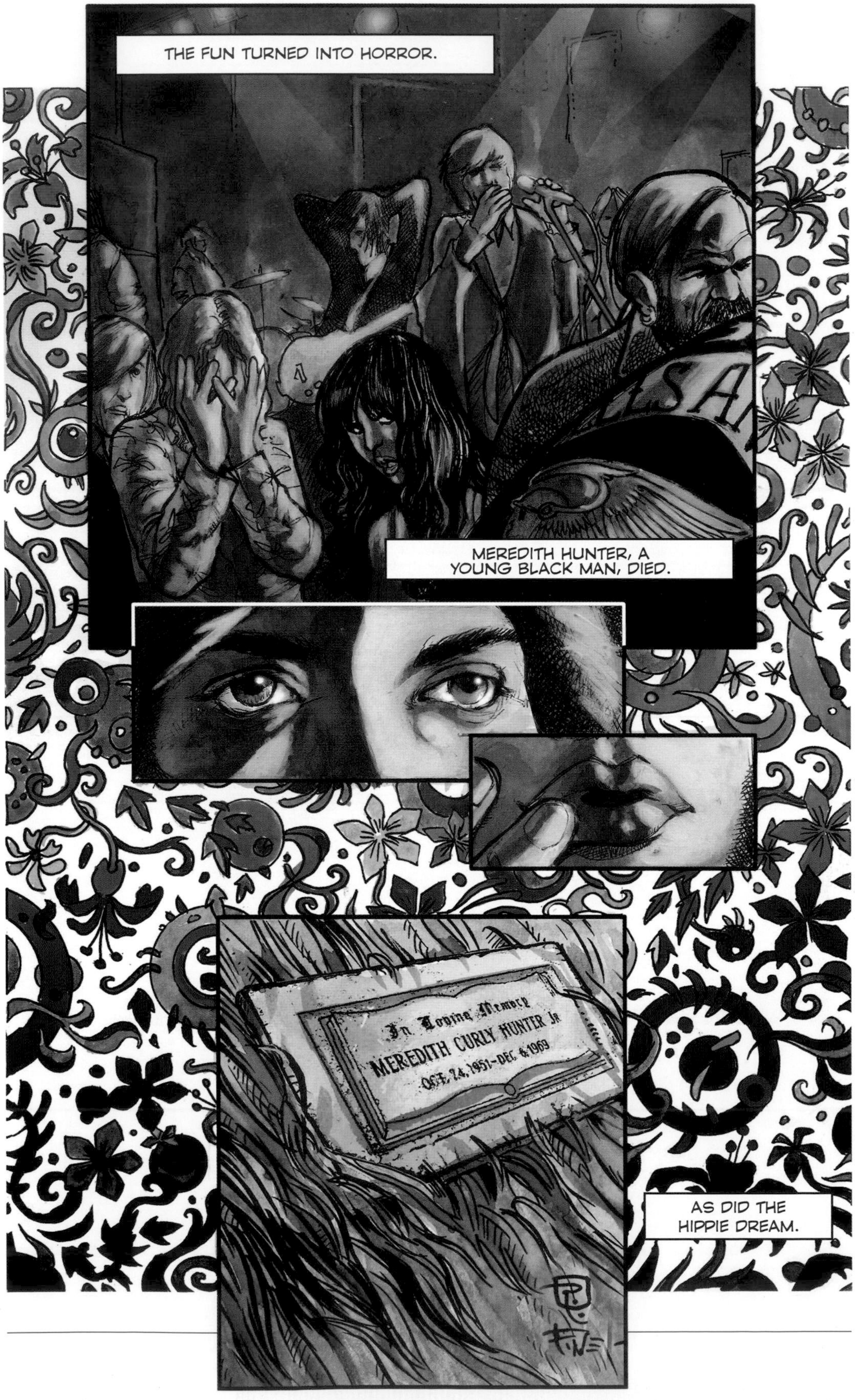
THE FUN TURNED INTO HORROR.
MEREDITH HUNTER, A YOUNG BLACK MAN, DIED.
In Loving Memory
MEREDITH CURLY HUNTER Jr
OCT. 24, 1951 - DEC. 6, 1969
AS DID THE HIPPIE DREAM.

Some Girls

SEX.

Carla Bruni-Sarkozy ©Remi Jouan CC BY-SA 3.0

In "Sex, drugs, and rock and roll," sex comes first, and the Rolling Stones certainly didn't hold back throughout their career, with the exception of Charlie Watts who, from the very start, lived a much tamer life. Shenanigans on the part of various bandmembers made their share of tabloid headlines and helped seal the Rolling Stones' reputation as partiers.

"SEX, FOR AN ARTIST, IS JUST ANOTHER FORM OF EXPRESSION."

Mick Jagger

Jerry Hall ©Piers Allardyce CC BY 2.0

Sex played a big part in forging the Rolling Stones' legend, namely under the impulse of Mick Jagger. The singer emancipated rock and roll via his increasingly sexualized stage performances and his openly sensual lyrics. And then there were the fans: hysterical groupies, faintings by the dozens and flying panties were common sights at their shows early on—not to mention people climbing naked on stage! It quickly became a tradition to end the night with a groupie. Or several. Ron Wood, Mick Taylor's future replacement, was nicknamed Woodpecker... not much ambiguity there... As Stu once joked regarding Mick Jagger: "He was no angel, but compared to the offers he received..." Mick, Keith and Brian had the reputation of being voracious, but the more self-effaced Bill Wyman wasn't suffering from deprivation either, far from it.

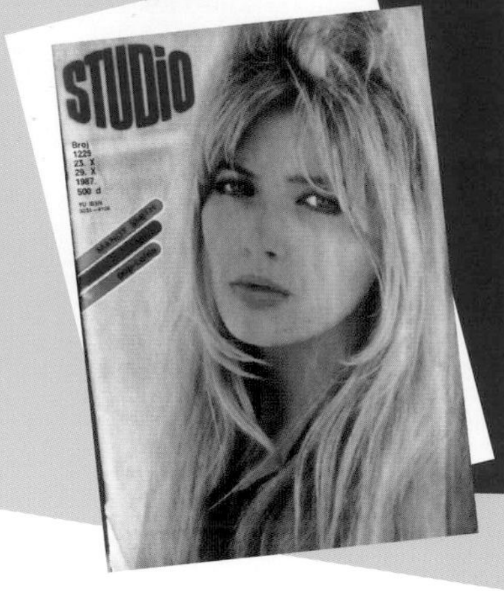
STUDIO

Mandy Smith ©Mishgan

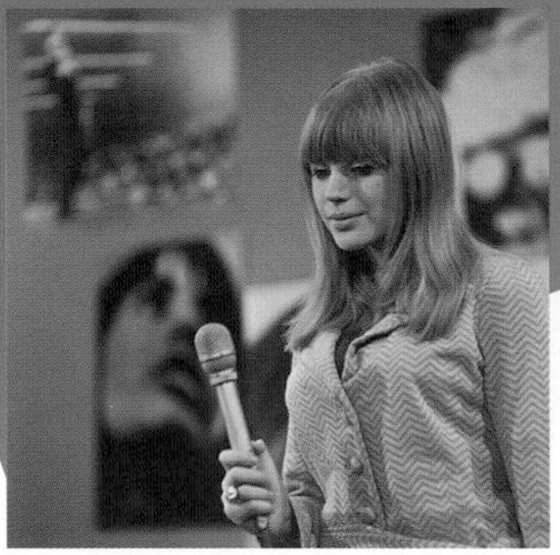

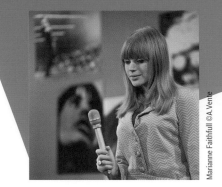

Marianne Faithfull ©A.Vente

They collected conquests at their shows. As they did in their private lives. Stability clearly wasn't their strong suit. They were "Wild Horses" who had a hard time keeping a ring on their finger. In fact, in an early attempt to maintain their bad-boy image and encourage groupie jealousy, the Stones cultivated their reputation as bachelors. An artist with a heart for the taking is just sexier... But that didn't stop Bill Wyman from eventually marrying, and Charlie Watts did the same in 1964. The others would also have long-term relationships, but only Shirley and Charlie would stick it out for the long run.

Mick Jagger scored the most notches on his bedpost: married twice, first to model Bianca Pérez-Mora Macias and then to model Jerry Hall; a philandering husband and lover, he had liaisons with Cleo Sylvestre, Chrissie Shrimpton, Marianne Faithfull, Patti d'Arbanville, Bebe Buell, Pamela Des Barres, Janice Dickinson, Carla Bruni, Carly Simon, Sophie Dahl and Linda Ronstadt, among others. According to some rumors, he also had trysts with David Bowie and Rudolph Nureyev. Bianca once said: "I'll be frank. Mick wanted to reach the ultimate sexual experience: making love to himself." Whether he achieved that goal is anyone's guess.

The bandmembers' sexual shenanigans brought scandal upon them more than once, as in the Trudeau incident, for instance. In 1977, Margaret Trudeau, wife of the Canadian Prime Minister at the time, went to a Stones concert and then spent the night partying with them. This led to a major diplomatic scandal. As Bill Wyman later commented, bemused: "That lady managed to rekindle relations between Britain and Canada." Speaking of Bill, he was behind the Mandy Smith incident in 1986. He was allegedly involved with a minor who was only thirteen when their affair began. As for Mandy's mother, she was involved with Bill Wyman's son, who was sixteen years her junior! Blaming it on a midlife crisis, Bill ended up marrying Mandy only to divorce her shortly afterwards.

Songs like "Parachute Woman" or "Under My Thumb," as well as the documentary *Cocksucker Blues*, drive home the point that **the Rolling Stones have unbridled sexual appetites and, at times, arguably sexist attitudes toward women.**

M. Cooper: M. Jagger, M. Faithfull, Al Vandenberg, B. Jones, Mahesh Yogi (1967) ©CC BY-SA Netherlands Archives-BenMerk

CK 'N' ROLL

"AND THEN THERE WERE THE GIRLS. THERE'S NOTHING LIKE THREE THOUSAND GIRLS THROWING THEMSELVES AT YOU TO MAKE YOUR HEAD SPIN, ESPECIALLY THE BAND OF HORNDOGS I WORK WITH..."

Keith Richards

Margaret Trudeau © ORLANDO LOPE

Performance

Artist: Anthony Audibert

Fidelity: Not a
Mick Jagger Thing.

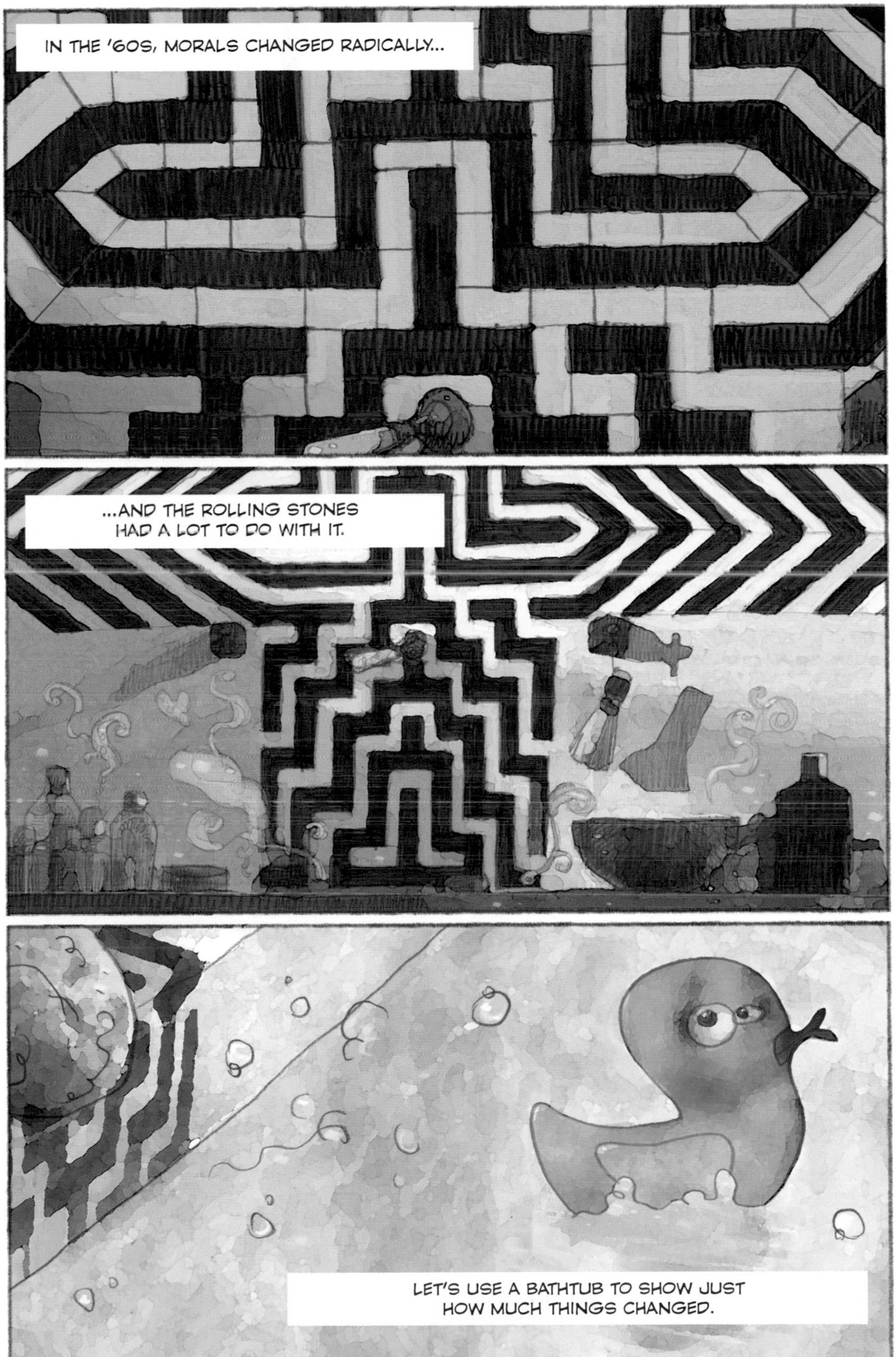
IN THE '60S, MORALS CHANGED RADICALLY...
...AND THE ROLLING STONES HAD A LOT TO DO WITH IT.
LET'S USE A BATHTUB TO SHOW JUST HOW MUCH THINGS CHANGED.

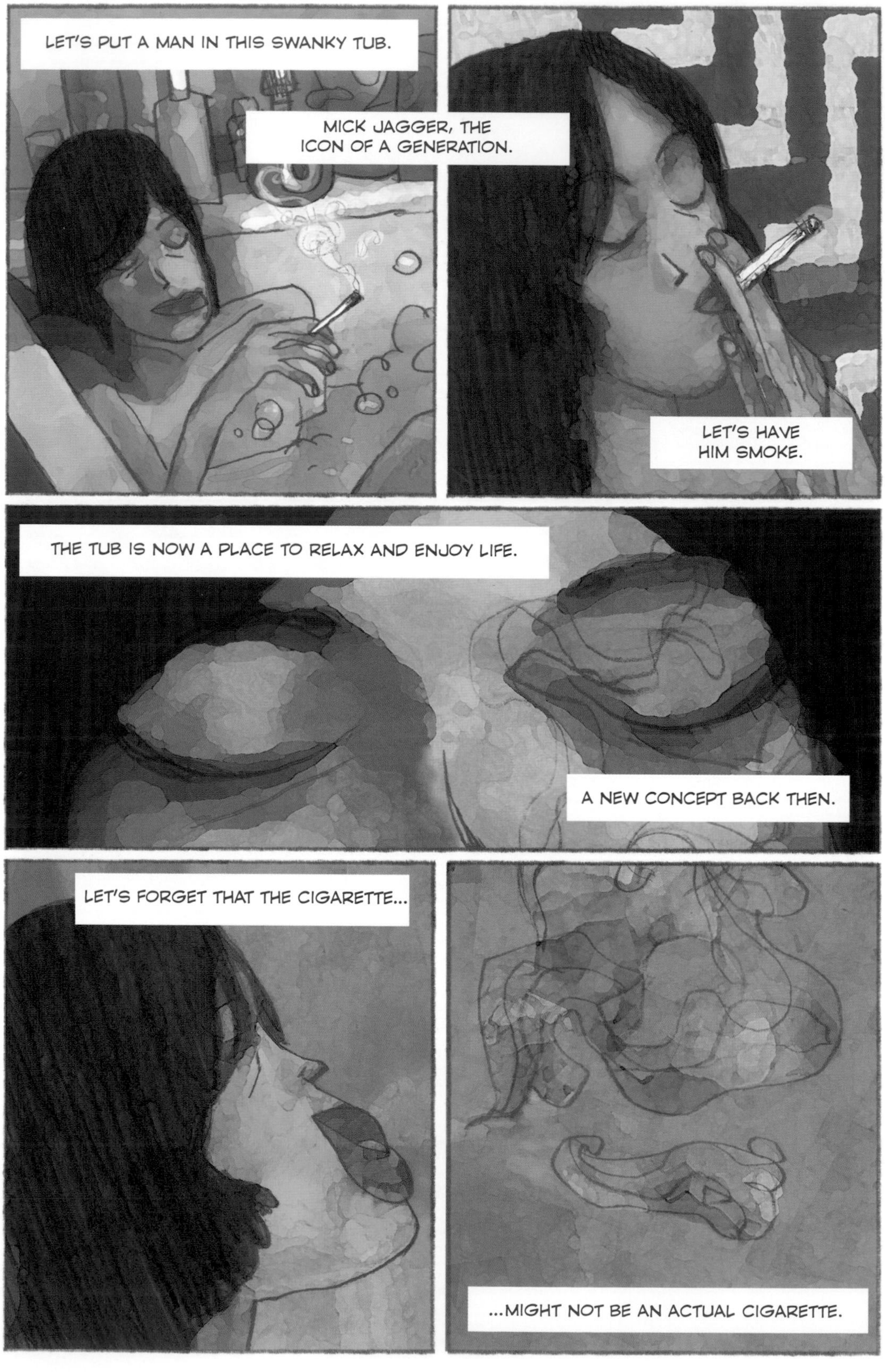
LET'S PUT A MAN IN THIS SWANKY TUB.
MICK JAGGER, THE ICON OF A GENERATION.
LET'S HAVE HIM SMOKE.
THE TUB IS NOW A PLACE TO RELAX AND ENJOY LIFE.
A NEW CONCEPT BACK THEN.
LET'S FORGET THAT THE CIGARETTE...
...MIGHT NOT BE AN ACTUAL CIGARETTE.

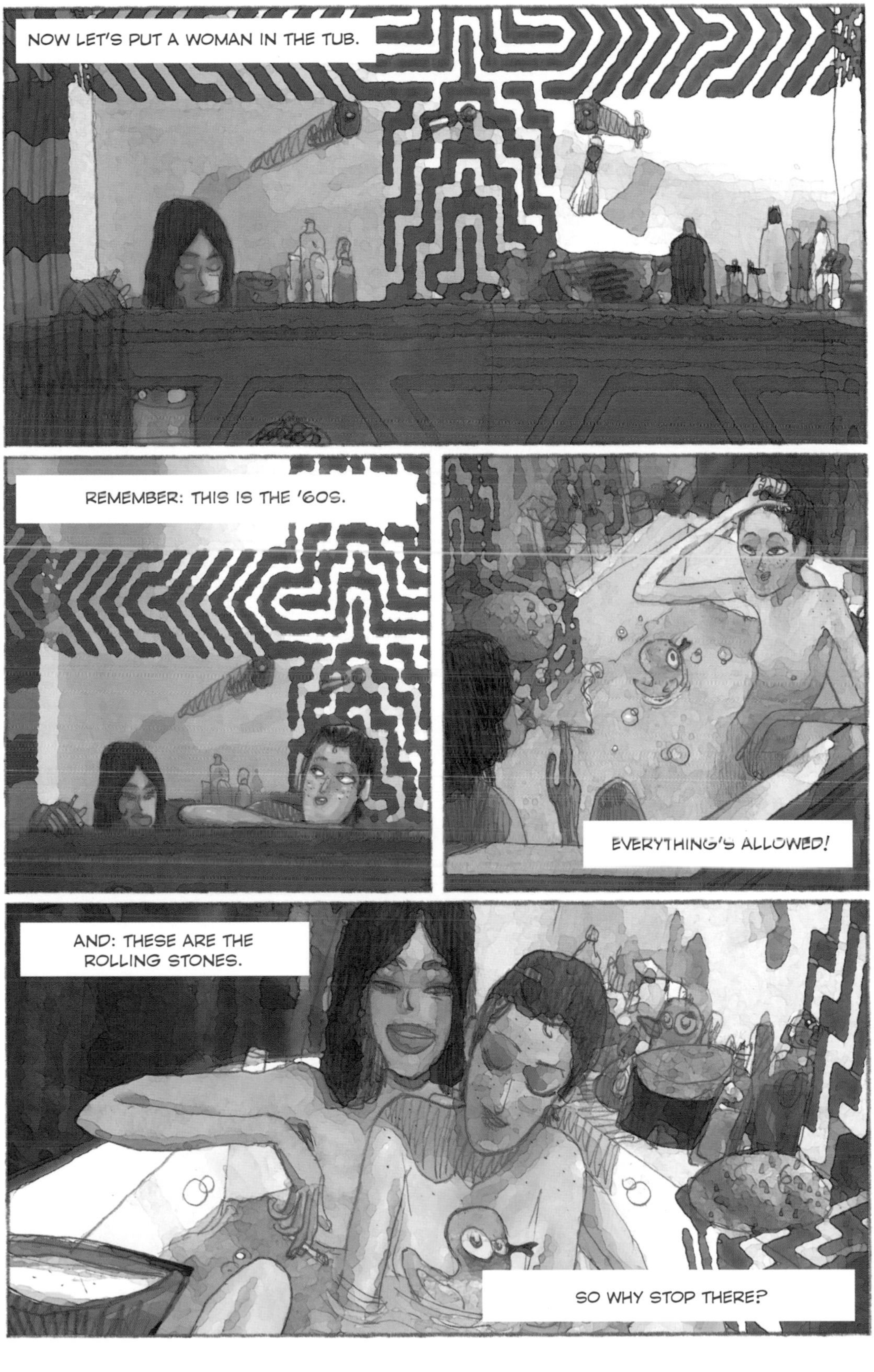
NOW LET'S PUT A WOMAN IN THE TUB.
REMEMBER: THIS IS THE '60S.
EVERYTHING'S ALLOWED!
AND: THESE ARE THE ROLLING STONES.
SO WHY STOP THERE?

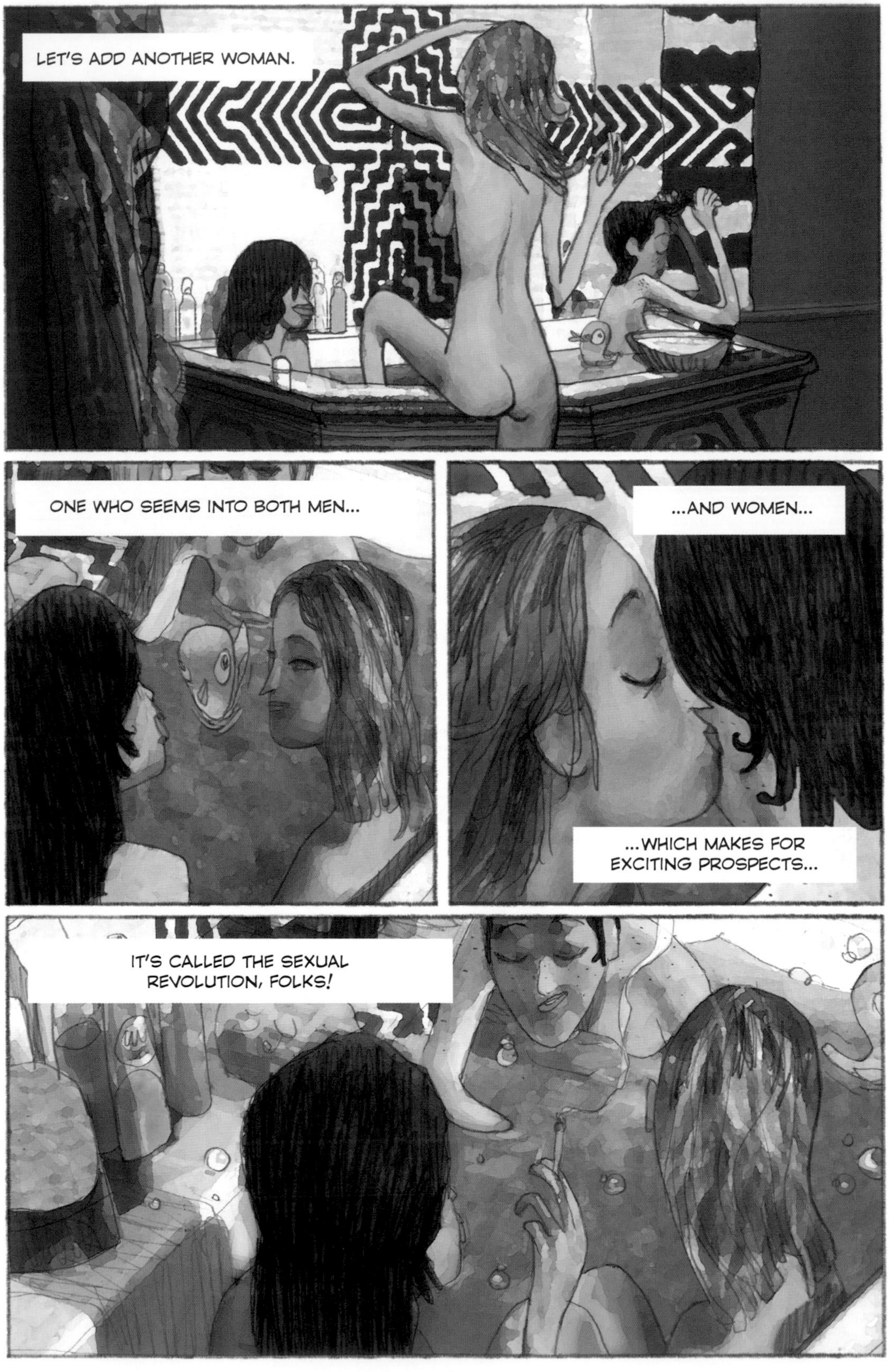
LET'S ADD ANOTHER WOMAN.
ONE WHO SEEMS INTO BOTH MEN...
...AND WOMEN...
...WHICH MAKES FOR EXCITING PROSPECTS...
IT'S CALLED THE SEXUAL REVOLUTION, FOLKS!

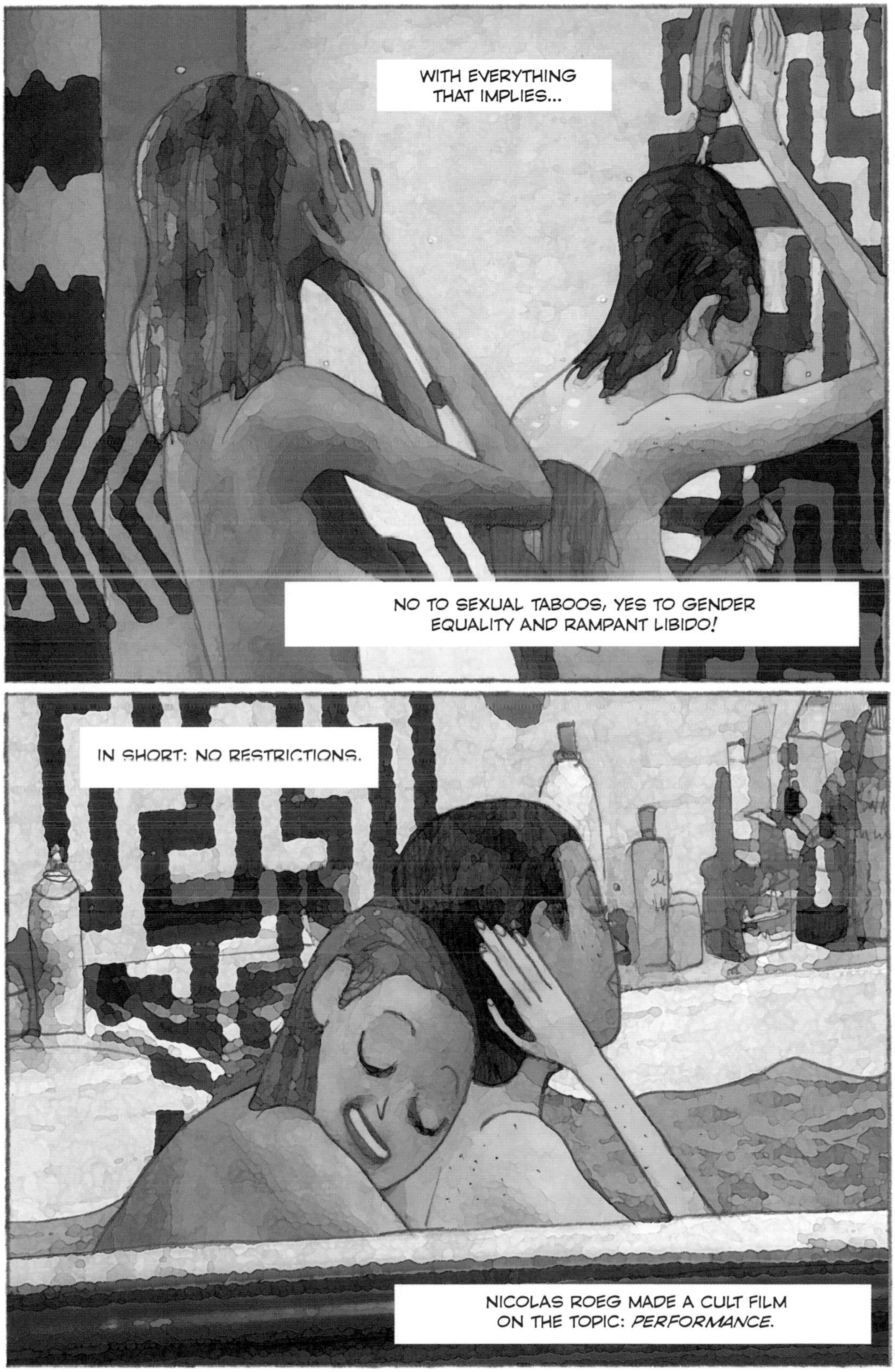
WITH EVERYTHING THAT IMPLIES...
NO TO SEXUAL TABOOS, YES TO GENDER EQUALITY AND RAMPANT LIBIDO!
IN SHORT: NO RESTRICTIONS.
NICOLAS ROEG MADE A CULT FILM ON THE TOPIC: *PERFORMANCE*.

LET'S MENTION IN PASSING THAT IT STARRED
ANITA PALLENBERG, KEITH RICHARDS' LOVER...

... IN TOTALLY NON-SIMULATED SEX SCENES...

...AND THAT JAGGER'S THEN-LOVER MARIANNE
FAITHFULL WAS PREGNANT AT THE TIME.

IT WAS THE SIXTIES.

IT WAS SWINGING
LONDON.

Harmonica, Sitar, etc.

The Rolling Stones? They're rhythm & blues first and foremost, and they're rock, too, of course, but not just that. The Rolling Stones are a whole different kind of alchemy, because they found a way to invent a whole different sound, partly thanks to the instrumental experimentation they've been doing since the start of their career, first under the impulse of Brian Jones, and then other bandmembers too.
One, two… one, two, three…

"AND IN THAT MOMENT, I HEARD THE INTOXICATING SOUNDS OF THE FUTURE OF ROCK MUSIC BEING PLAYED BY MY FAVORITE BAND."

Rob Bowman

Bill Wyman, Mick Jagger and Keith Richards in concert in 1981 ©Patricia Fitzgerald CC-BY SA 2.0

From the get-go, the Stones used an original approach to their lineup, with a preeminent rhythmic base section by Watts and Wyman that drove the interlocking guitars of Jones and Richards. Brian Jones soon enhanced this lineup by introducing a series of instruments that were never or rarely used in that kind of music: the sitar, the organ, the mellotron, the harpsichord, the harp, the marimbas, etc. In just a few quick hours, Mr. Shampoo had the uncanny ability to learn how to play a new instrument well enough to draw out its magic. **And so, for instance, in "Lady Jane," he had the idea of adding the dulcimer, without which the piece wouldn't be "Lady Jane."**

But the other bandmembers tried new things as well. In addition to his bass guitar, Bill Wyman experimented with the vibraphone and the autoharp, the glockenspiel and other percussion instruments. As for Charlie Watts, his training as a jazzman gave the band that highly personal groove and sound. Look at him, he still holds his drumsticks like a jazz percussionist. Even Mick Jagger contributed musical originality to the band: beyond his voice, which enhanced the band's rugged sound, he introduced the harmonica early on, an instrument inherited from the blues and one he grew to excel at. We won't even bother mentioning Keith Richards, inventor of five-string open tuning and riffs that belong in the annals of history...

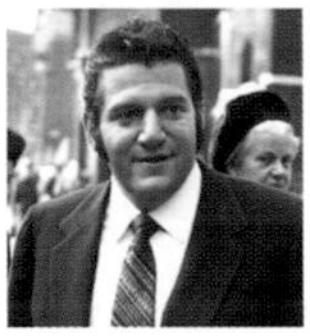
Allen Klein

The early '70s were a period of rebirth for the Stones. But before you can rebuild, you have to demolish, of course! The first casualty was Andrew Loog Oldham, their manager and career strategist. He spinelessly avoided the Stones during their brushes with the law in 1967... bad move on his part. Additionally, the band seemed to have gotten as much out of him professionally as they could. As Bill Wyman dryly summed it up: "We could do without Andrew's creative talents. Same goes for his talents as a producer." So they decided to call it quits. As a result, the production of *Satanic Majesties* turned out to be one big joyful mess, even though they recruited the help of ace producer Jimmy Miller.

Next step: resolve the issue with Klein, the Stones' financial manager. He was great at managing money, but mostly his own, as part of ABKCO Industries, Inc. The band calculated that Klein had taken about twenty-nine million dollars of their money for himself, thanks to his creative accounting. Because of him, and despite the massive amounts of money accumulated over the past years, the band was having cash flow problems and was even on the verge of ruin. Their European tour helped them stay afloat, but on July 29, 1970, the Rolling Stones decided that Klein and his company "would no longer have the power to negotiate artistic contracts on their behalf."

In the legal battle that followed, the band lost the master tapes of the '60s and the accompanying recording rights, which were held by Klein. It was a risky choice that turned out to be the right one.

Final step: the Stones decided to leave Decca when their contract expired in 1970. When the label refused to greenlight cover art for the *Beggars Banquet* album that showed a bathroom wall tagged with the song titles, it was the last straw. If there was to be censorship, they didn't want it coming from their own label, which was supposed to have their back. They already had to bend to radio and TV censors that refused to play songs like "(I Can't Get No) Satisfaction" and "Street Fighting Man" on the air. They were contractually bound to produce one last album and one last song with Decca before they left; this turned out to be the live album *Get Yer Ya-Ya's Out!*, which, to this day, is considered the best live album of all time. And, as a farewell "screw you," the last song they recorded for Decca was "Cocksucker Blues." It's not too hard to figure out why that title was never released.

That defiant attitude toward show biz led the Stones to launch their own label: Rolling Stones Records. Marshall Chess, son of Chess Records co-founder Leonard Chess, was hired as CEO. Inspired by the Shell logo, he tried to find a logo just as immediately recognizable for the band: the famous lapping tongue. It was designed by a young art student by the name of John Pasche. Iconoclastic and highly sexual, the logo remains the epitome of modernity to this day. Record companies wooed the band for distribution rights. They ended up signing with Ahmet Ertegun at the Kinney National Company, which owned Atlantic, Warner, Reprise and Elektra records. They hit the ground running with the album *Sticky Fingers* and its famous cover featuring a real trouser zipper opening on a...

Yep, it was back to sex, drugs and rock and roll!

"TO THIS DAY, I STILL MARVEL AT THE DIFFERENT STYLES FROM ONE SINGLE TO THE NEXT: THE INDIAN RAGA SOUNDS OF "PAINT IT BLACK," THE SLIGHTLY B-GRADE MUSIC HALL STYLE OF "MOTHER'S LITTLE HELPER," THE PURE ELIZABETHAN STYLE OF "LADY JANE," THE INCREDIBLE PARANOIA OF "HAVE YOU SEEN YOUR MOTHER, BABY, STANDING IN THE SHADOW?," THE STOIC "RUBY TUESDAY," AND THE DANCEHALL PIANO OF "LET'S SPEND THE NIGHT TOGETHER."

Rob Bowman

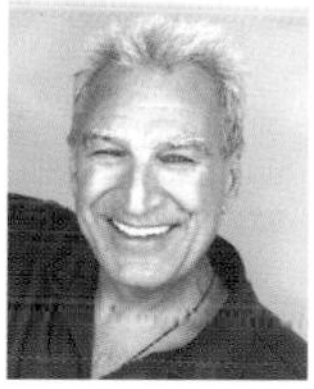

Marshall Chess ©Jamar Chess CC BY-SA 2.0

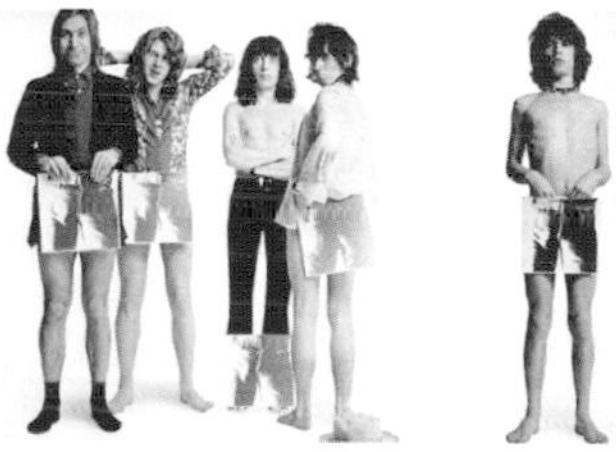

The 1971 Sticky Fingers album ©Rolling Stones Records

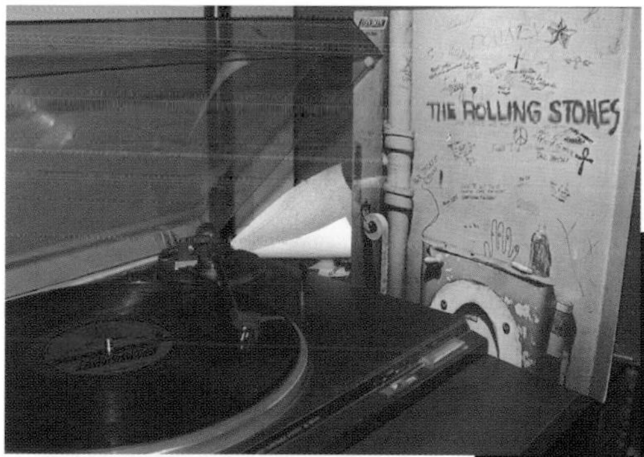
THE ROLLING STONES

©Charlie and Cassie Bennet CC BY-SA 2.0

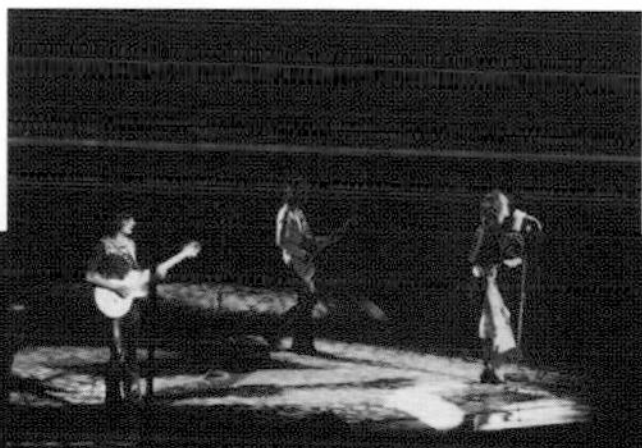

Concert in 1975 ©CC BY SA 2.0

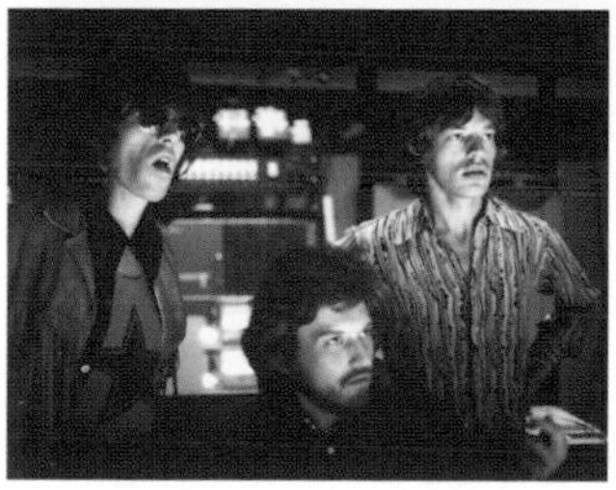

Keith, Mick and Jimmy Miller in 1980

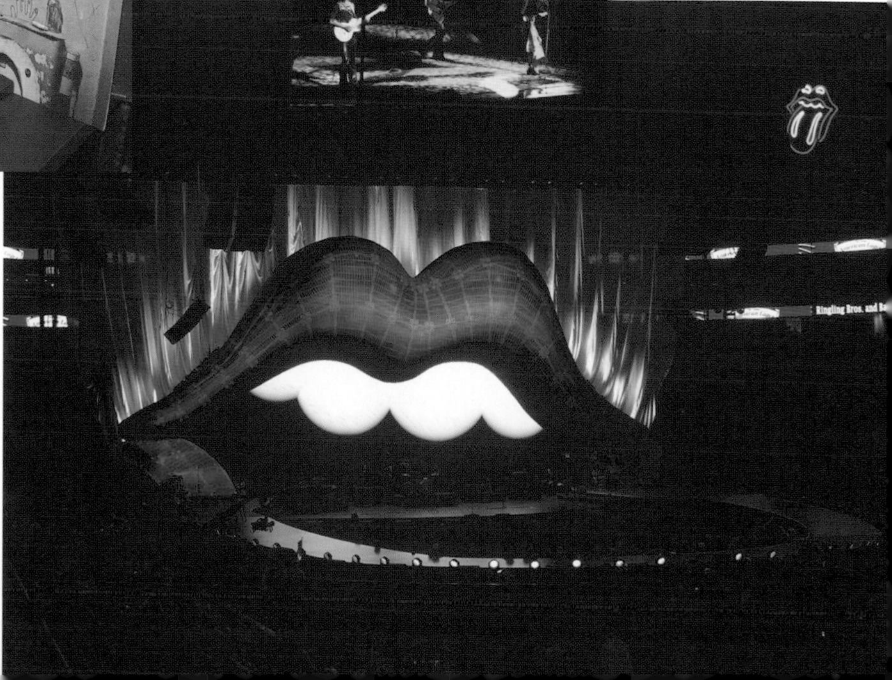

The stage at the Prudential Center, in Newark, 2013 © Solar Scott CC BY 2.0

Keith and His Electric Guitars

Artist: Bruno Loth

More Than Just a Passion:
A True Love Story.

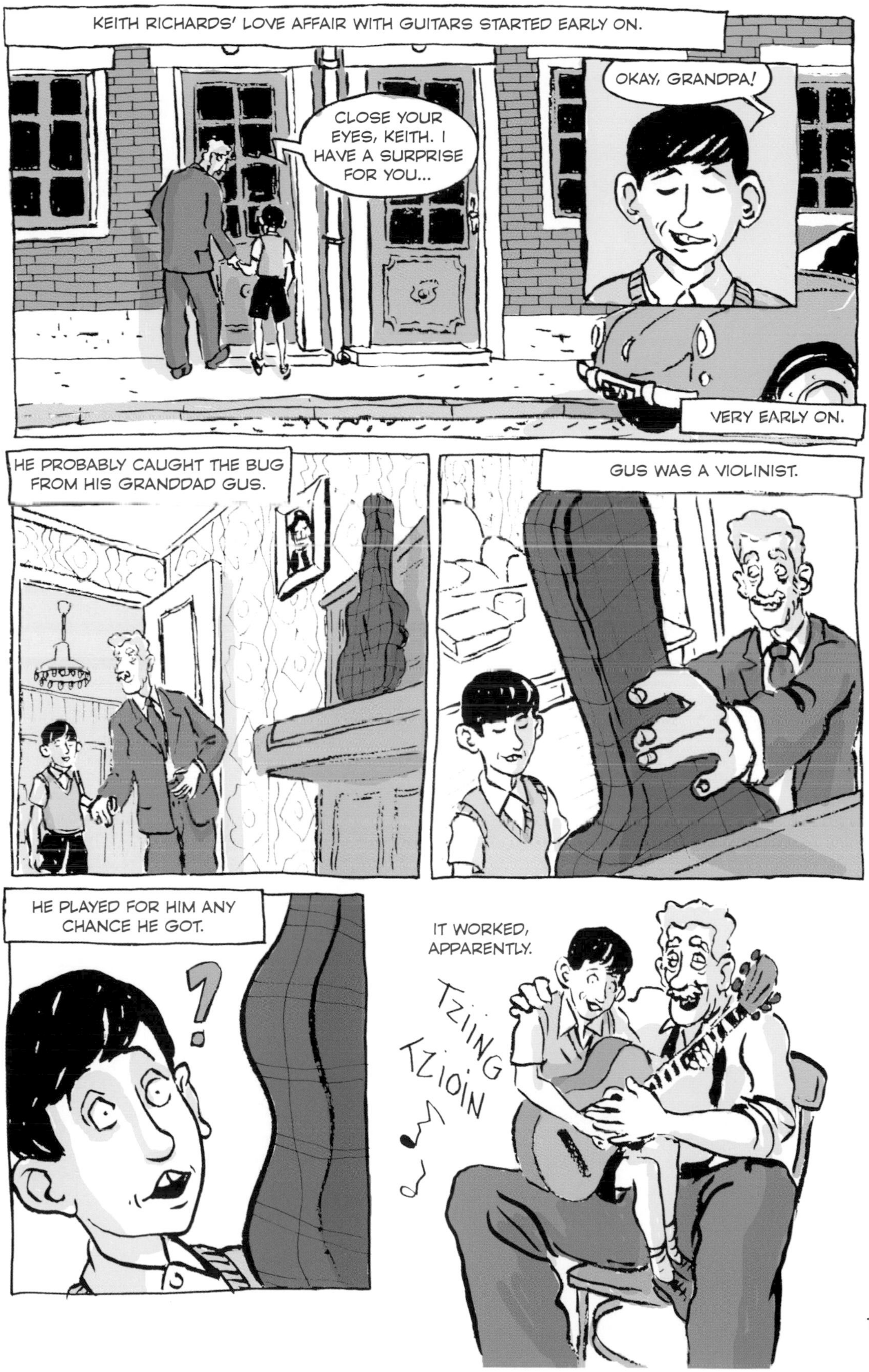
KEITH RICHARDS' LOVE AFFAIR WITH GUITARS STARTED EARLY ON.
CLOSE YOUR EYES, KEITH. I HAVE A SURPRISE FOR YOU...
OKAY, GRANDPA!
VERY EARLY ON.
HE PROBABLY CAUGHT THE BUG FROM HIS GRANDDAD GUS.
GUS WAS A VIOLINIST.
HE PLAYED FOR HIM ANY CHANCE HE GOT.
?
IT WORKED, APPARENTLY.
TZIING
TZIOIN

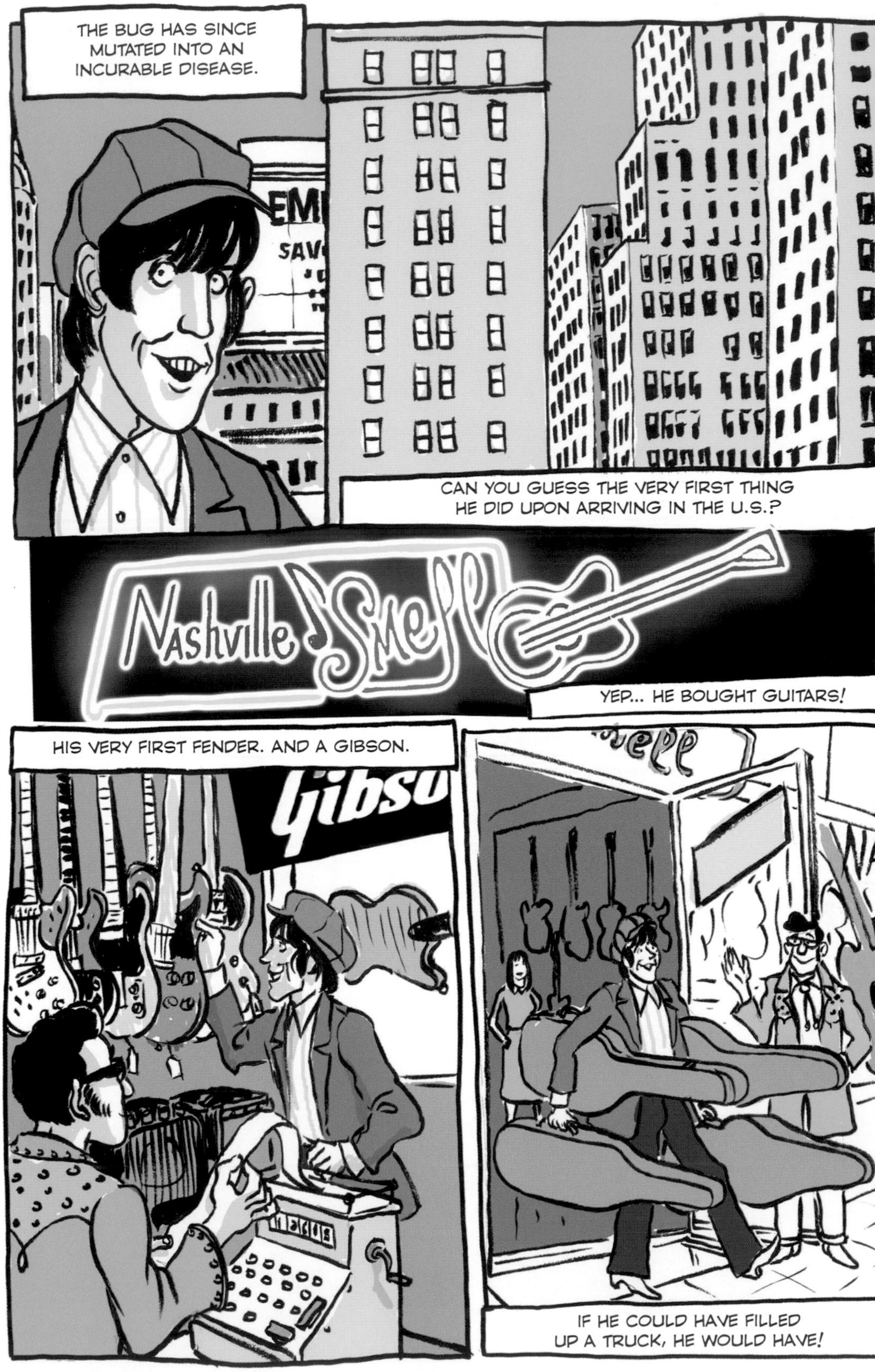
THE BUG HAS SINCE MUTATED INTO AN INCURABLE DISEASE.
CAN YOU GUESS THE VERY FIRST THING HE DID UPON ARRIVING IN THE U.S.?
YEP... HE BOUGHT GUITARS!
HIS VERY FIRST FENDER. AND A GIBSON.
IF HE COULD HAVE FILLED UP A TRUCK, HE WOULD HAVE!

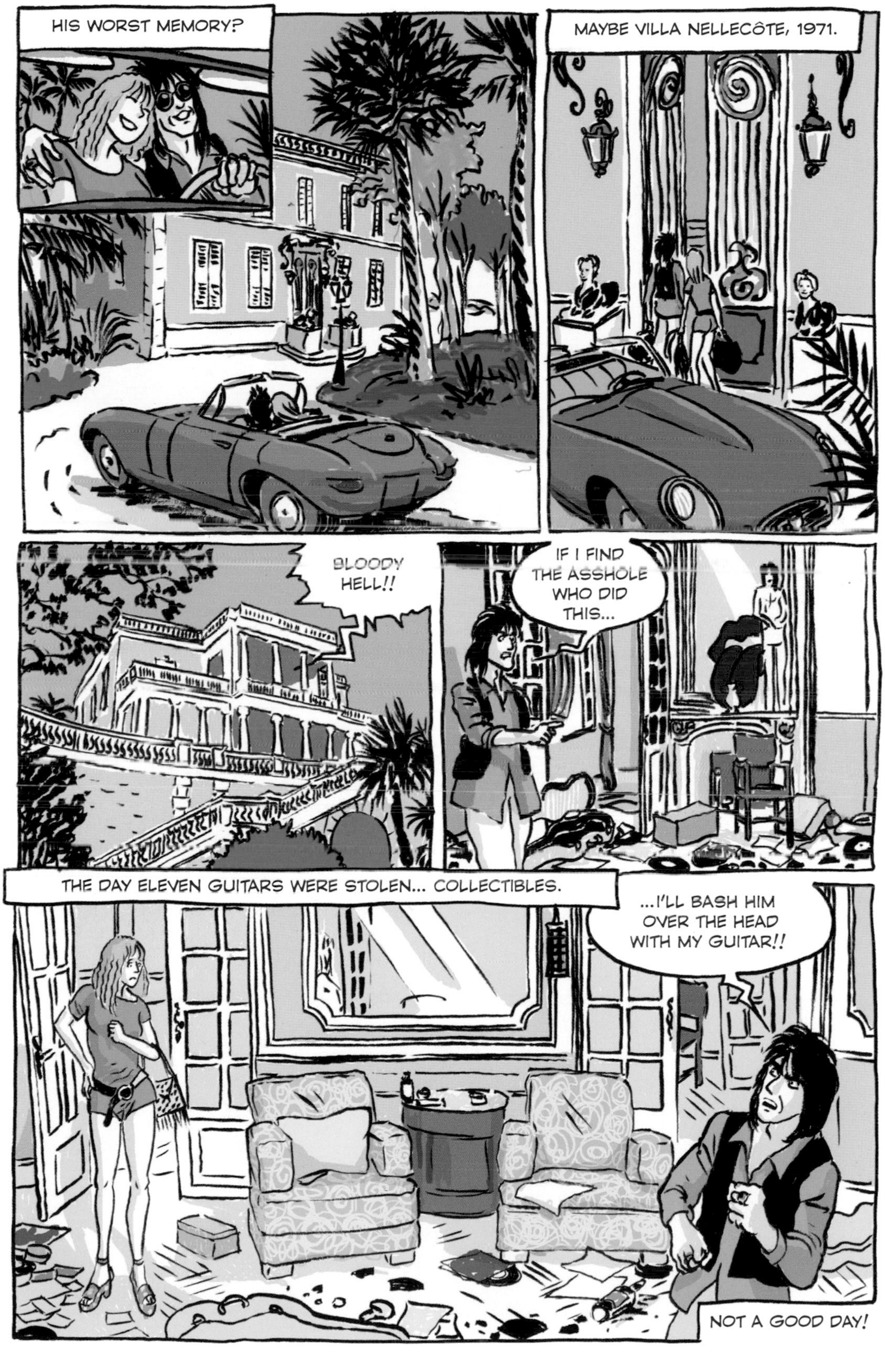
HIS WORST MEMORY?
MAYBE VILLA NELLECÔTE, 1971.
BLOODY HELL!!
IF I FIND THE ASSHOLE WHO DID THIS...
THE DAY ELEVEN GUITARS WERE STOLEN... COLLECTIBLES.
...I'LL BASH HIM OVER THE HEAD WITH MY GUITAR!!
NOT A GOOD DAY!

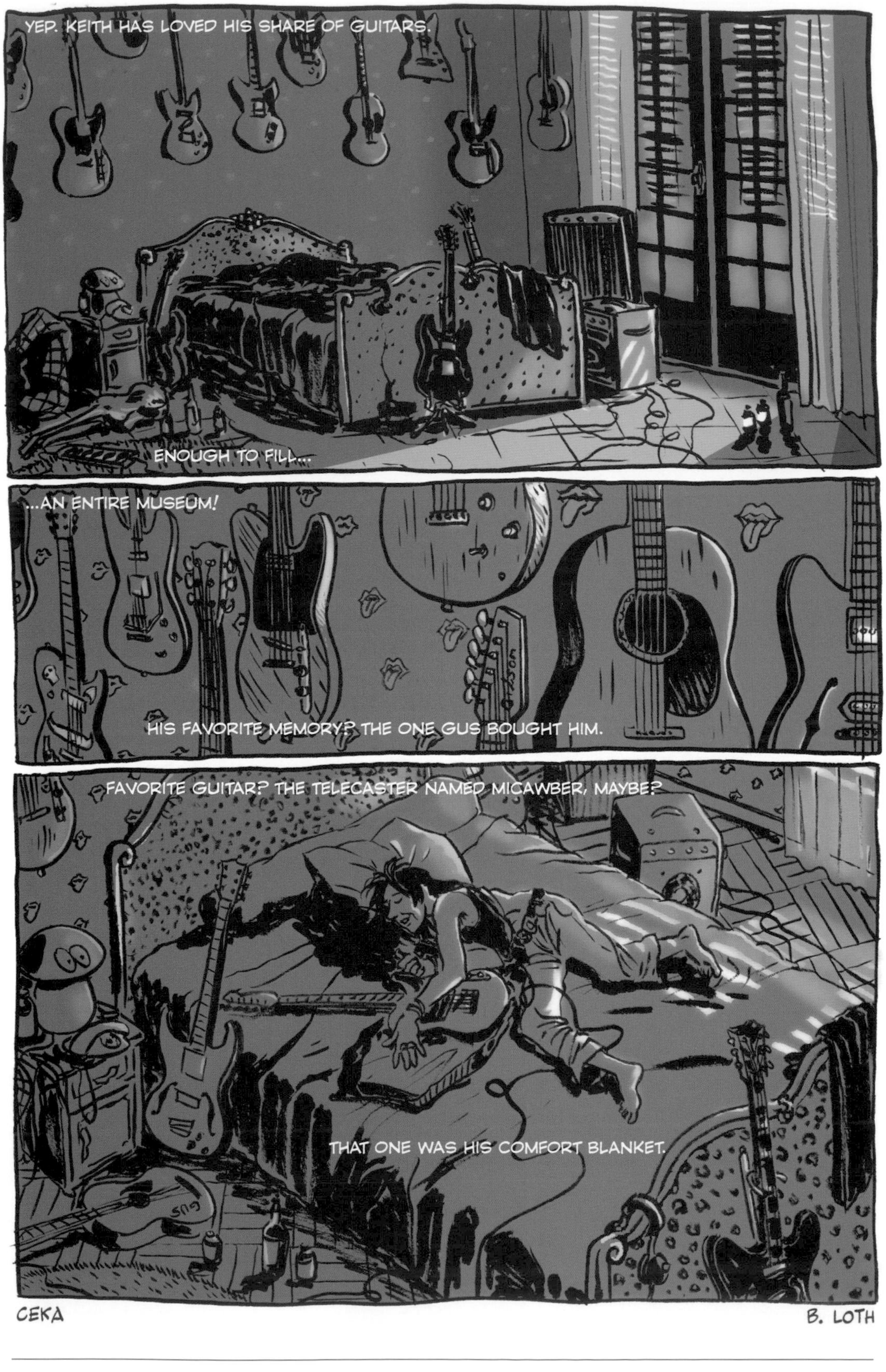
YEP. KEITH HAS LOVED HIS SHARE OF GUITARS.
ENOUGH TO FILL...
...AN ENTIRE MUSEUM!
HIS FAVORITE MEMORY? THE ONE GUS BOUGHT HIM.
FAVORITE GUITAR? THE TELECASTER NAMED MICAWBER, MAYBE?
THAT ONE WAS HIS COMFORT BLANKET.

CEKA B. LOTH

Smog Over Stone Land

Keith Richards and Mick Jagger in concert in Rotterdam, 1982 ©Marcel Antonisse CC BY SA 3.0

After the euphoria of rebirth in the early '70s came the downfall. Keith Richards got hooked on drugs, Mick on the jetset lifestyle. There were tensions among the bandmembers who now only saw each other on tour and in the recording studio. Mick Taylor had some concerns. As did the fans.
Could this be the end of the greatest rock band in the world?

San Francisco, 1972 ©Larry Rogers CC BY-SA 2.0

"WHAT I FOUND DISAPPOINTING ABOUT MICK TAYLOR WAS THAT HE HAD THE OPPORTUNITY TO REALLY GO FOR IT AND DO HIS OWN THING BUT HE DIDN'T TAKE ADVANTAGE OF THAT. HE WANTED TO WRITE, PRODUCE, DO LOTS OF BIG PROJECTS—BUT HE DID NOTHING."

Keith Richards

Picasso had his blue period. The Stones went through their gray period. And it wouldn't be just the one. More drug and legal problems, this time in France. Keith Richards took off for Switzerland, where he was still welcome, to live off the grid for a while. His chalet had extensive security and nobody could get near him... except for his drug dealers, of course. Doctors gave him six months to live... Mick went off on his own. The Glimmer Twins grew apart.

It was around this time that they discovered Jamaica, where there were good recording studios and good musicians. Kingston went on to become a second home base for them, and it wasn't long before Keith bought a house there. He no doubt preferred Jamaica's grass over Switzerland's alpine pastures! It was there that they recorded *Goats Head Soup*, with the single "Angie" going on to become a money-making hit. *It's Only Rock 'n' Roll* followed in 1974, but both albums met with only relative success.

While Keith was spinning out of control, Mick Taylor carved out a place for himself, unquestionably leaving his mark as a skilled guitarist on the albums and concerts. So it came as a big shock when, on December 14, 1974, the virtuoso musician left the Stones. Why? To get off the drugs he too had fallen prey to? Was he tired of not getting any royalties while making increasingly significant contributions to their music? It was the wrong decision, as time would tell, but as he himself said, **he was "the only guitarist to ever leave the Stones alive."**

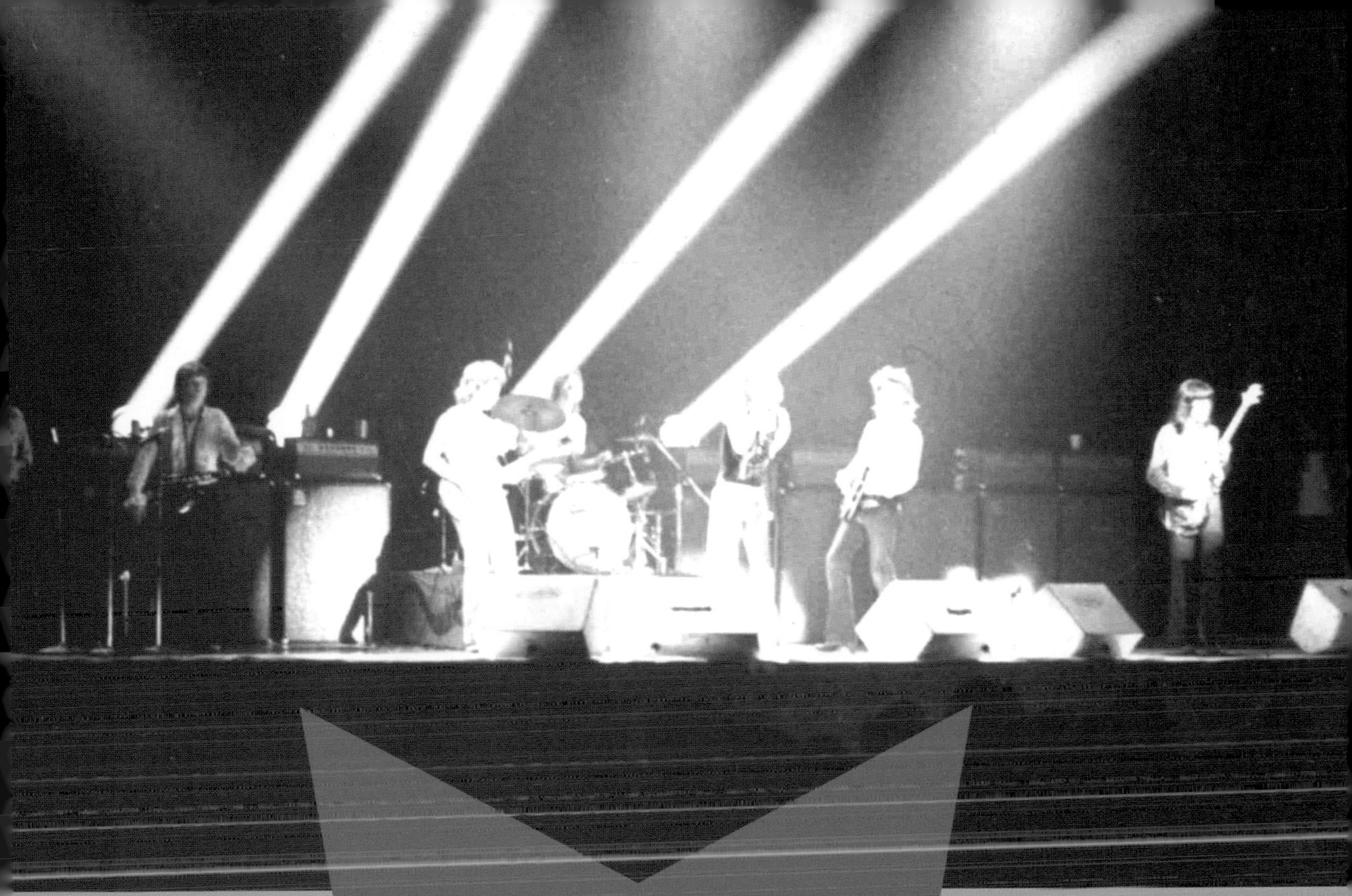

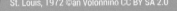

St. Louis, 1972 ©an Volonnino CC BY SA 2.0

"AFTER WE SPLIT UP, I STARTED TRAVELING MY OWN PATH, AND IT WAS THE DOWNWARD PATH TO DRUGSVILLE, WHILE MICK FLEW OFF WITH THE JET-SET CROWD."

Keith Richards

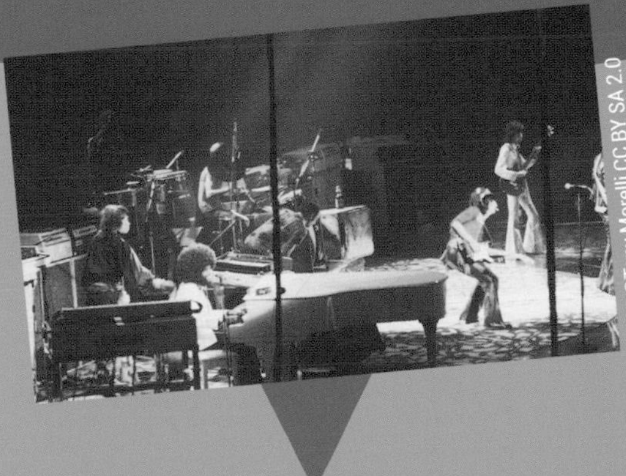

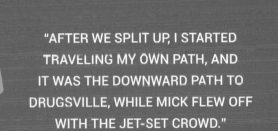

1975 ©Tony Morelli CC BY SA 2.0

Summer of '73

Artist: Aurélie Neyret

"Angie": The Best Slow Song of All Time.

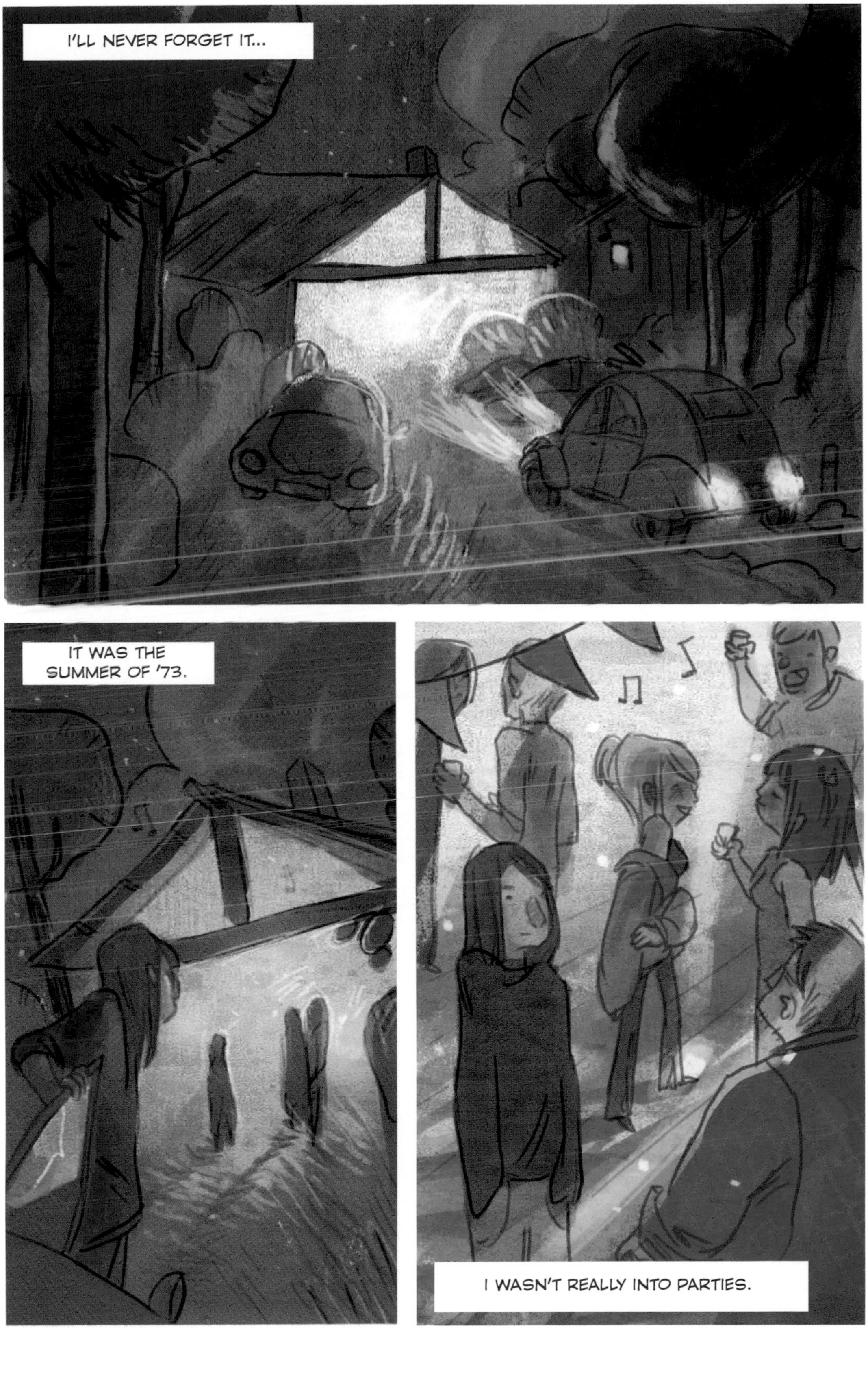
I'LL NEVER FORGET IT...
IT WAS THE SUMMER OF '73.
I WASN'T REALLY INTO PARTIES.

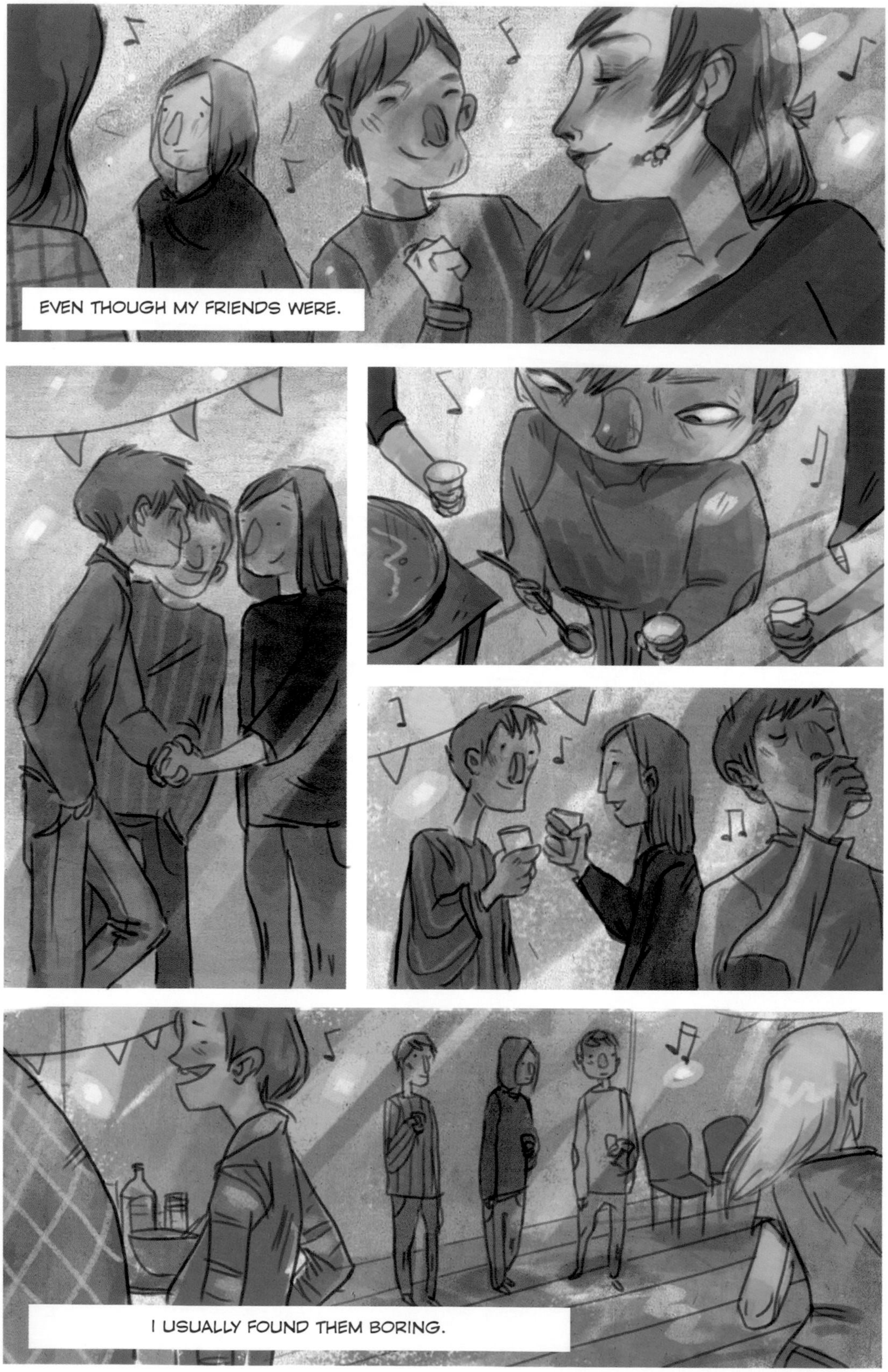
EVEN THOUGH MY FRIENDS WERE.
I USUALLY FOUND THEM BORING.

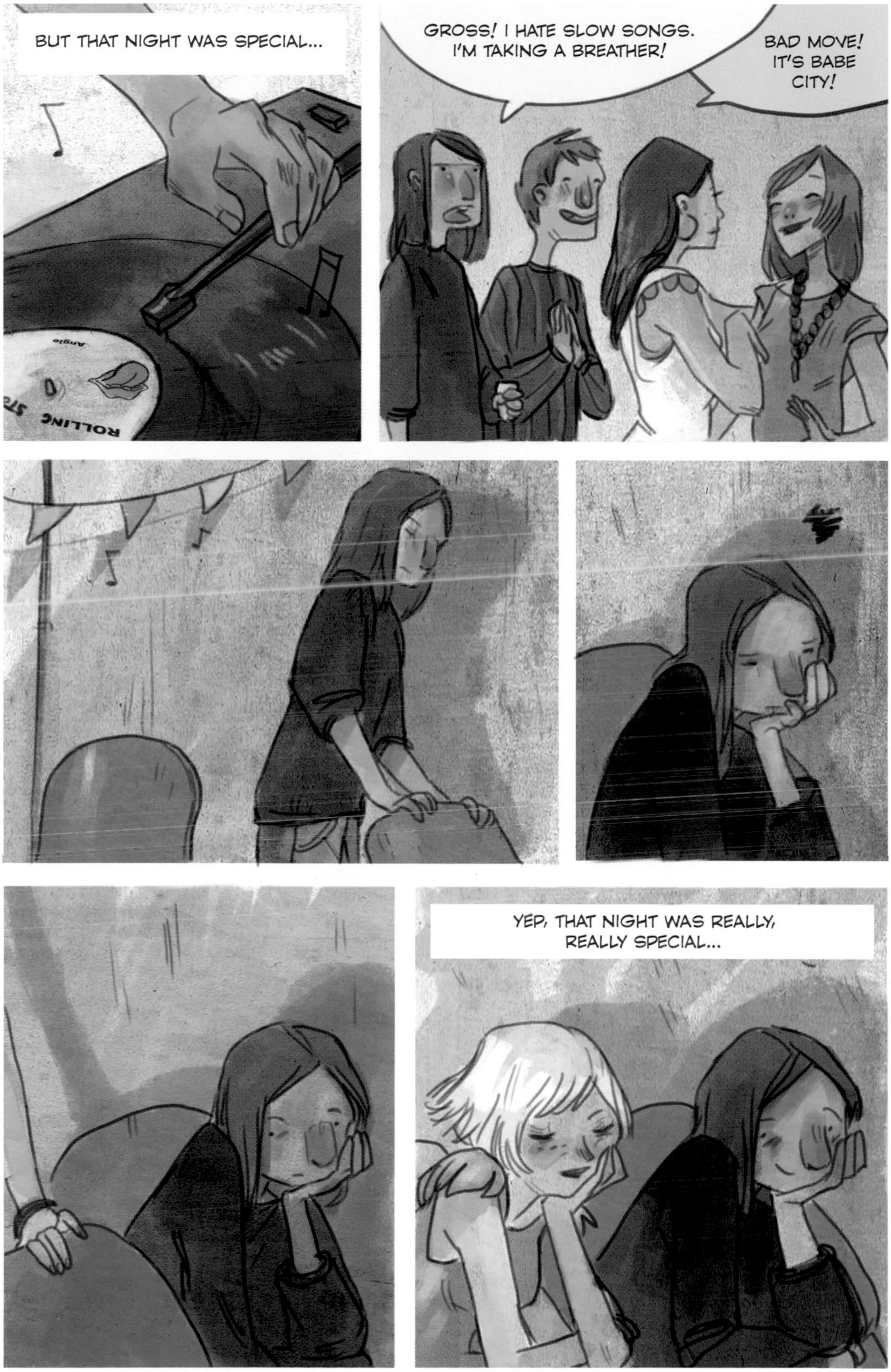
BUT THAT NIGHT WAS SPECIAL...
ROLLING STO
Angie
GROSS! I HATE SLOW SONGS. I'M TAKING A BREATHER!
BAD MOVE! IT'S BABE CITY!
YEP, THAT NIGHT WAS REALLY, REALLY SPECIAL...

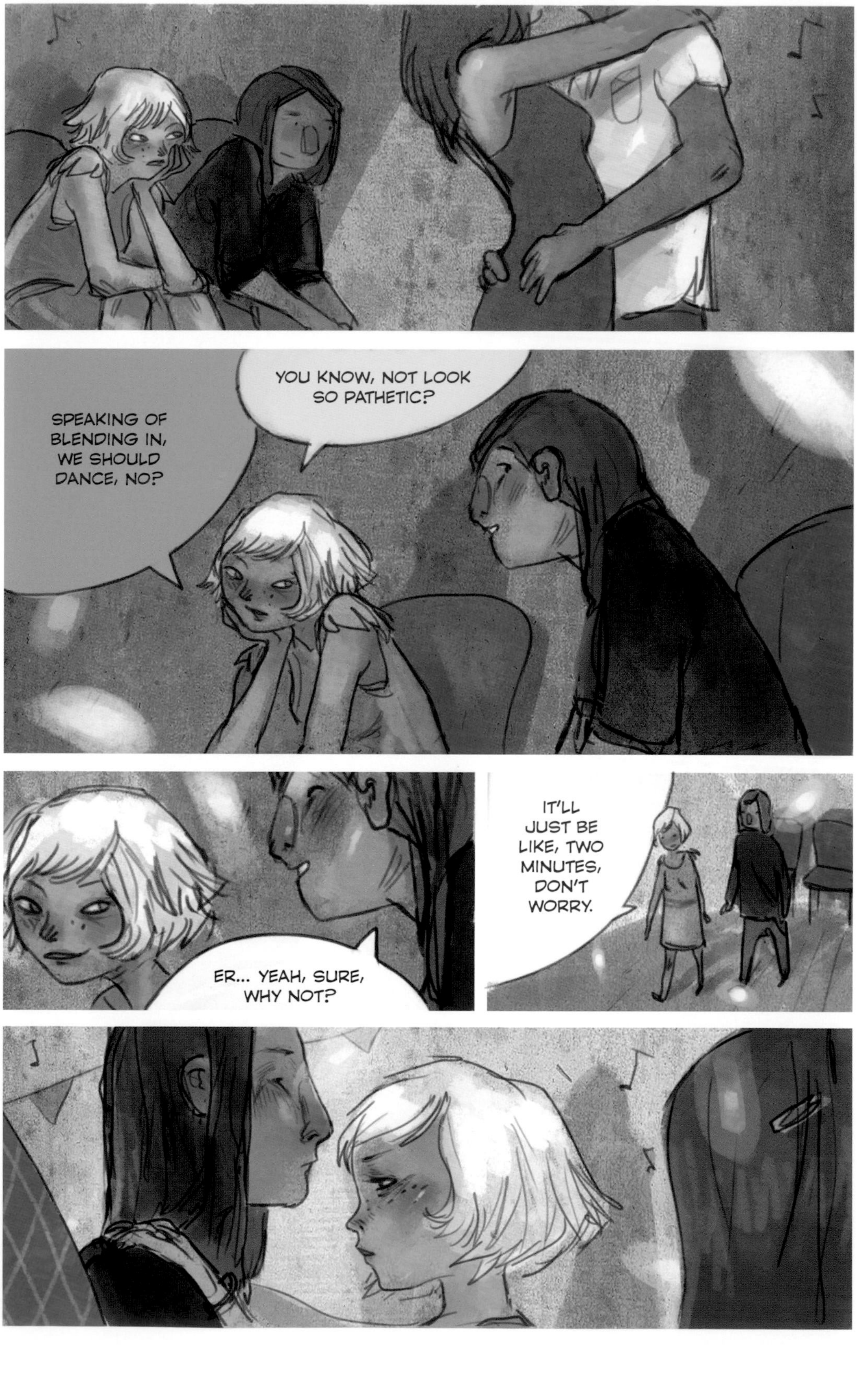
SPEAKING OF BLENDING IN, WE SHOULD DANCE, NO?
YOU KNOW, NOT LOOK SO PATHETIC?
ER... YEAH, SURE, WHY NOT?
IT'LL JUST BE LIKE, TWO MINUTES, DON'T WORRY.

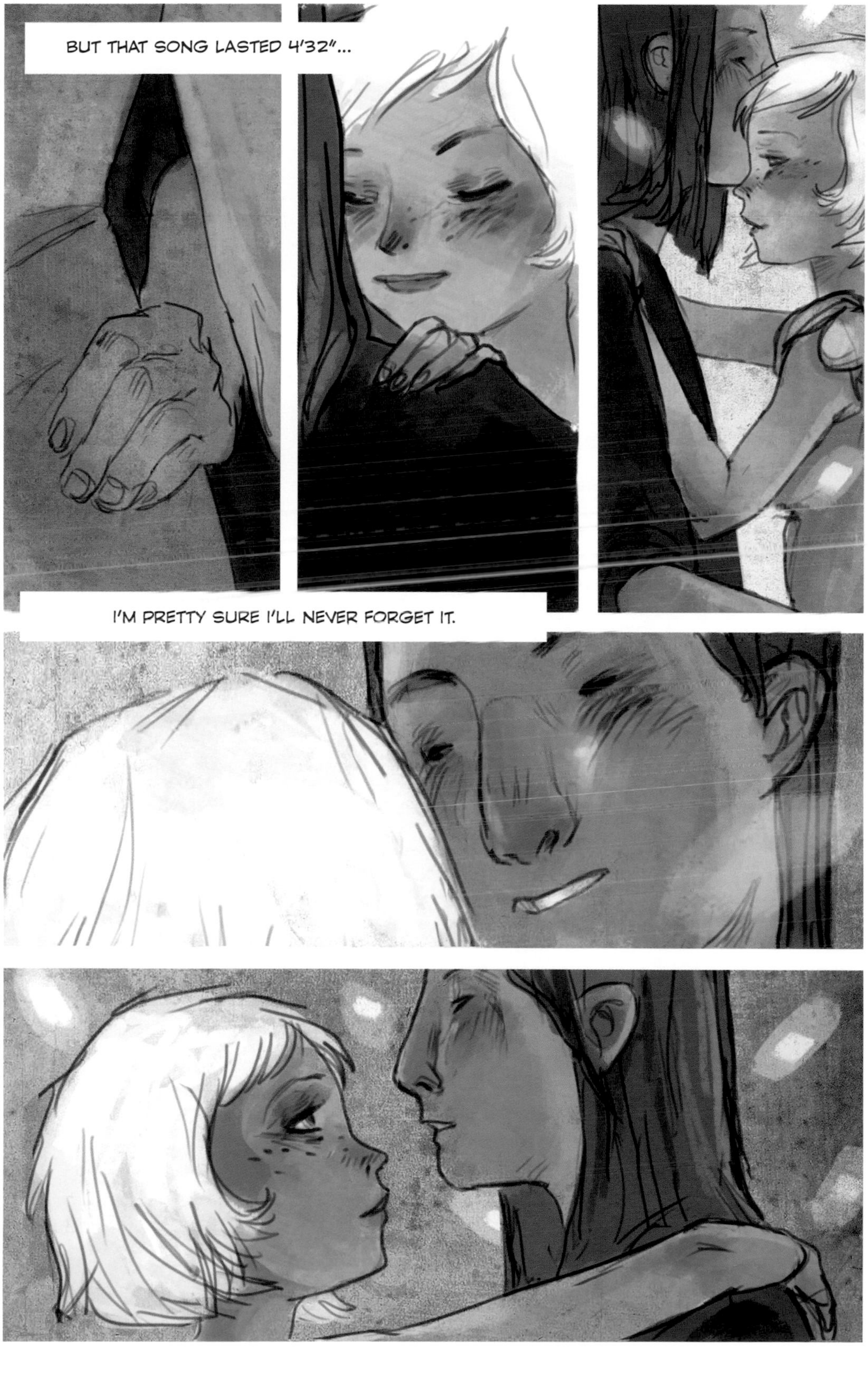
BUT THAT SONG LASTED 4'32"...
I'M PRETTY SURE I'LL NEVER FORGET IT.

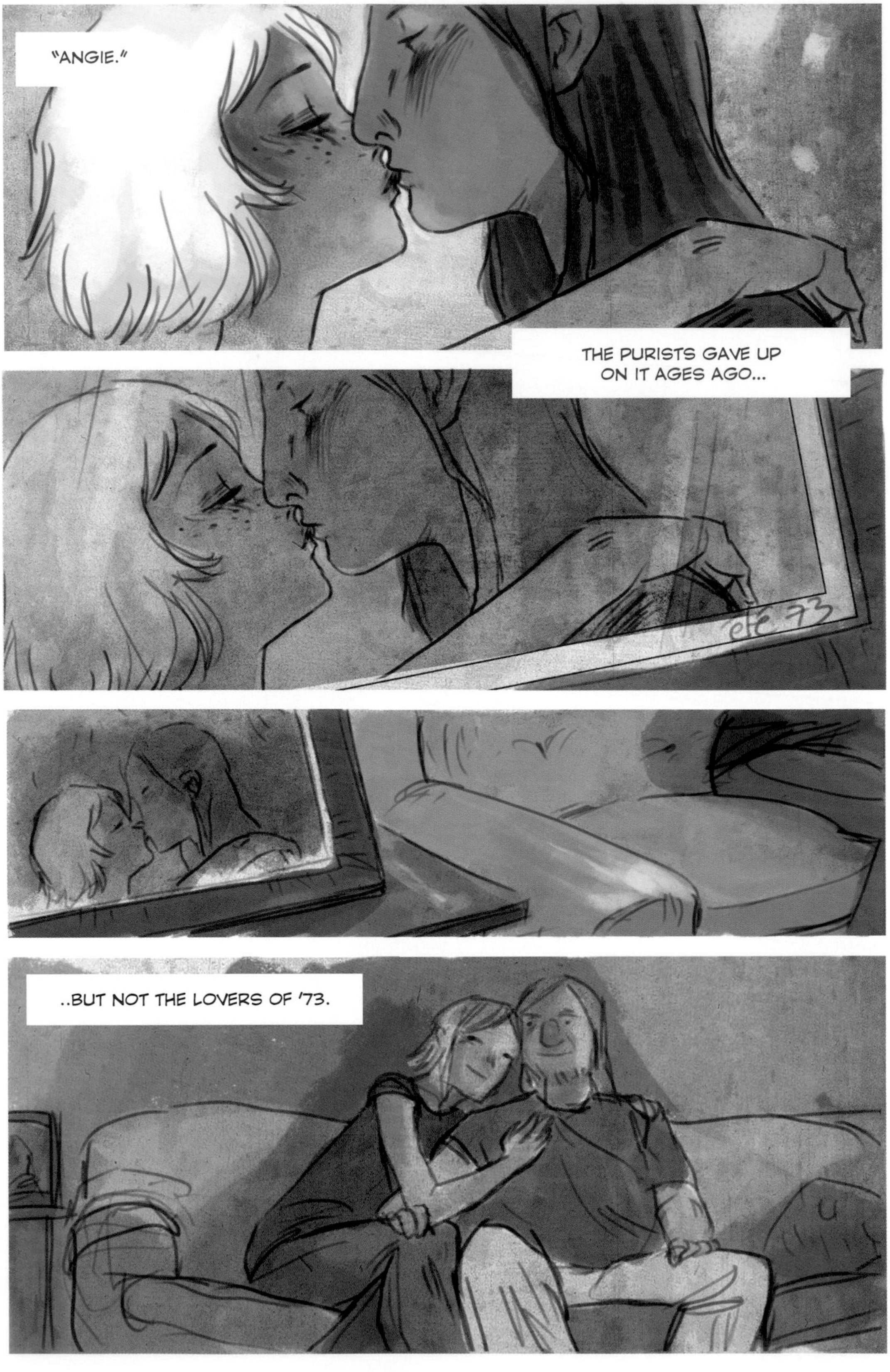
"ANGIE."
THE PURISTS GAVE UP ON IT AGES AGO...
..BUT NOT THE LOVERS OF '73.

Bye Bye The Kid, Hello Ronnie!

Replacing a Stone: in and of itself, not a problem. The best musicians of the day came in droves to try to get their foot in the door. No, the problem was that this time, the criteria had to extend beyond mere musical talent. The Rolling Stones needed someone they could really connect with. **And it was on the human level that Ron Wood stood out.**

"THERE'S ONE THING RONNIE DOES REALLY WELL THAT MICK TAYLOR WAS UTTERLY INCAPABLE OF DOING: SIMPLY SHOWING UP AND PLAYING FOR THE NEXT THIRTY YEARS."

Charlie Watts

Chicago - 1975 ©Jim Summaria CC BY SA 3.0

Ron Wood and Mick Jagger in concert in Chicago in 1975 ©Jim Summaria CC BY SA 3.

Musically, Ronnie—or Woody, as he was called—promptly began playing in a way that supported Keith and reinforced his guitar, without putting himself forward the way Mick Taylor used to do. On a personal level, Ron Wood turned out to be a very nurturing person, which was something Keith Richards, whom the press had called "the world's most elegantly wasted human being," desperately needed.

On top of that, he had a pleasant and contagious personality. On tour, he could be seen jumping around on stage, even getting a reaction out of stoic Bill Wyman. A true miracle!

In concert in Lexington, Kentucky, 1981 ©Michale E. Conen CC BY SA 2.0

Thanks to Ron Wood, the Rolling Stones began to enjoy being together again. Initially "on loan" from The Faces, the guitarist soon became a full-fledged Stone in his own right!

Keith Richards and Ron Wood in concert in Turin 1982 ©Gorup de Basanez CC BY SA 3.0

Ron Wood in concert in San Francisco in 1981 ©Catherine Anderson CC BY-SA 2.0

"PLUS, WITH MICK TAYLOR, I WASN'T PLAYING THE WAY I WANTED. I FELT LIKE WE WERE HEADING TOWARDS A DIVIDE BETWEEN LEAD GUITAR AND RHYTHM GUITAR, AND THAT WAS NEVER MY THING. I WAS ALWAYS MORE INTERESTED IN "THE ANCIENT ART OF WEAVING," AS RONNIE AND I CALL IT."

Keith Richards

Dr. Wood

Artist: Sanzito

The Arrival of Ron Wood,
New Guitarist and
Keith Richards' Savior.

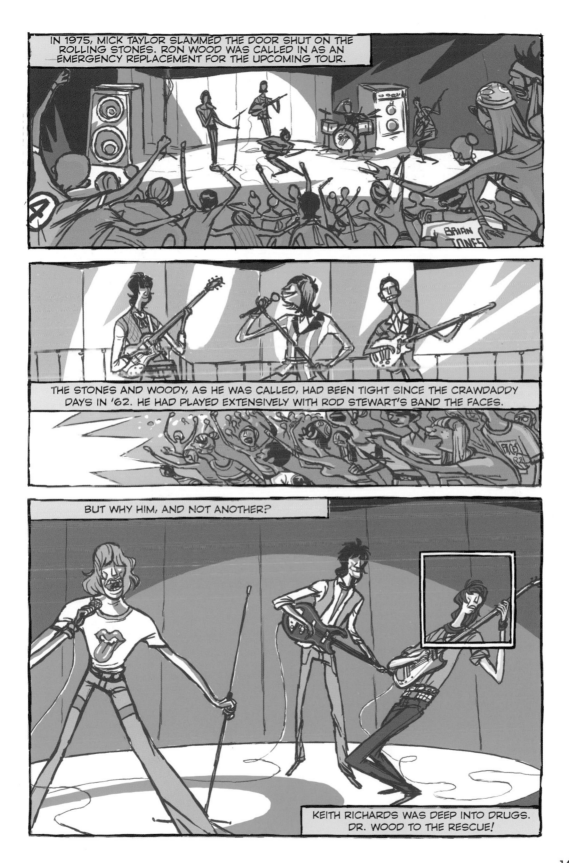

IN 1975, MICK TAYLOR SLAMMED THE DOOR SHUT ON THE ROLLING STONES. RON WOOD WAS CALLED IN AS AN EMERGENCY REPLACEMENT FOR THE UPCOMING TOUR.

THE STONES AND WOODY, AS HE WAS CALLED, HAD BEEN TIGHT SINCE THE CRAWDADDY DAYS IN '62. HE HAD PLAYED EXTENSIVELY WITH ROD STEWART'S BAND THE FACES.

BUT WHY HIM, AND NOT ANOTHER?

KEITH RICHARDS WAS DEEP INTO DRUGS. DR. WOOD TO THE RESCUE!

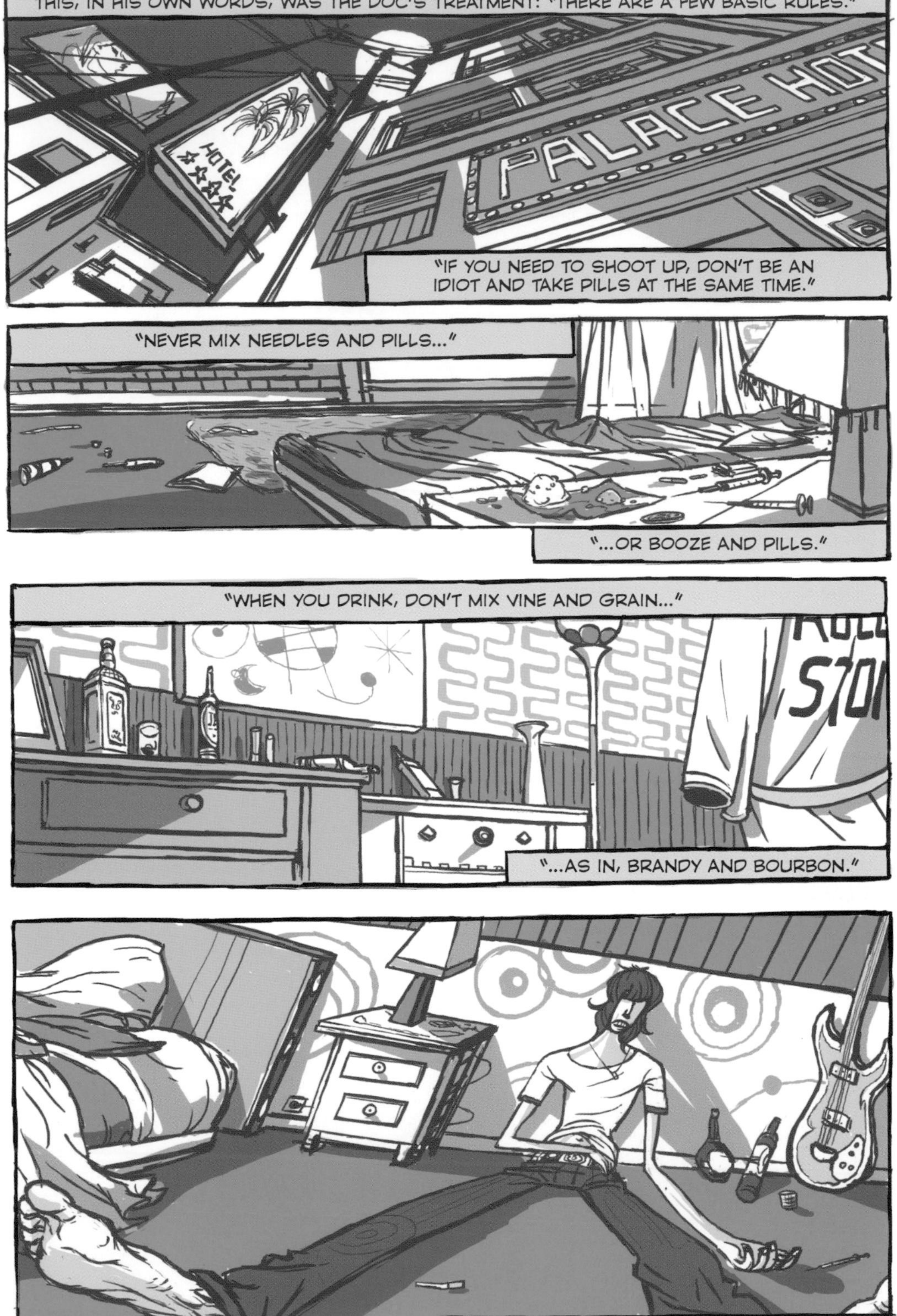
THIS, IN HIS OWN WORDS, WAS THE DOC'S TREATMENT: "THERE ARE A FEW BASIC RULES."
"IF YOU NEED TO SHOOT UP, DON'T BE AN IDIOT AND TAKE PILLS AT THE SAME TIME."
"NEVER MIX NEEDLES AND PILLS..."
"...OR BOOZE AND PILLS."
"WHEN YOU DRINK, DON'T MIX VINE AND GRAIN..."
"...AS IN, BRANDY AND BOURBON."
"THAT'S SAVED MY LIFE MORE THAN ONCE."

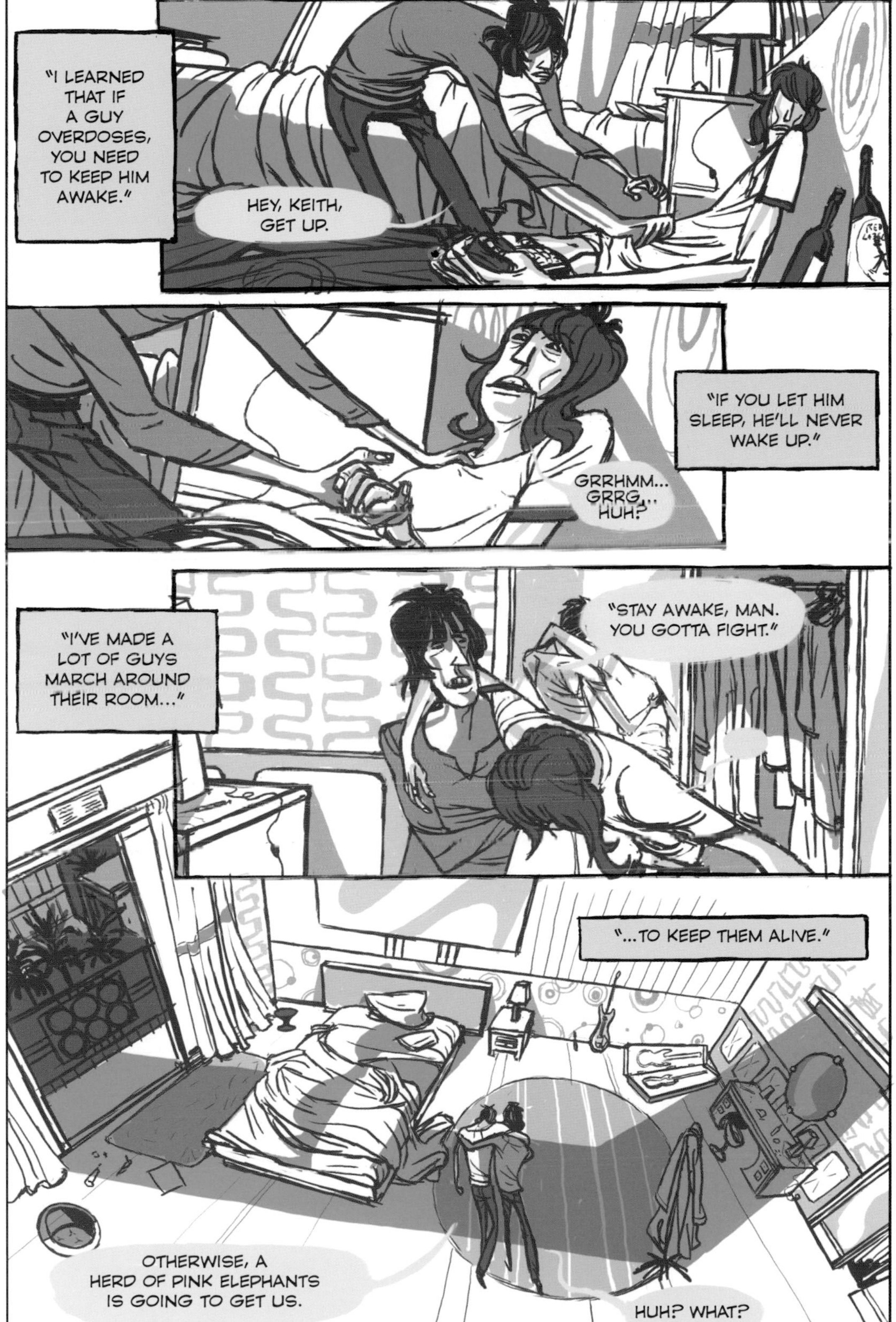
"I LEARNED THAT IF A GUY OVERDOSES, YOU NEED TO KEEP HIM AWAKE."
HEY, KEITH, GET UP.
"IF YOU LET HIM SLEEP, HE'LL NEVER WAKE UP."
GRRHMM... GRRG... HUH?
"I'VE MADE A LOT OF GUYS MARCH AROUND THEIR ROOM..."
"STAY AWAKE, MAN. YOU GOTTA FIGHT."
"...TO KEEP THEM ALIVE."
OTHERWISE, A HERD OF PINK ELEPHANTS IS GOING TO GET US.
HUH? WHAT?

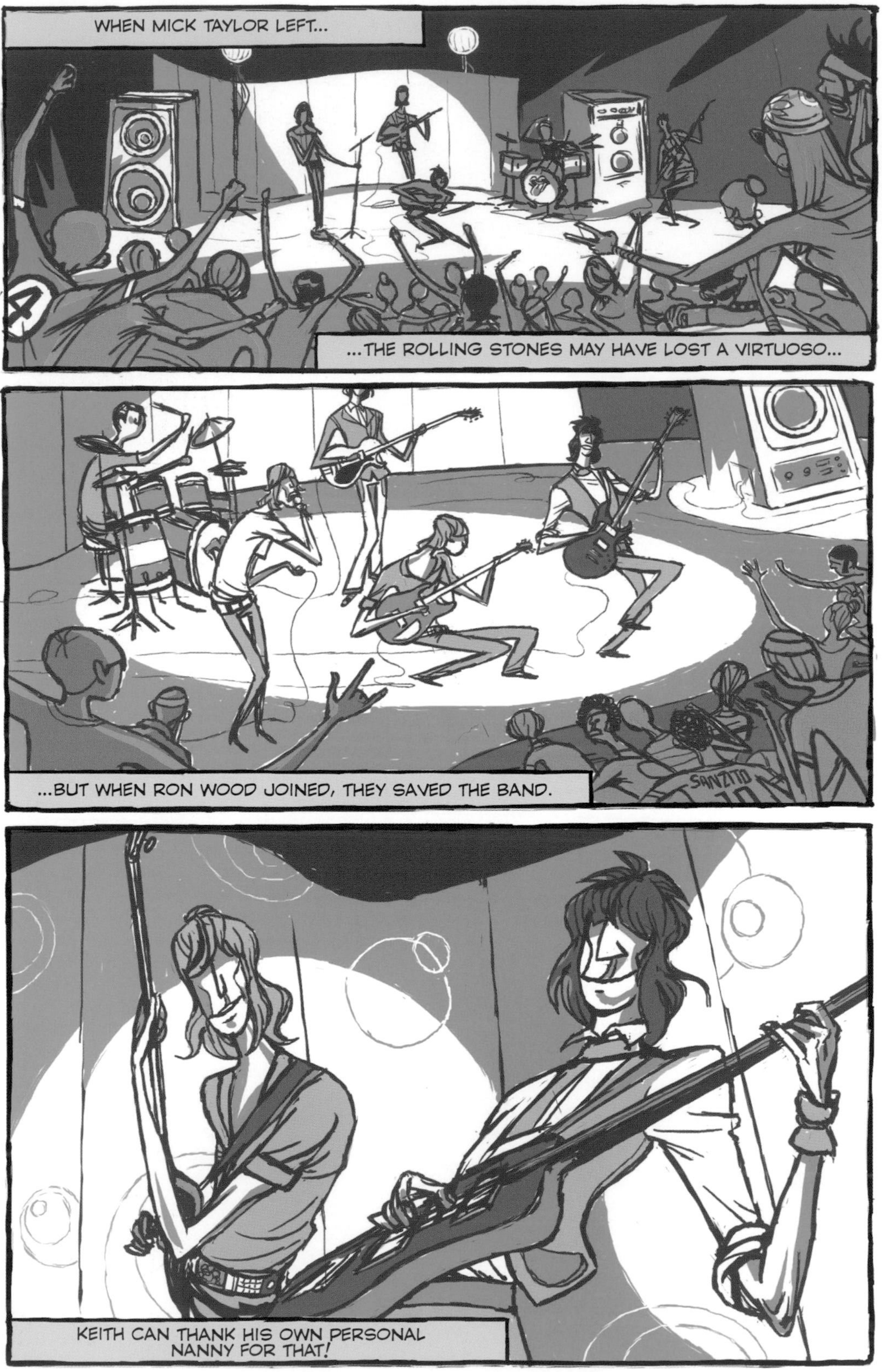
WHEN MICK TAYLOR LEFT...
...THE ROLLING STONES MAY HAVE LOST A VIRTUOSO...
...BUT WHEN RON WOOD JOINED, THEY SAVED THE BAND.
KEITH CAN THANK HIS OWN PERSONAL NANNY FOR THAT!

Oh, Solo Mio

In 1982 in Rotterdam ©Marcel Antonisse CC BY-SA 3.0

"I CALL THAT TIME PERIOD WORLD WAR THREE—
IT WAS A HIATUS IN THE HISTORY OF THE ROLLING STONES.
I WAS ENRAGED THAT MICK SIGNED A CONTRACT FOR SOLO ALBUMS
AND TIED IT IN WITH A STONES' CONTRACT WITHOUT TELLING ANYONE.
AT THE TIME, I THOUGHT THAT WAS A REALLY SHITTY THING TO DO."

Keith Richards

When things aren't going well in a band, there are two solutions: either split up for good, whether on friendly terms or not, or take a break from each other. When he and Keith Richards went through their rough patch, Mick Jagger chose the second option by pursuing a solo career, unaware that by doing so he was fanning the flame of conflict...

Bill Wyman and Mick Taylor in 2008 ©Eddie Janssens CC BY-SA 3.

"THE STONES' SYNERGY WAS BASED ON CONFLICT."

Edna Gundersen

Years went by and the Stones were still rolling, though not always necessarily in the same direction.

They needed another shock to the system to figure out whether or not they still made sense as a band. Mick Jagger provided just that. In early 1984, he was in contract negotiations with Walter Yetnikoff, the CEO of CBS, who agreed to sign them on one condition: that Mick also release solo albums at the same time. He was a crafty strategist and knew that while the future of the Stones seemed uncertain, Mick was a sure thing. Jagger also viewed that as an opportunity to revive his career. When Keith Richards got wind of that secret arrangement, he was furious and accused Mick of putting his own needs before the band's. Yet other Rolling Stones had already gone that route, starting with Brian Jones, who produced an album in 1967 with Jajouka musicians from Morocco, which is now considered one of the very first World Music albums. In 1974, Bill Wyman also embarked on a solo career, meeting with a small degree of success with his song "(Si Si) Je Suis Un Rock Star." Charlie Watts followed suit in 1981, rekindling his love for jazz with, among others, a Charlie Parker tribute album.

But Mick Jagger's decision carried greater consequences, as he was one of the band's two leaders (the other being Keith Richards). If he did well, what would that mean for the band's future? *She's the Boss*, his first album, was relatively successful. Keith Richards counter-attacked with solo albums of his own, on the Virgin label, which, ironically... were bigger hits! This solo album competition between them did not, however, cause the band to implode. **On the contrary, it made them realize they might require a little time apart sometimes to enjoy playing together again!**

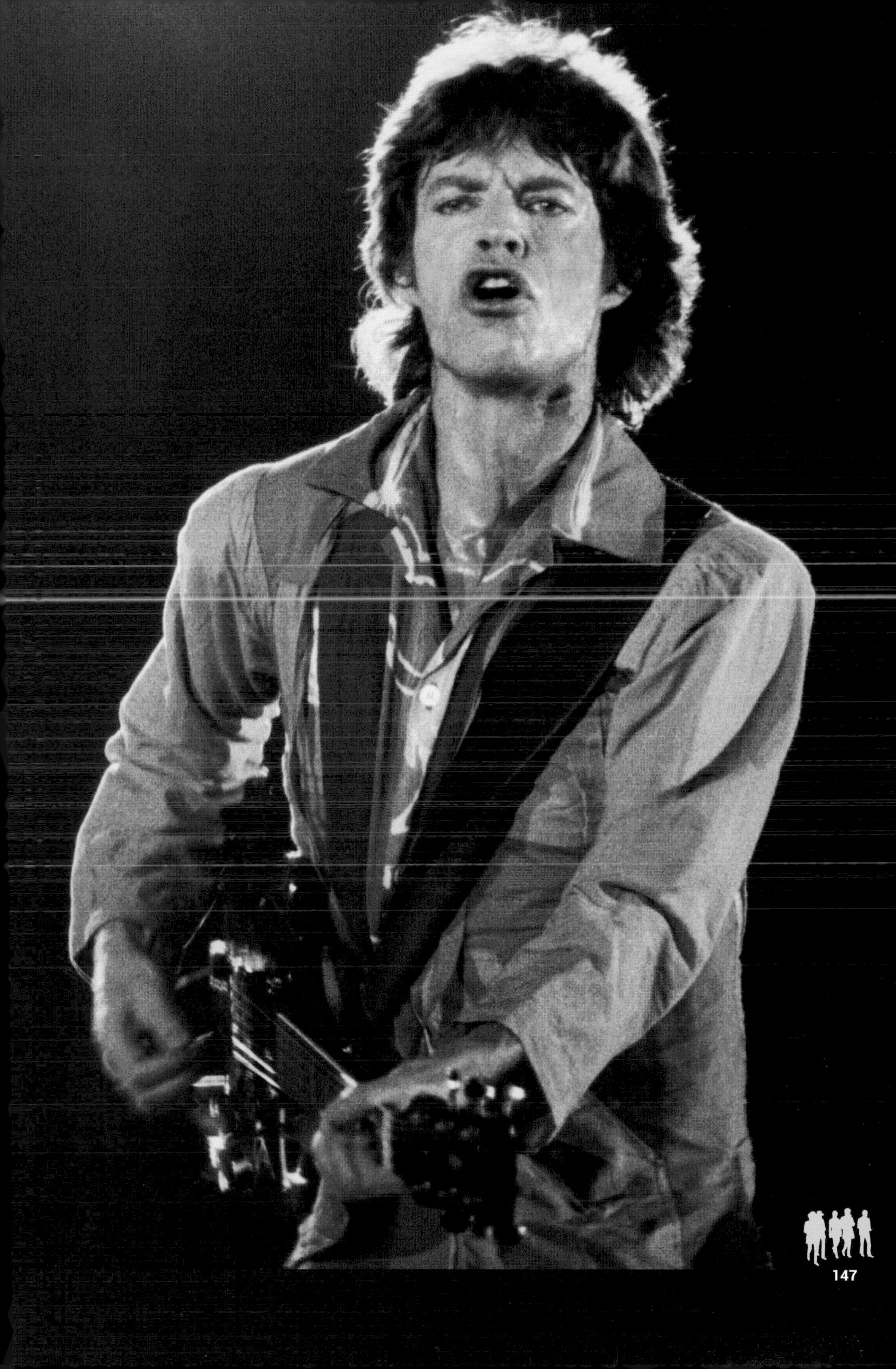

In 1982 in Rotterdam

Erase It!

Artist: Sarah Williamson

Mick Jagger's
Solo Adventure.

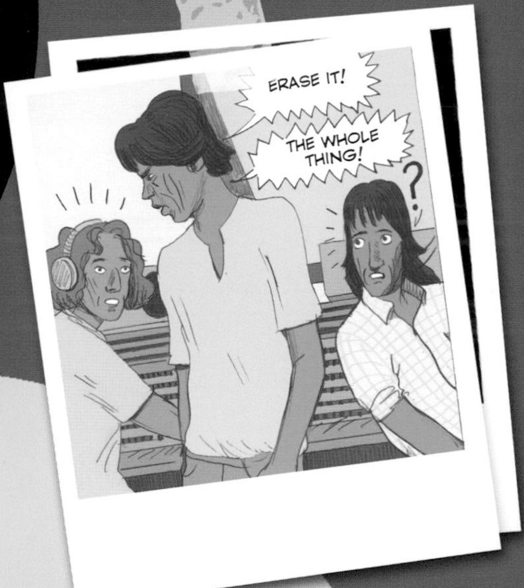
ERASE IT!
THE WHOLE THING!
?

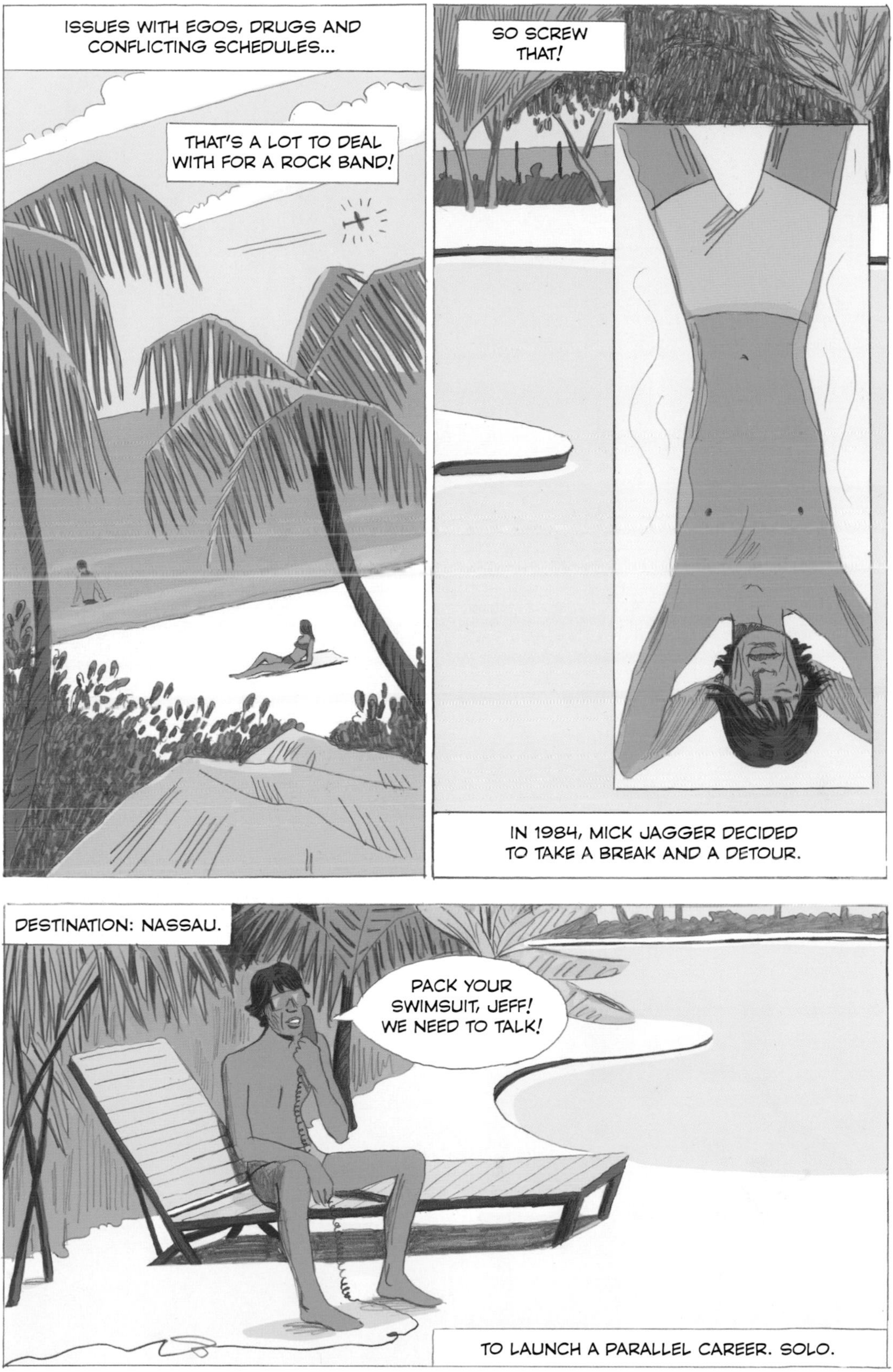
ISSUES WITH EGOS, DRUGS AND CONFLICTING SCHEDULES...
THAT'S A LOT TO DEAL WITH FOR A ROCK BAND!
SO SCREW THAT!
IN 1984, MICK JAGGER DECIDED TO TAKE A BREAK AND A DETOUR.
DESTINATION: NASSAU.
PACK YOUR SWIMSUIT, JEFF! WE NEED TO TALK!
TO LAUNCH A PARALLEL CAREER. SOLO.

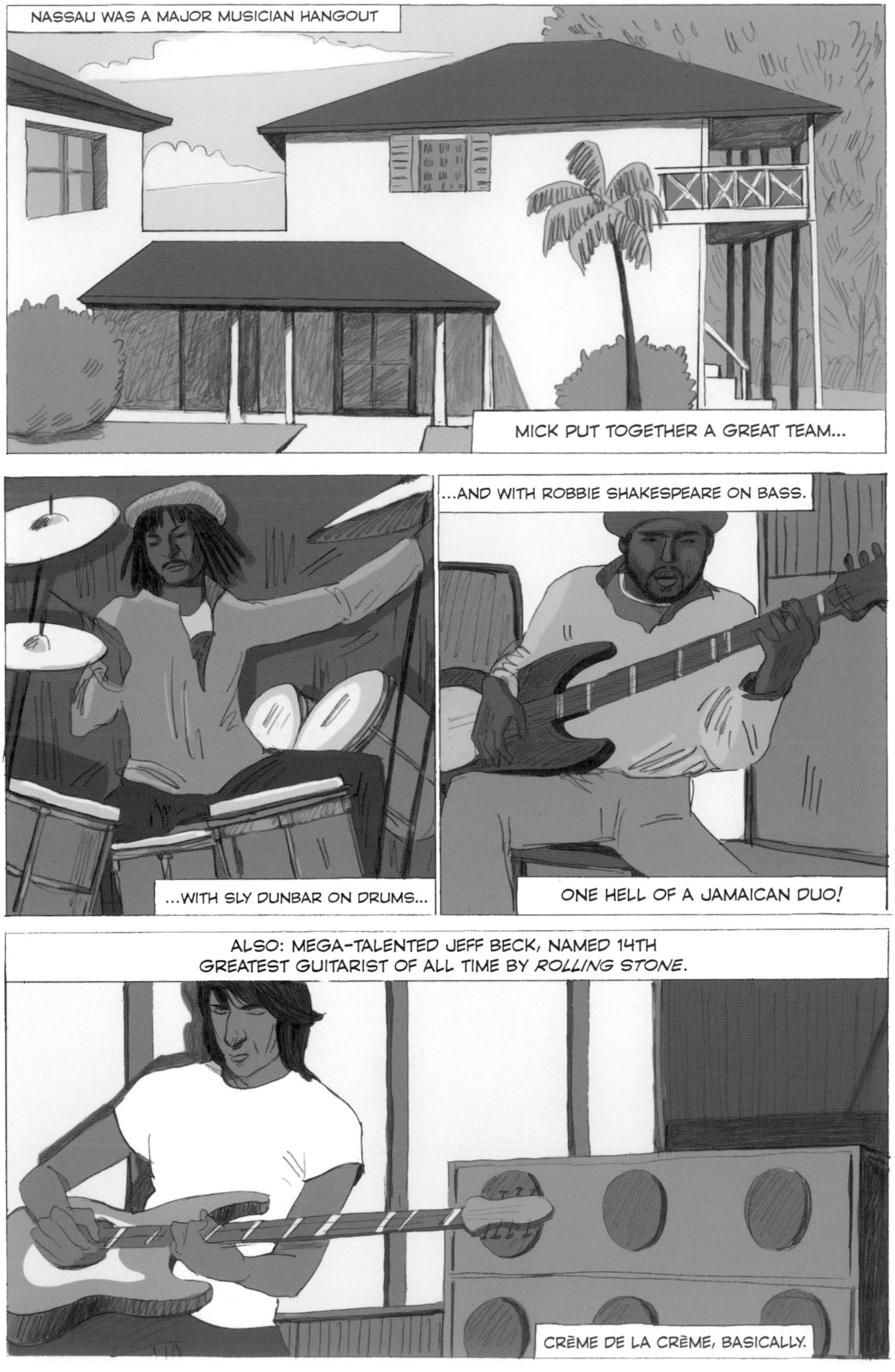
NASSAU WAS A MAJOR MUSICIAN HANGOUT
MICK PUT TOGETHER A GREAT TEAM...
...WITH SLY DUNBAR ON DRUMS...
...AND WITH ROBBIE SHAKESPEARE ON BASS.
ONE HELL OF A JAMAICAN DUO!
ALSO: MEGA-TALENTED JEFF BECK, NAMED 14TH GREATEST GUITARIST OF ALL TIME BY *ROLLING STONE*.
CRÈME DE LA CRÈME, BASICALLY.

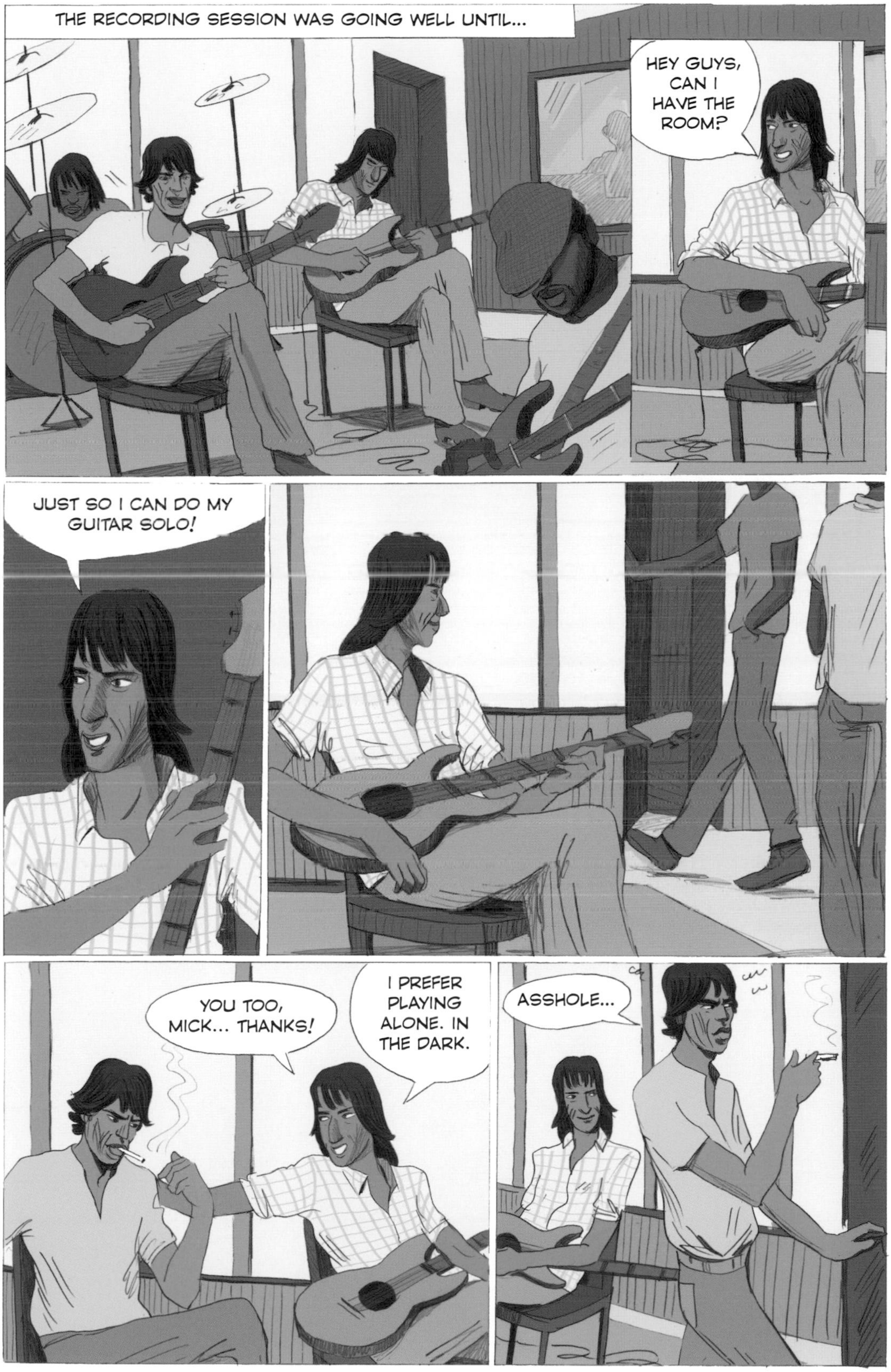
THE RECORDING SESSION WAS GOING WELL UNTIL...
HEY GUYS, CAN I HAVE THE ROOM?
JUST SO I CAN DO MY GUITAR SOLO!
YOU TOO, MICK... THANKS!
I PREFER PLAYING ALONE. IN THE DARK.
ASSHOLE...

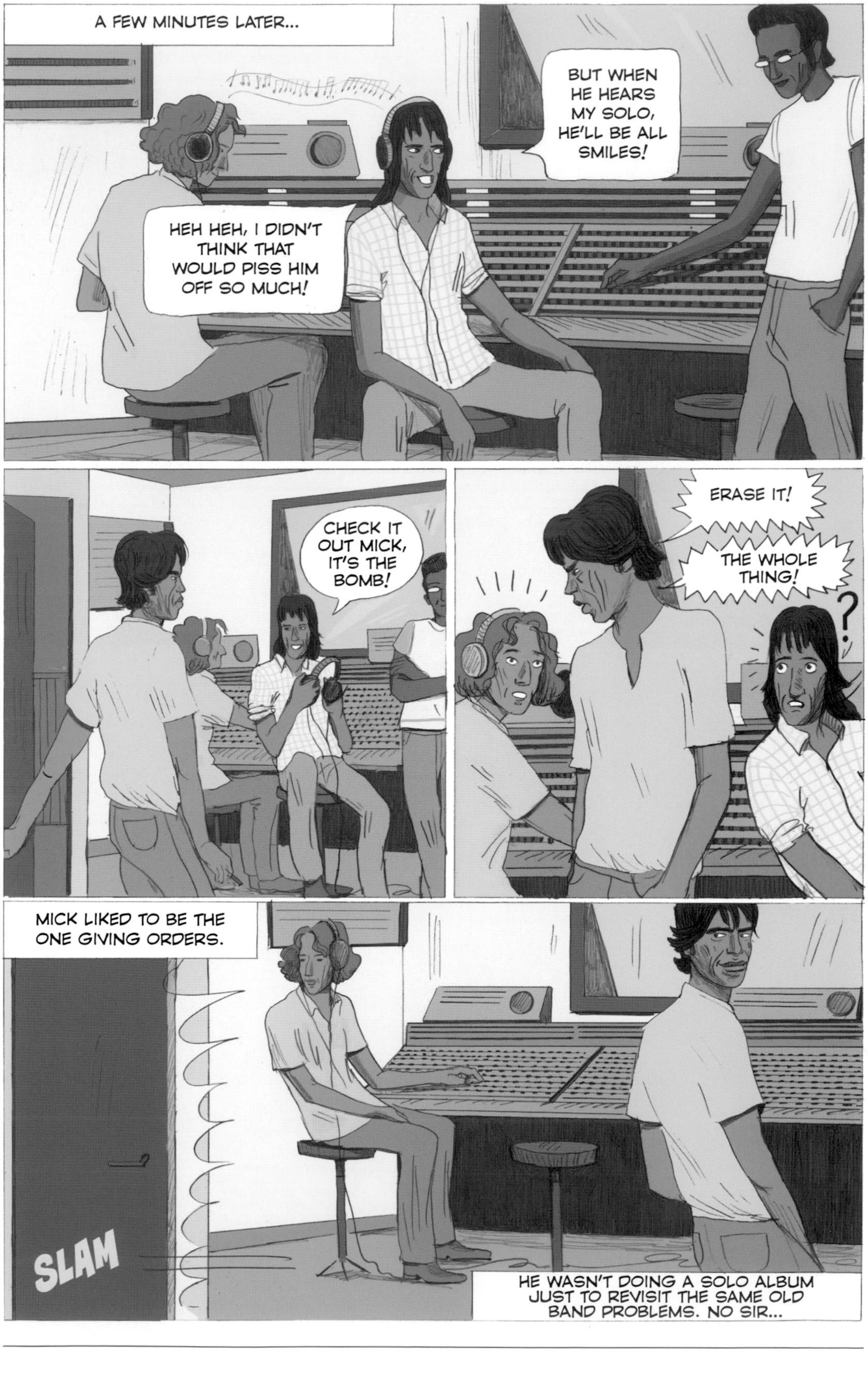
A FEW MINUTES LATER...
BUT WHEN HE HEARS MY SOLO, HE'LL BE ALL SMILES!
HEH HEH, I DIDN'T THINK THAT WOULD PISS HIM OFF SO MUCH!
CHECK IT OUT MICK, IT'S THE BOMB!
ERASE IT!
THE WHOLE THING!
?
MICK LIKED TO BE THE ONE GIVING ORDERS.
SLAM
HE WASN'T DOING A SOLO ALBUM JUST TO REVISIT THE SAME OLD BAND PROBLEMS. NO SIR...

Thrills and Chills

The Rolling Stones are a live band par excellence. On stage is where they feel at home and it's where they return when things aren't going well. If they've acquired the reputation as the greatest rock band in the world, it's also thanks to the top-notch quality of their concerts, where grandiose excess is guaranteed—**as are the fans.**

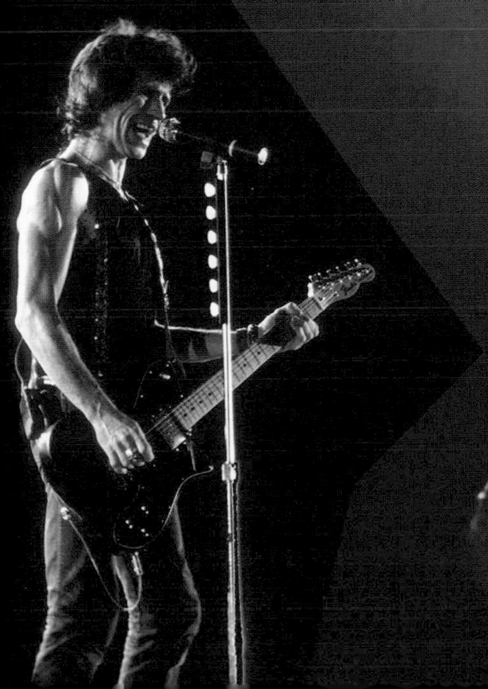

Concert in Turin (1982) ©Gorup De Besanez - CCBYSA3.0

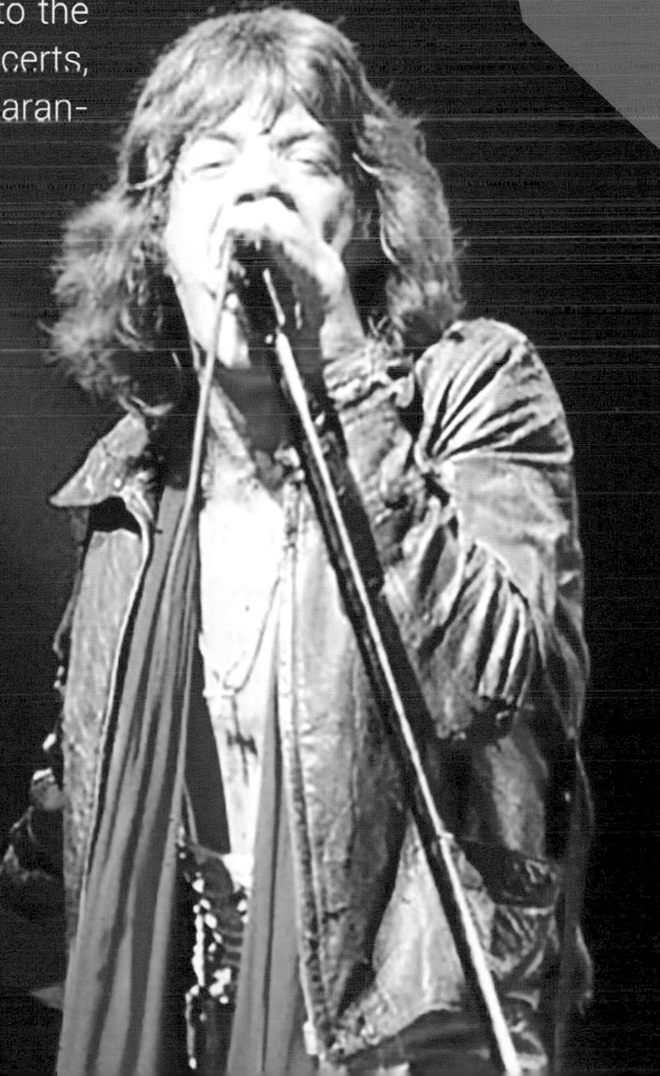

Mick Jagger of the Rolling Stones - NYC show, taken with a Nikon F ©Dina RegineCC-BY-SA

Concert in Toronto (2005) ©Exettra CC BY 2

"WHEN THE LIGHTS GO
ON AND THE MUSIC STARTS,
IT FEELS LIKE YOU'RE HOME.
THAT'S WHEN YOU HAVE TOTAL
CONTROL. YOU'RE ZEUS, THE
EMPEROR OF THE WORLD."

Keith Richards

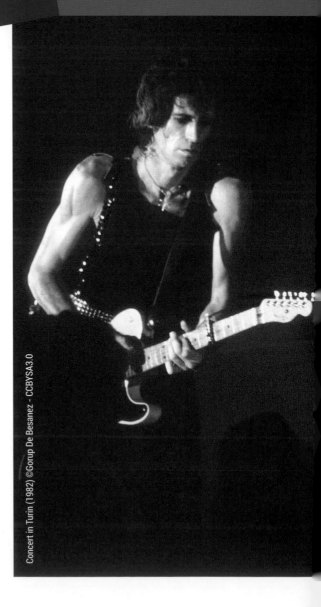

Concert in Turin (1982) ©Gorup De Besanez - CCBYSA3.0

They had come a long way from the Crawdaddy days, when their gear was barely loud enough to drown out the cries of the groupies. Over the years, Rolling Stones tours became enormous, intricately planned and well-oiled machines. As Charlie Watts once said: "The main thing is that if you don't do it right, the people who paid to come and see you get the raw end of the deal, and that's not fair. So the only way to do it, we found out, was to organize this like in the army. As rigorously as that." Yet while Keith Richards loved those huge shows, he still enjoyed the occasional open mic night at smaller venues, like the night he ended up on a stage in New York with singer Jim Carroll's band!
Good times, good times...

Concert in Turin (1932) ©Gorup De Besanez - CCBYSA3.0

> "THE HARDEST PART IS
> MAKING FIFTY THOUSAND PEOPLE
> FEEL LIKE THERE ARE ONLY
> FIVE HUNDRED OF THEM."
>
> **Keith Richards**

Concert at Twickenham, 2006 © Egghead

While technology has taken over their stage in the form of giant screens and speakers and while the concerts keep getting bigger and bigger, with light shows and dazzling pyrotechnics, the Rolling Stones themselves haven't changed one bit. The same thrill of performing live on stage before fans is still there.

As Keith Richards said: "It's a sanctuary. Those two and a half hours, man, you can do whatever you want with them. For us, it's a question of honor, to give it all we've got." The playlist changes every night so as to keep the audience and themselves on their toes. Yep... their last concert won't be happening any time soon. As long as Mick ends the show drenched in sweat, as long as Keith is having a blast with his riffs, Bill and Charlie are in sync, and Ronnie's as happy as a clam, **there's no danger of them calling it quits!**

Sex, Drugs and ...Ping-Pong

Artist and colorist: Joël Alessandra
Storyboard by Carine Becker

The Band's Little Rituals
Before the Big Show.

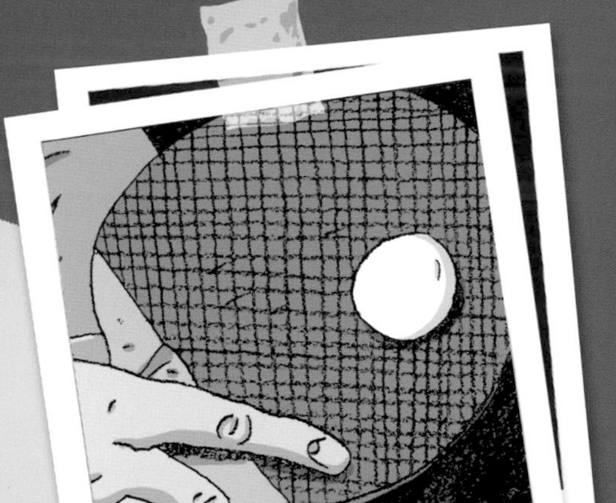

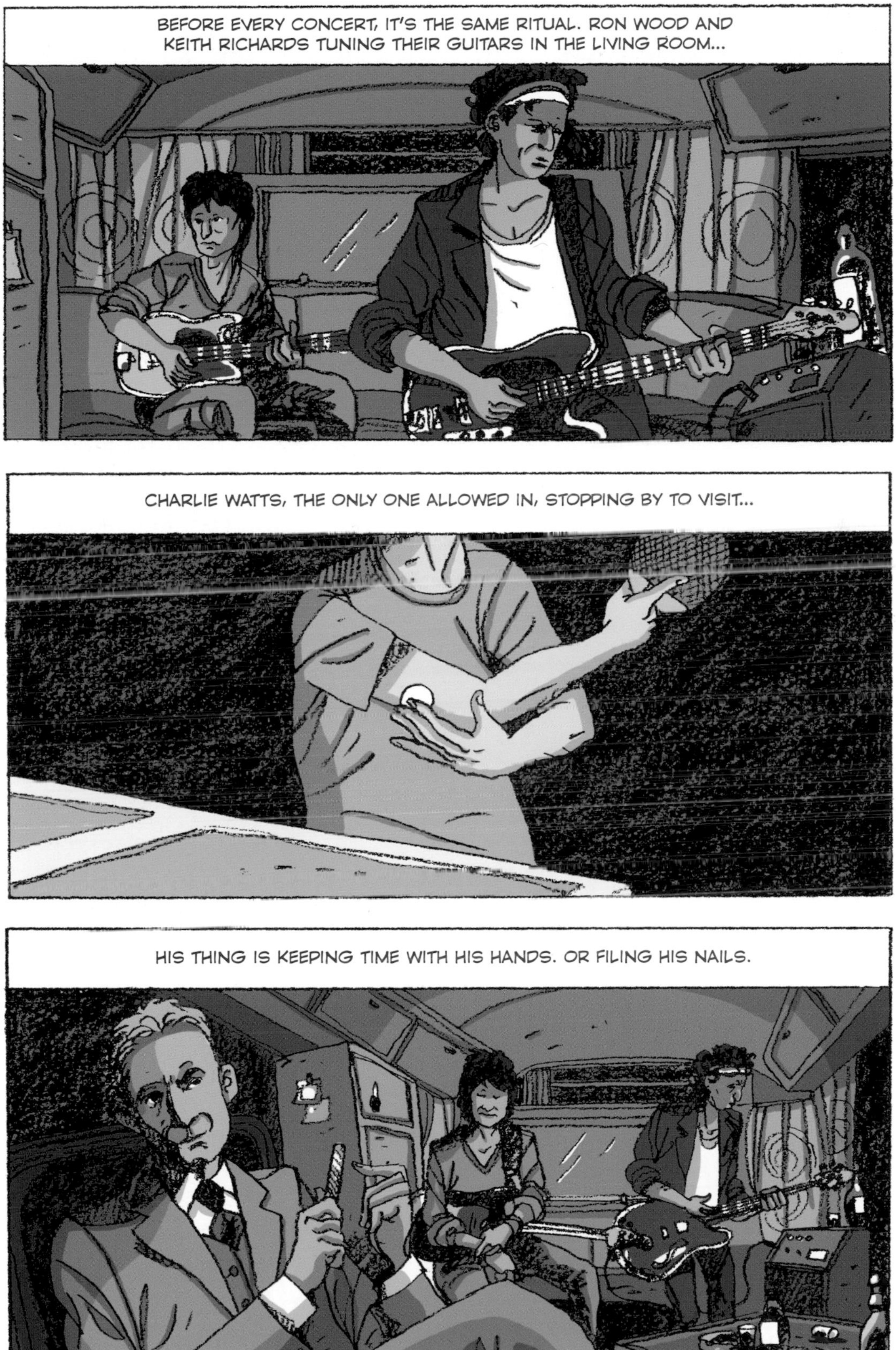
BEFORE EVERY CONCERT, IT'S THE SAME RITUAL. RON WOOD AND KEITH RICHARDS TUNING THEIR GUITARS IN THE LIVING ROOM...
CHARLIE WATTS, THE ONLY ONE ALLOWED IN, STOPPING BY TO VISIT...
HIS THING IS KEEPING TIME WITH HIS HANDS. OR FILING HIS NAILS.

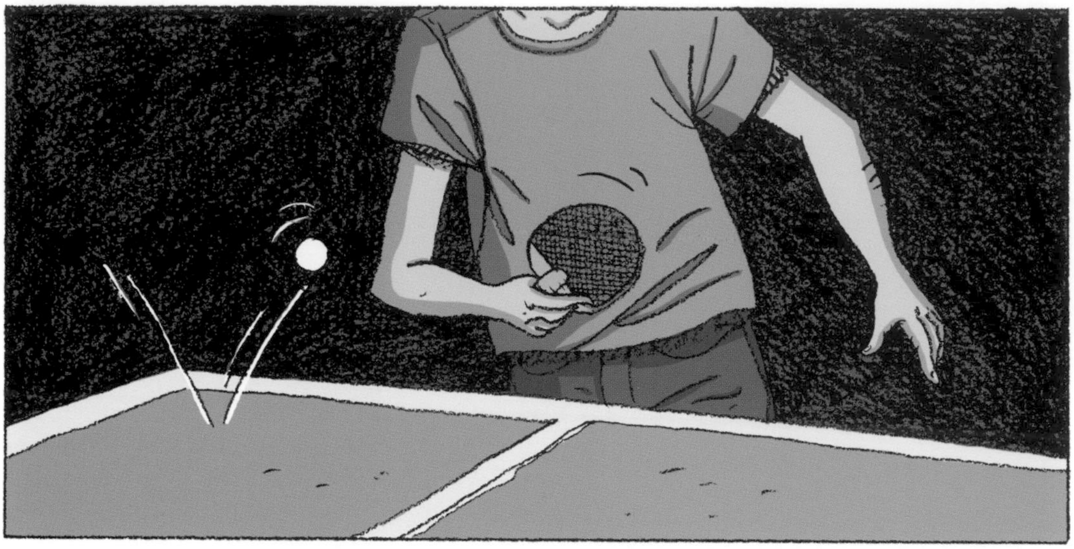

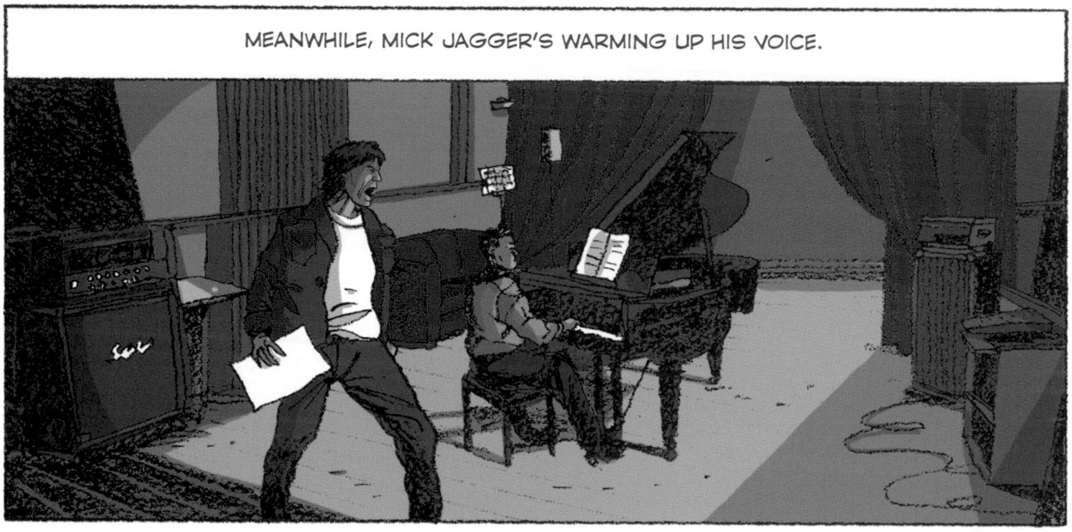
MEANWHILE, MICK JAGGER'S WARMING UP HIS VOICE.

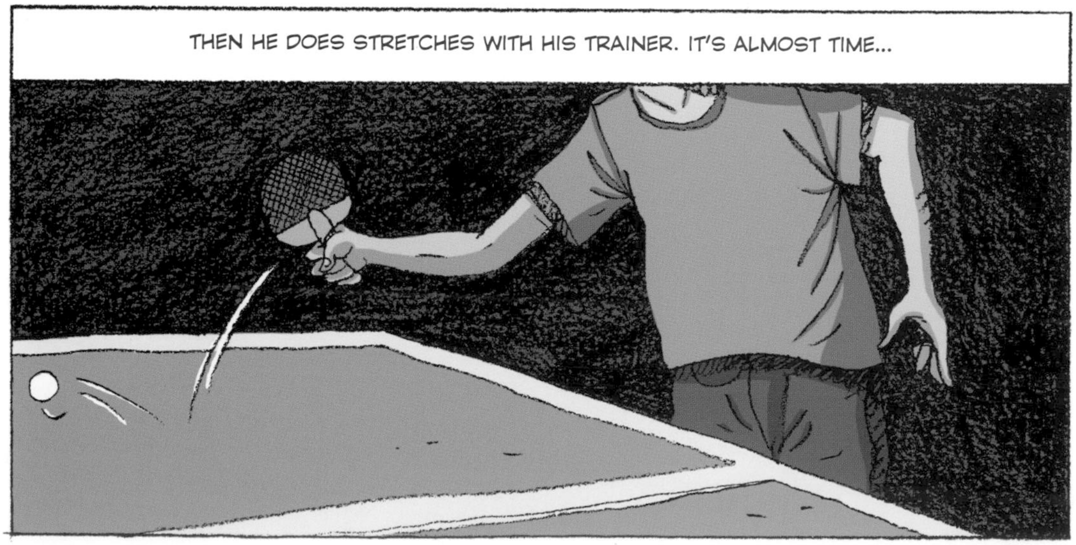
THEN HE DOES STRETCHES WITH HIS TRAINER. IT'S ALMOST TIME...

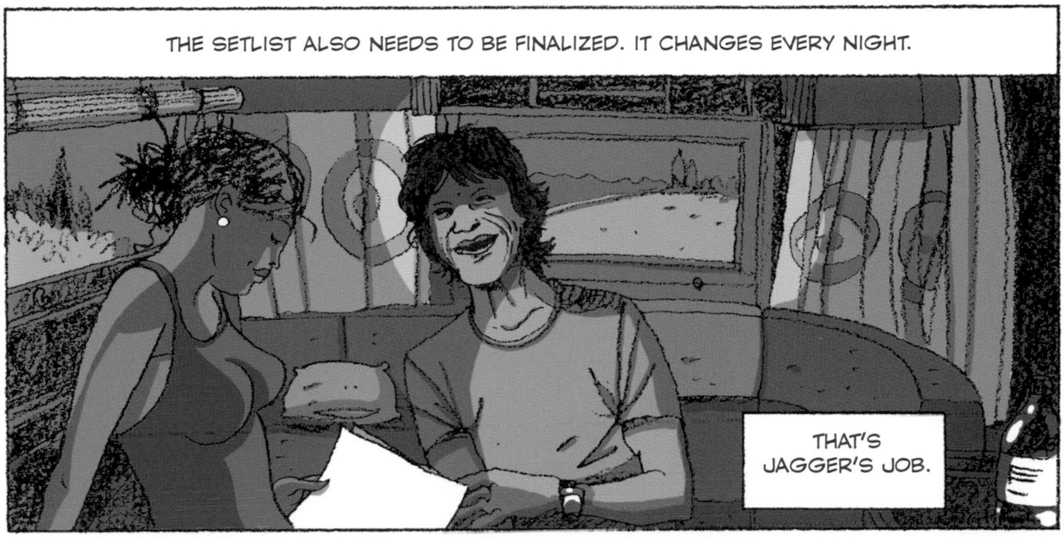
THE SETLIST ALSO NEEDS TO BE FINALIZED. IT CHANGES EVERY NIGHT.
THAT'S JAGGER'S JOB.

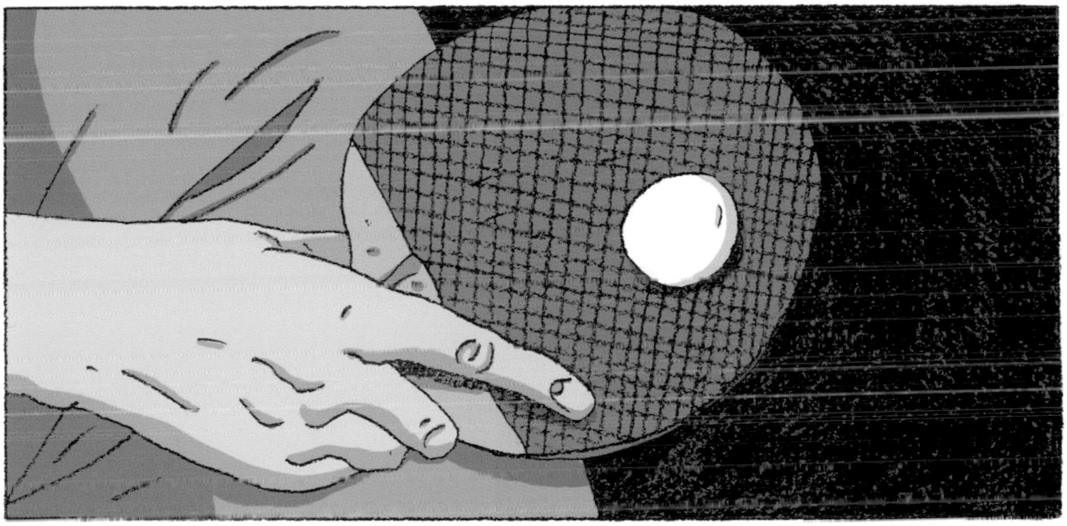

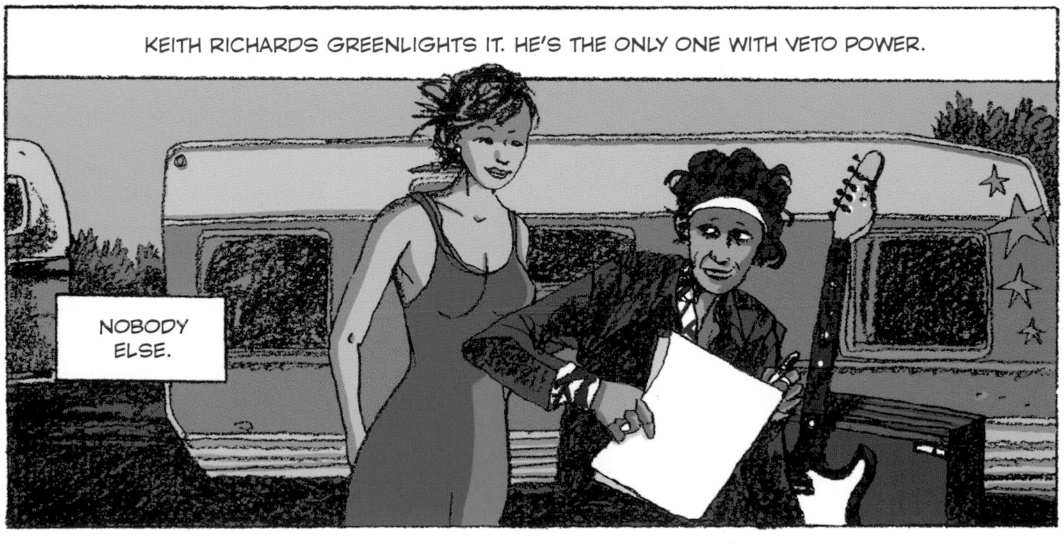
KEITH RICHARDS GREENLIGHTS IT. HE'S THE ONLY ONE WITH VETO POWER.
NOBODY ELSE.

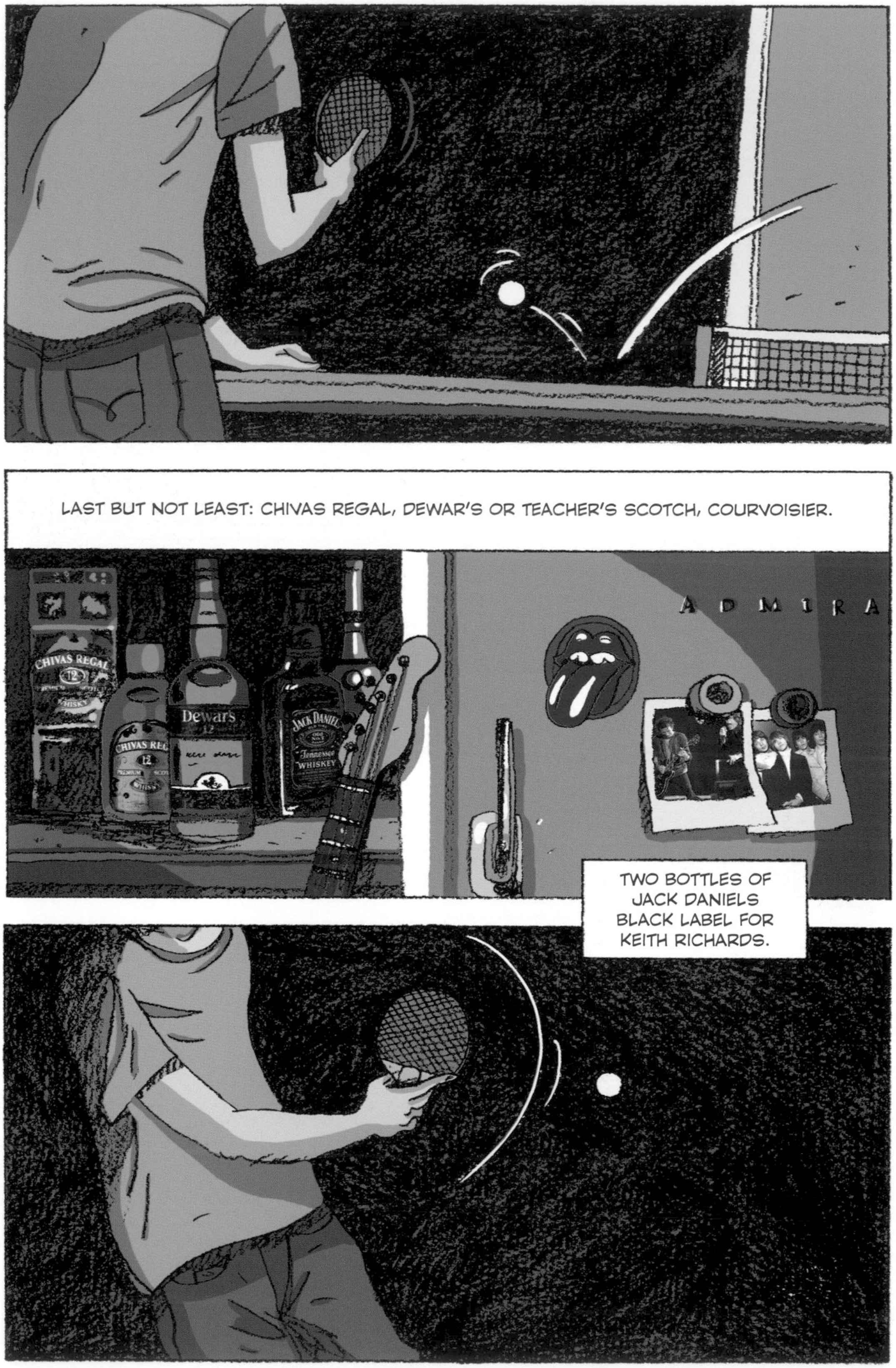
LAST BUT NOT LEAST: CHIVAS REGAL, DEWAR'S OR TEACHER'S SCOTCH, COURVOISIER.
ADMIRA
TWO BOTTLES OF JACK DANIELS BLACK LABEL FOR KEITH RICHARDS.

AND TEQUILA FOR MICK JAGGER. ANOTHER FAVE. WITH LIME AND SALT, NATURALLY.

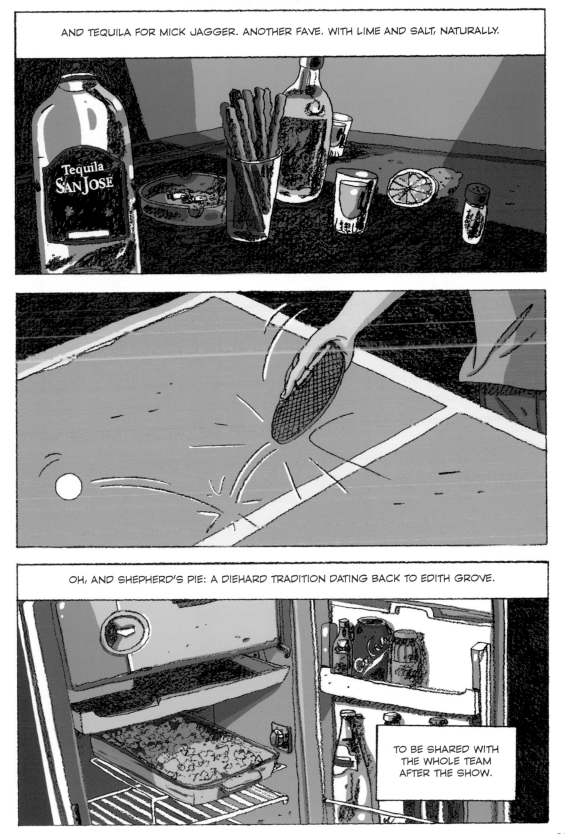

OH, AND SHEPHERD'S PIE: A DIEHARD TRADITION DATING BACK TO EDITH GROVE.

TO BE SHARED WITH THE WHOLE TEAM AFTER THE SHOW.

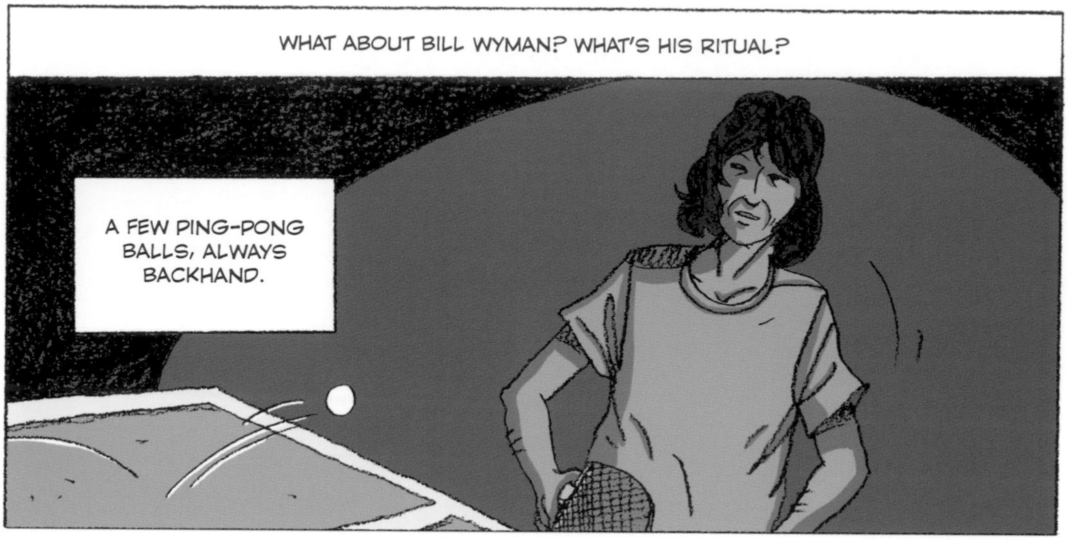
WHAT ABOUT BILL WYMAN? WHAT'S HIS RITUAL?
A FEW PING-PONG BALLS, ALWAYS BACKHAND.

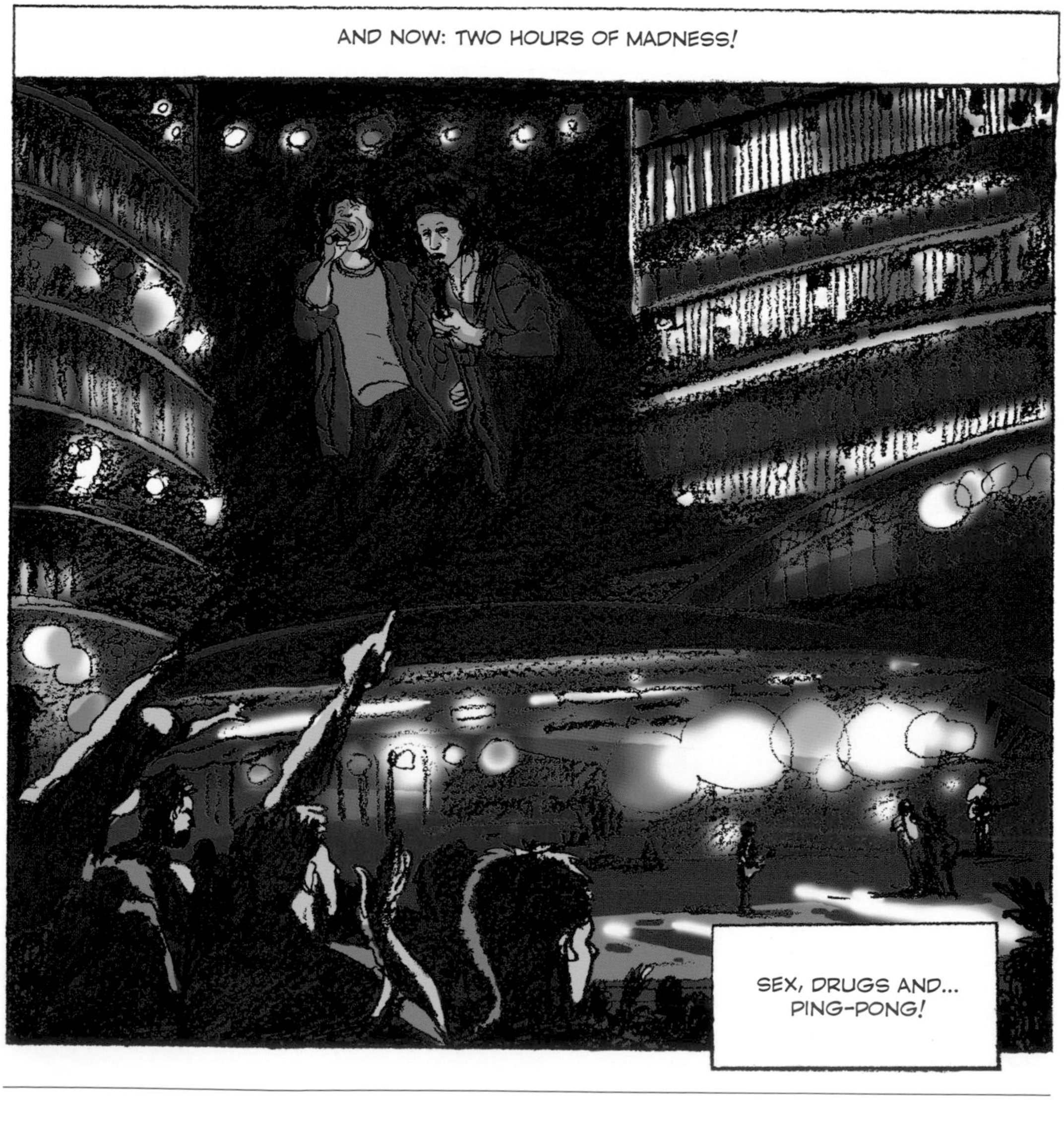
AND NOW: TWO HOURS OF MADNESS!
SEX, DRUGS AND... PING-PONG!

The Rolling Stones, Minus Two

Two milestones in the Rolling Stones timeline: the departure of Ian Stewart, the sixth Stone, who had a good excuse: he passed away in 1985; and the departure of Bill Wyman, who had a terrible excuse: his growing fear of flying. It was the end of a chapter, but the Rolling Stones aren't the type to dwell on the past.

With Ian Stewart ©TELEGRAPH

Ian Stewart died of a heart attack on December 12, 1985. He would be sorely missed, and not just out of nostalgia for the days when Stu used to schlep the band around in his old, hand-painted VW van to godforsaken places all across the UK. No, Ian would be missed for his boogie-woogie piano, his musical integrity and his energy. As Charlie Watts said fondly: "Now there's nobody to boss us around." Though he wasn't officially a Stone, he certainly was one unofficially—as evidenced by his posthumous induction into the Rock & Roll Hall of Fame in 1989 alongside the rest of the band.

Darryl Jones ©P Baumbach

"IN STARK CONTRAST
WITH THE FIERY JAGGER, YOU
ONLY SEE BILL WYMAN MOVE
WHEN HE BREATHES."

Tom Squitieri

Another bit of the cookie crumbled with the departure of Bill Wyman, aka The Quiet One. He split in 1993, tired of air travel, or... of getting so little credit? His influence on "Paint It Black" and his riff on "Jumpin' Jack Flash"—totally ignored!

Of course, he was the one who wrote "In Another Land" in 1967 and "Downtown Suzie" in 1975, but that's not very much, over a period of thirty years... So Bill Wyman figured maybe it was time to break free.

The bass player wanted to go back to playing music from the '50s, and in fact, the others had taken to calling him Mr. Formica. His new band, the Rhythm Kings, had no other objective than to have a good time... something probably missing from the Stones at the time of his departure. The low-key Englishman was replaced by a young American bass player nicknamed "The Munch."

A non-Brit in the band: that was a first!

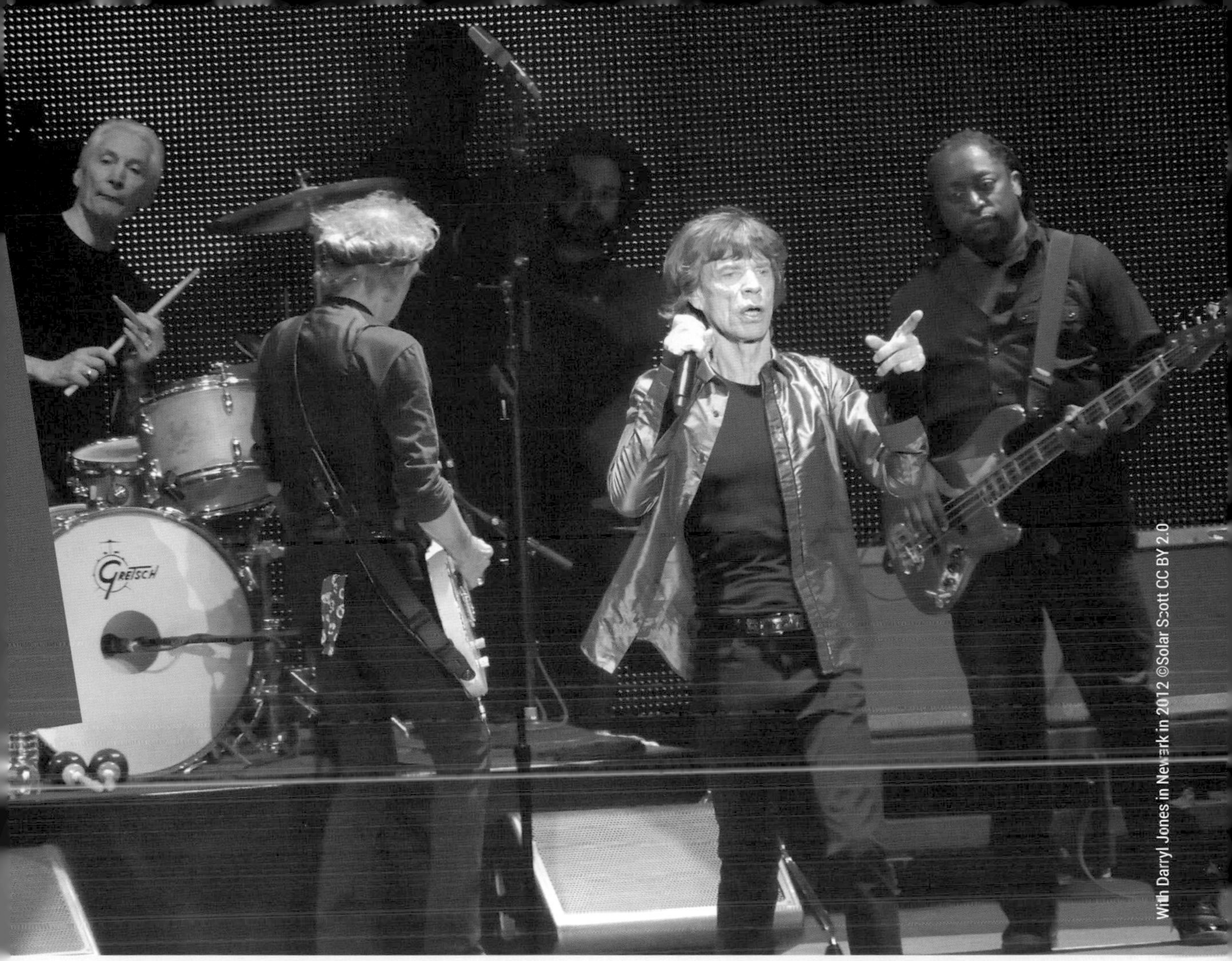
GRETSCH

With Darryl Jones in Newark in 2012 ©Solar Scott CC BY 2.0

"AT THE END OF THE *URBAN JUNGLE TOUR*, BILL SAID HE WAS LEAVING THE BAND. I GOT REALLY PISSED WITH HIM. I THREATENED TO DO EVERYTHING IN THE WORLD TO HIM, INCLUDING DEATH AT DAWN—AS I ALWAYS SAY, NOBODY LEAVES THIS BAND EXCEPT IN A COFFIN."

Keith Richards

Stone Alone

Artist: Sanzito

Bill Wyman,
the Solitary Stone.

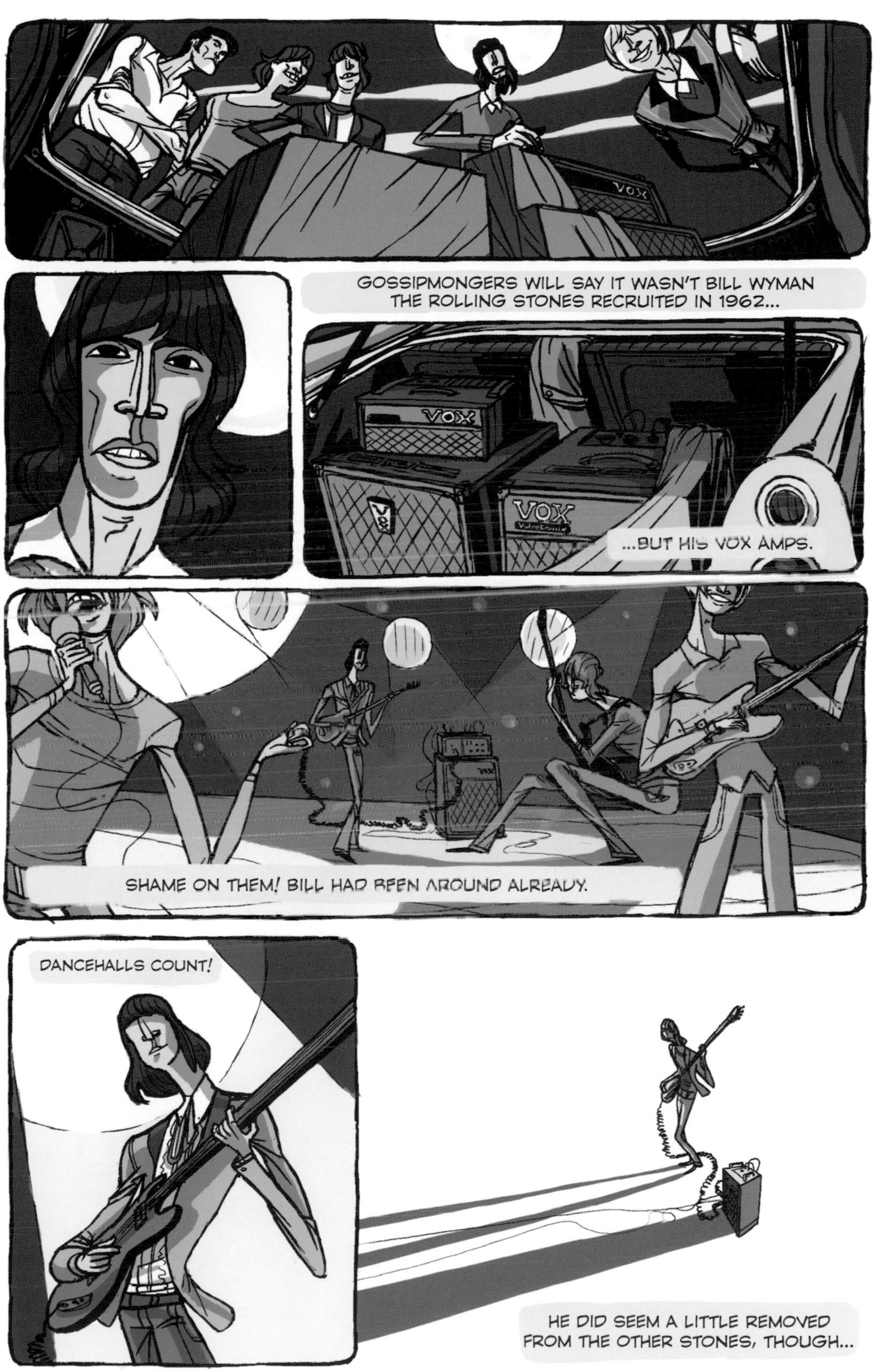
GOSSIPMONGERS WILL SAY IT WASN'T BILL WYMAN THE ROLLING STONES RECRUITED IN 1962...
...BUT HIS VOX AMPS.
SHAME ON THEM! BILL HAD BEEN AROUND ALREADY.
DANCEHALLS COUNT!
HE DID SEEM A LITTLE REMOVED FROM THE OTHER STONES, THOUGH...

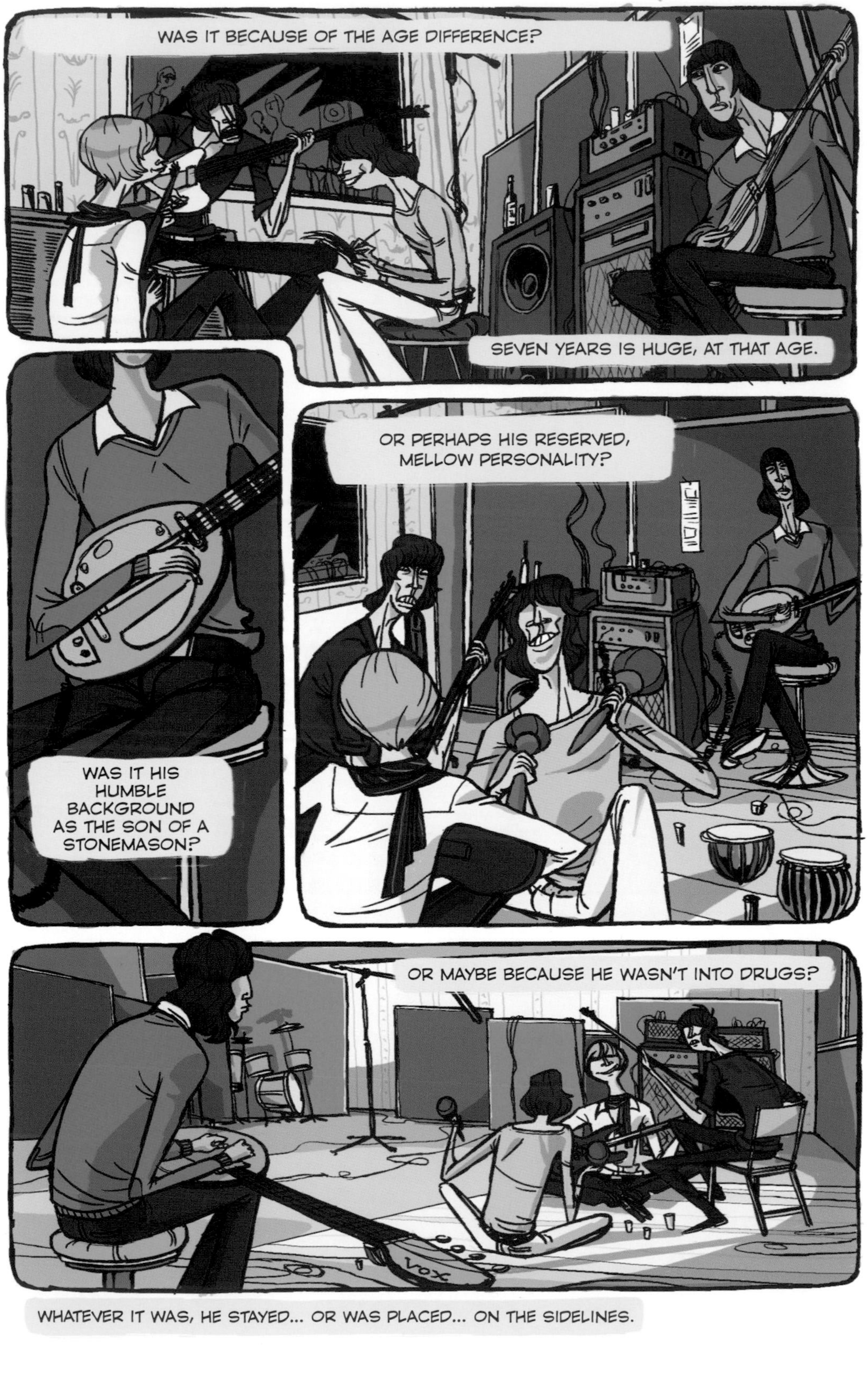
WAS IT BECAUSE OF THE AGE DIFFERENCE?
SEVEN YEARS IS HUGE, AT THAT AGE.
WAS IT HIS HUMBLE BACKGROUND AS THE SON OF A STONEMASON?
OR PERHAPS HIS RESERVED, MELLOW PERSONALITY?
OR MAYBE BECAUSE HE WASN'T INTO DRUGS?
VOX

WHATEVER IT WAS, HE STAYED... OR WAS PLACED... ON THE SIDELINES.

BUT HE PUT UP WITH IT STOICALLY, DESPITE ALL THE TEASING.

AS HE ONCE SUMMED IT UP:
"SOME LEAD, OTHERS FOLLOW."

SO BILL FOLLOWED.
THE WHOLE LONG WAY.

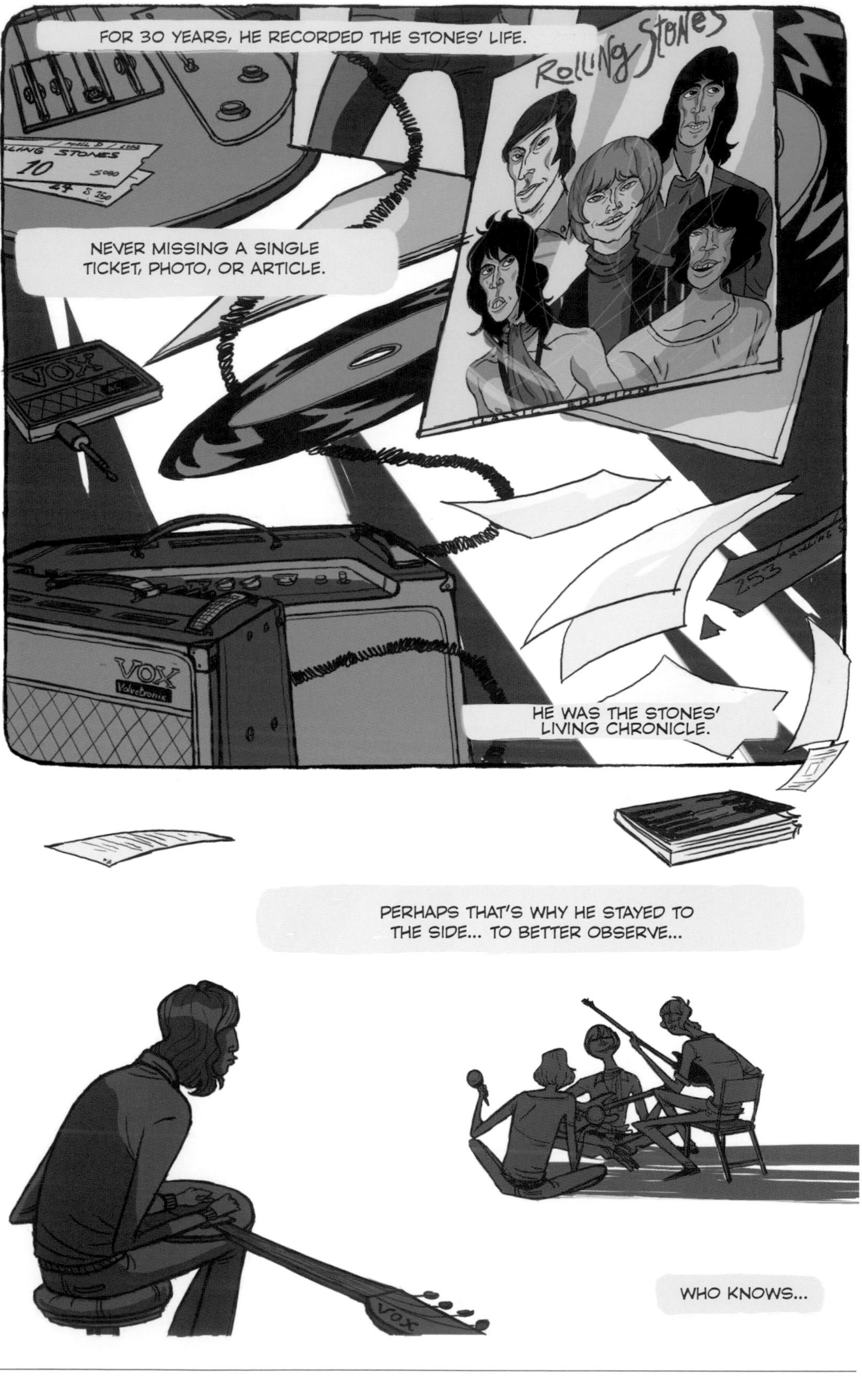
FOR 30 YEARS, HE RECORDED THE STONES' LIFE.
Rolling Stones
NEVER MISSING A SINGLE TICKET, PHOTO, OR ARTICLE.
VOX
VOX ValveTronix
HE WAS THE STONES' LIVING CHRONICLE.
PERHAPS THAT'S WHY HE STAYED TO THE SIDE... TO BETTER OBSERVE...
WHO KNOWS...

Who's the Guy in the Back?

Charlie Watts... we haven't said much about him so far. And yet Charlie Watts was the band's star member in the early days. To land Alexis Korner's drummer, now that was a coup. And if we haven't said much about him, it's simply because the man doesn't say much. As discreet as he is elegant, when he does speak, it tends to be with his drumsticks. And then.... respect!

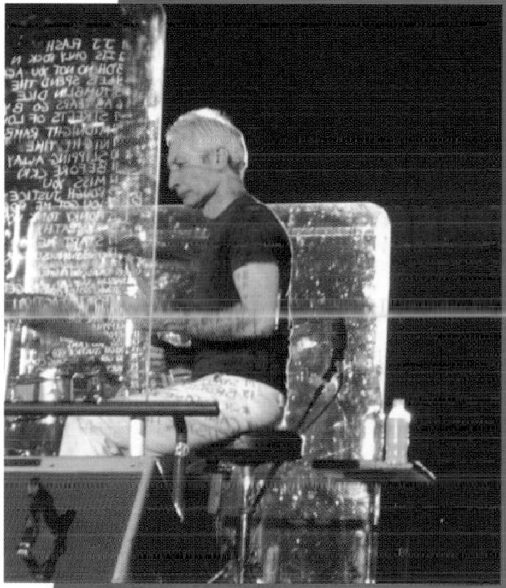

Charlie Watts in 2006 ©Dieband

As Keith Richards said in 1986 about the Rolling Stones: "It's Charlie Watts's band. Without him, we wouldn't have become a band." Charlie still cuts a dashing figure and plays as elegantly as ever. No going overboard. Fifty years in the band and not a single drum solo. He has always used his drumsticks exclusively in support of the band and the groove. A groove that drives everybody. Keith Richards knows that, and always turns to him before he starts playing, like a sunflower toward the sun. Then, the impassive Bill Wyman follows Charlie's lead, with a synchronicity that could make them pass for rhythm twins. Next to the Glimmer Twins are the Groover Twins. That's why Charlie stayed: for that innate harmony he has with Bill. **It was destiny calling.**

"THE DAY MY DRUMS EXPLODE WILL BE OUR LAST CONCERT."

Charlie Watts

> "I DON'T CARE WHAT PEOPLE SAY
> ABOUT ME. BUT I DO CARE WHAT THEY SAY
> ABOUT MY FAMILY, SO I DON'T REALLY
> TALK TO THE PRESS."
>
> **Charlie Watts**

2006 ©SEVERINO CC BY 2.0

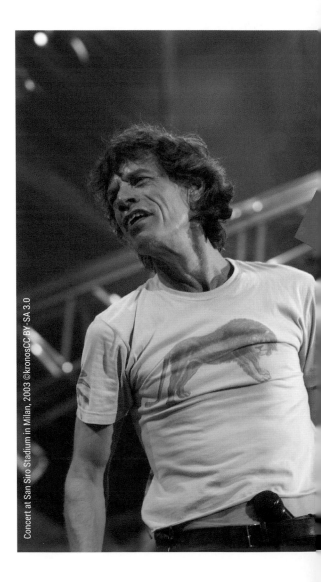

Concert at San Siro Stadium in Milan, 2003 ©kronosCC BY-SA 3.0

But what is Charlie Watts doing playing milli-metrically in a rock band? After all, his back-ground was in jazz, in improv, in effusion, in a genre where every individual can shine, doesn't he miss all that freedom? Undoubtedly. In fact, he once admitted to having joined the Stones primarily in the hope of traveling to the U.S. and seeing his musical idols. Meaning jazzmen. And when he embarked on a solo career in the '80s, it was naturally jazz that he turned to. A strang-er to rock and its universe, Charlie Watts seems to have become a Rolling Stone by mistake. But we forgive him that beautiful mistake and say... **Keep banging that drum!**

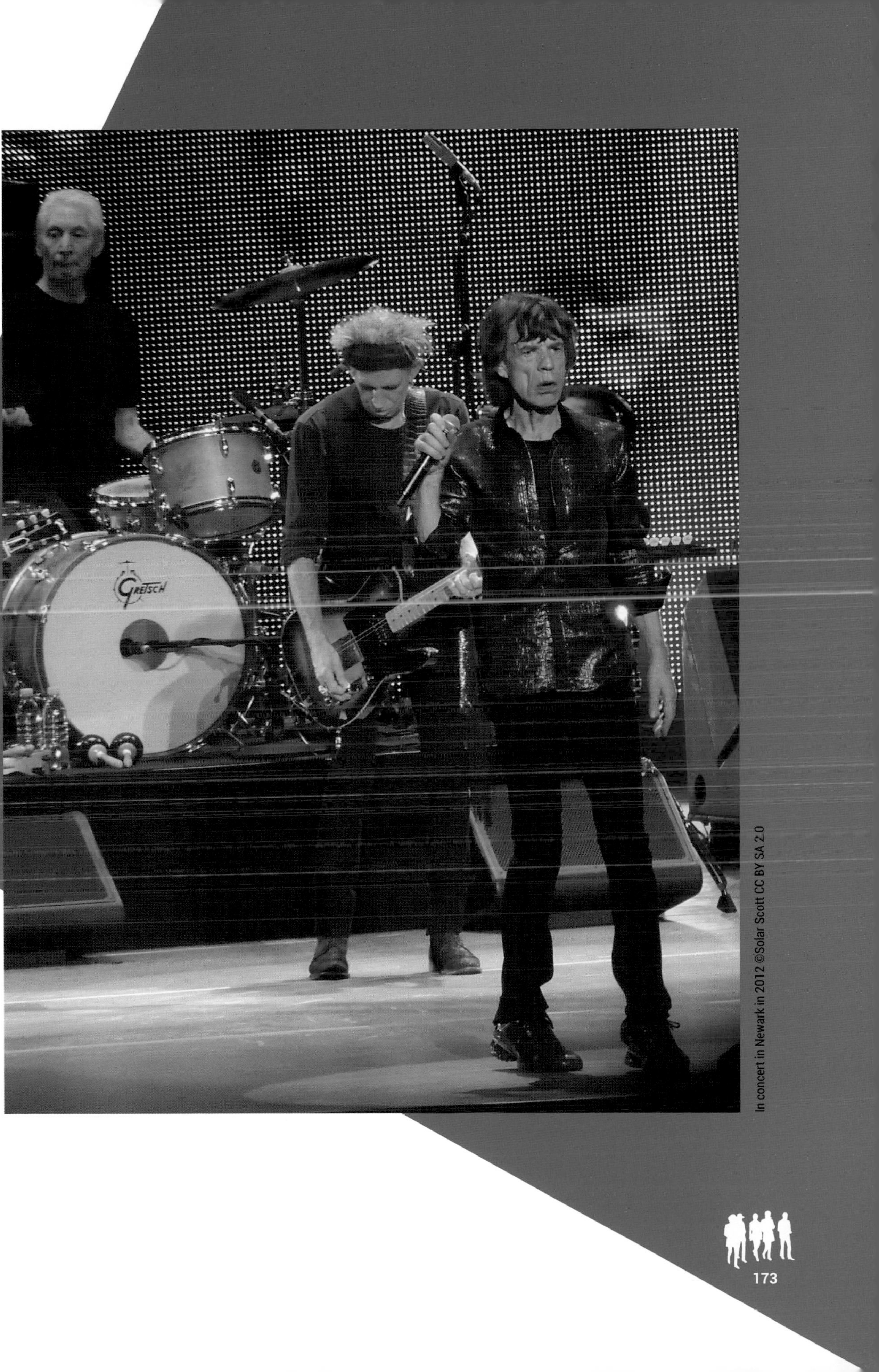
GRETSCH

In concert in Newark in 2012 ©Solar Scott CC BY SA 2.0

The Silent Stone

Artist: Patès

Charlie Watts,
Genius Drummer.

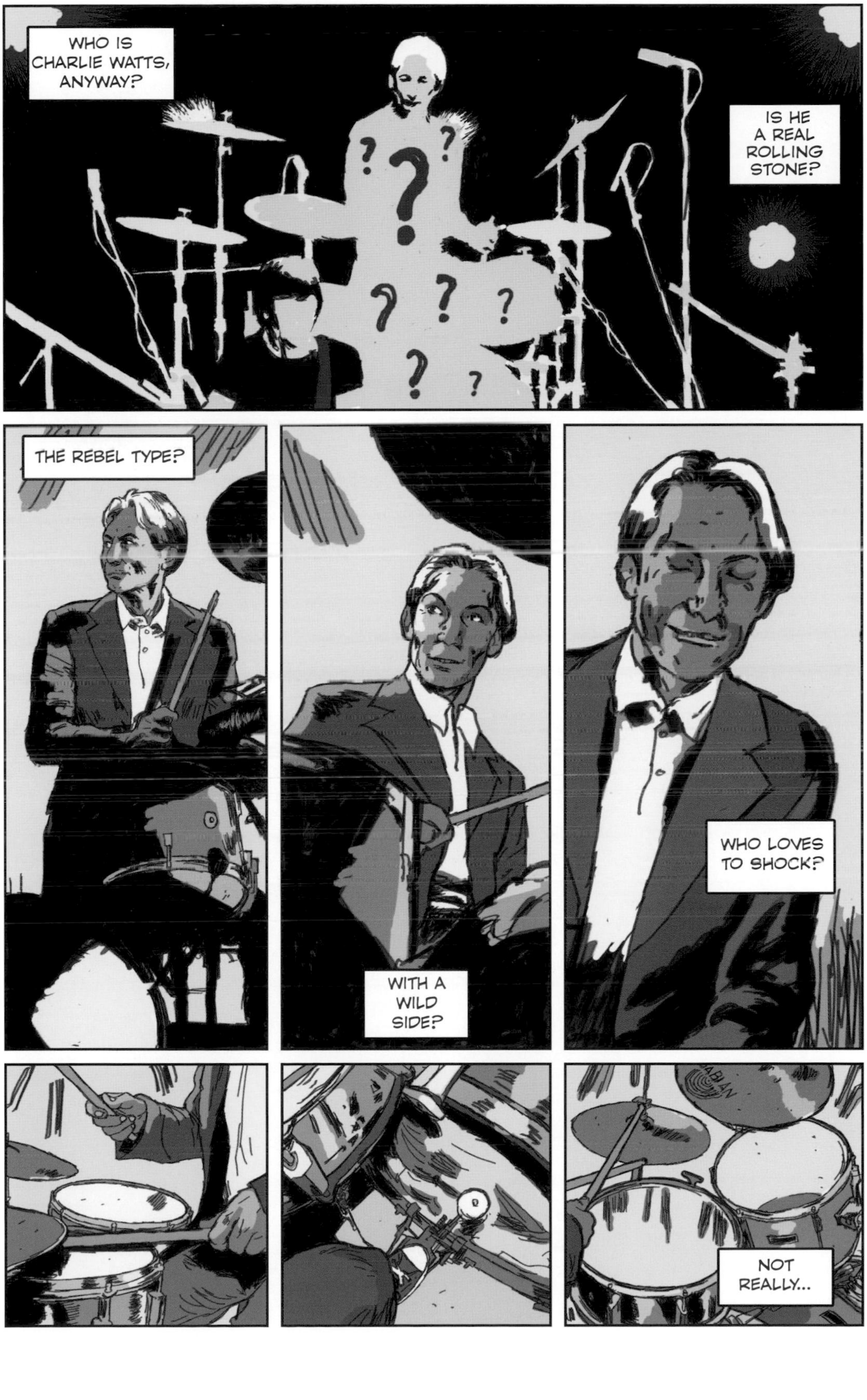
WHO IS CHARLIE WATTS, ANYWAY?
IS HE A REAL ROLLING STONE?
THE REBEL TYPE?
WITH A WILD SIDE?
WHO LOVES TO SHOCK?
NOT REALLY...

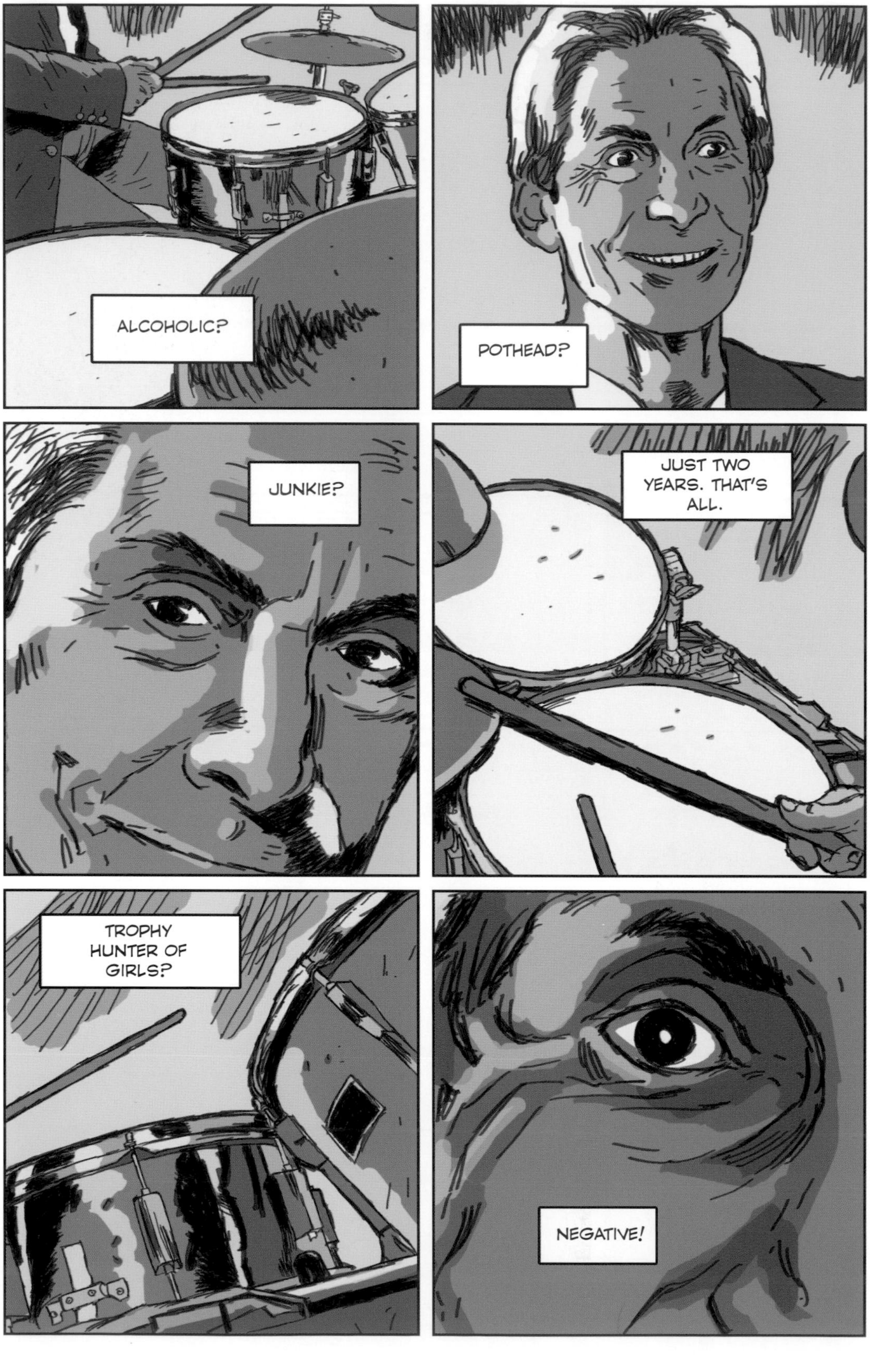
ALCOHOLIC?
POTHEAD?
JUNKIE?
JUST TWO YEARS. THAT'S ALL.
TROPHY HUNTER OF GIRLS?
NEGATIVE!

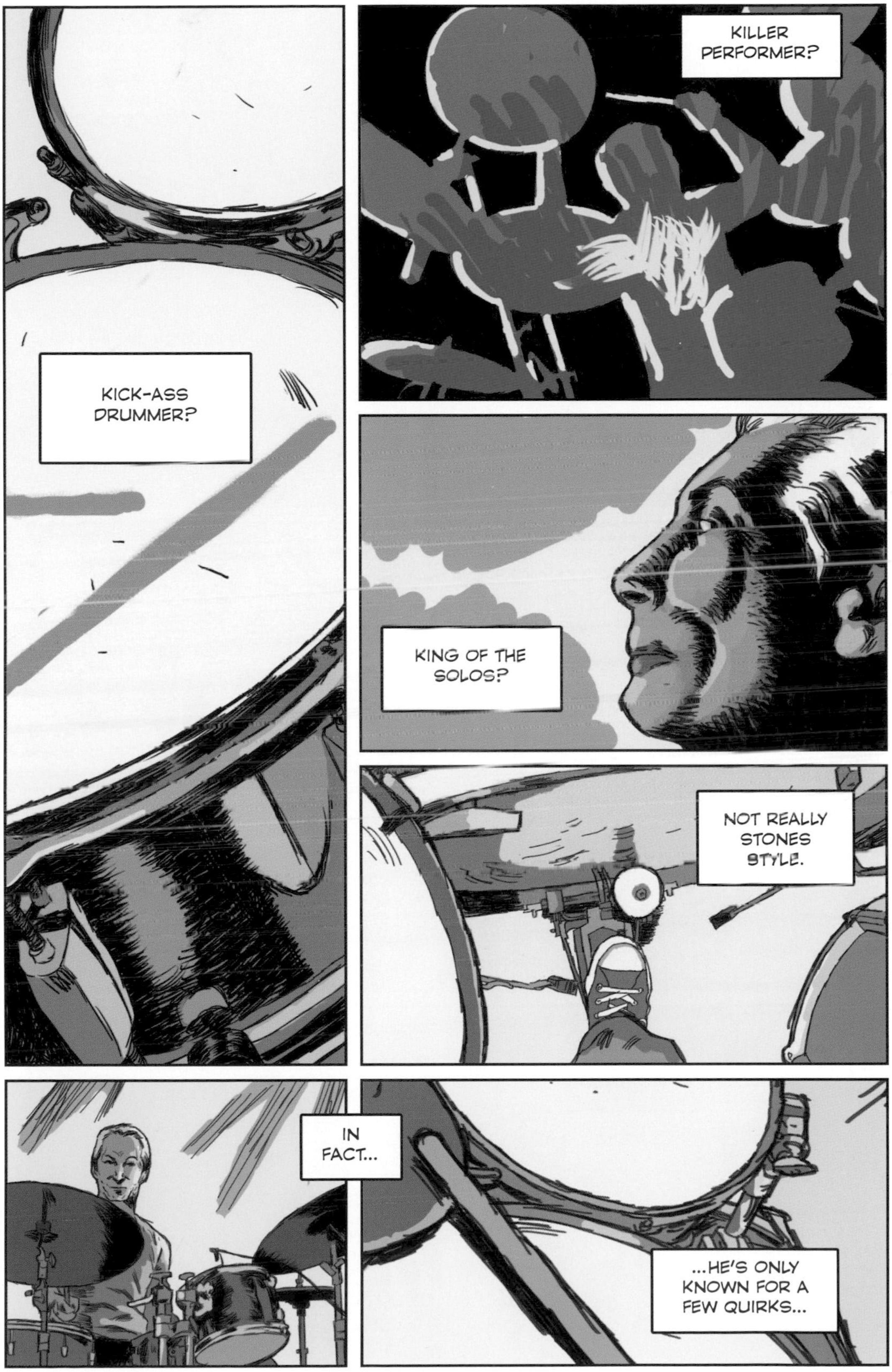
KICK-ASS DRUMMER?
KILLER PERFORMER?
KING OF THE SOLOS?
NOT REALLY STONES STYLE.
IN FACT...
...HE'S ONLY KNOWN FOR A FEW QUIRKS...

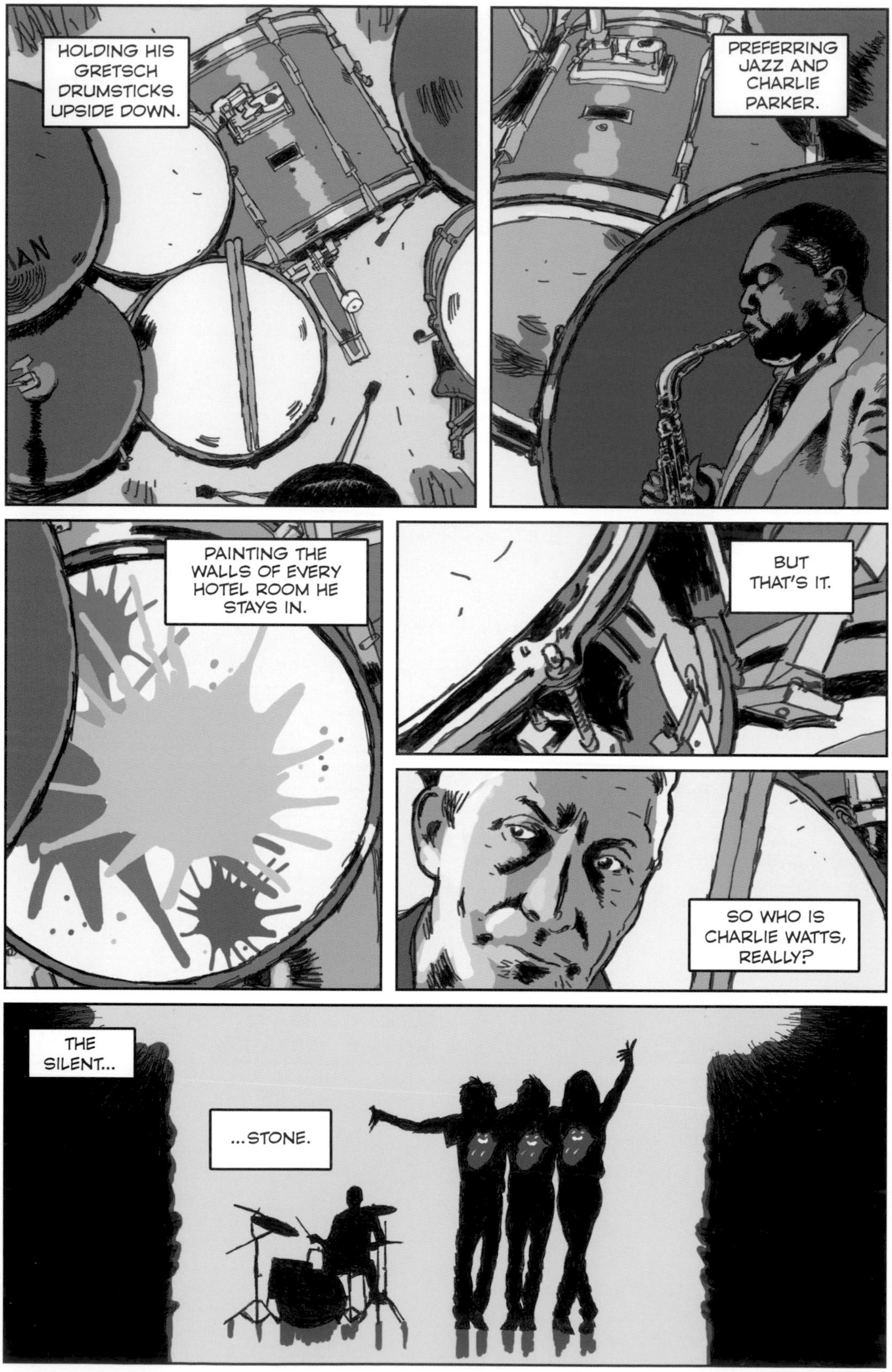
HOLDING HIS GRETSCH DRUMSTICKS UPSIDE DOWN.
PREFERRING JAZZ AND CHARLIE PARKER.
PAINTING THE WALLS OF EVERY HOTEL ROOM HE STAYS IN.
BUT THAT'S IT.
SO WHO IS CHARLIE WATTS, REALLY?
THE SILENT...
...STONE.

The Stones Are STILL Rolling

Yes, some have left, and yes, some have died; yes, there have been highs and lows and yes, time has passed. But one thing is sure: the Rolling Stones are still here, as jubilant as they were on day one. How many times did people wager they were over? As many times as they rose from the dead like gods. **Gods of rock.**

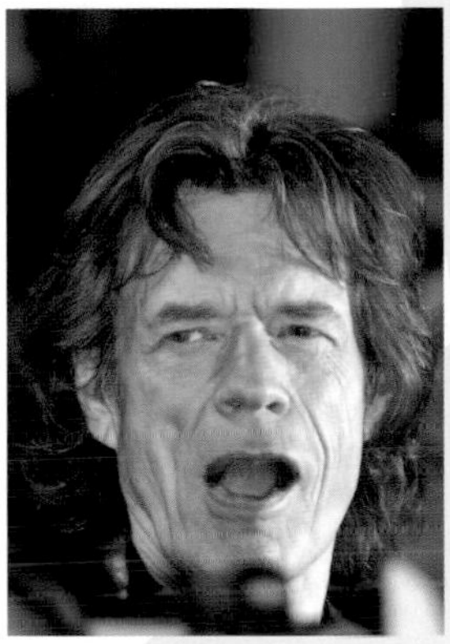

In Deauville in 2014 ©Georges Biard CC BY-SA 3.0

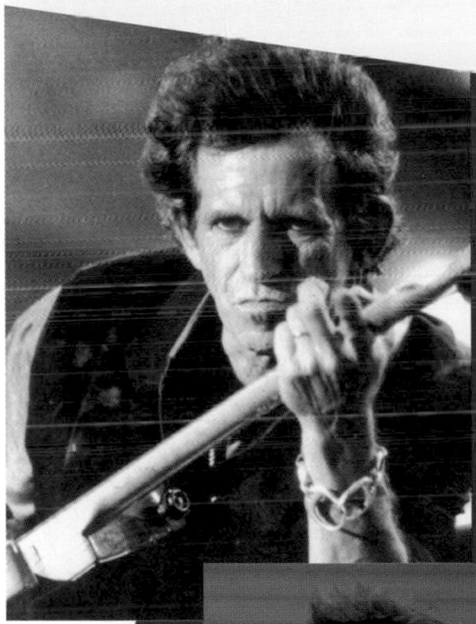

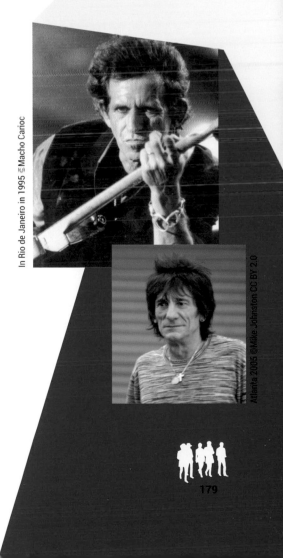

In Rio de Janeiro in 1995 ©Macho Carioc

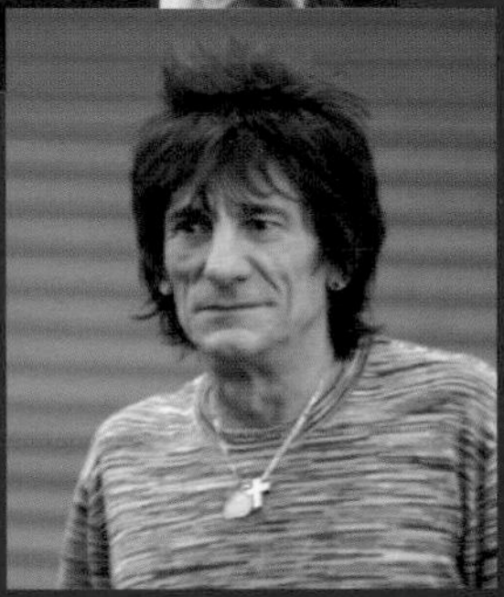

Atlanta 2005 ©Mike Johnston CC BY 2.0

They would be the first ones not to have wagered a shilling on their longevity. After all, Mick Jagger once vowed to stop at thirty-three, "not wanting to be a rock star [his] whole life." True, a rebel with wrinkles and gray hair was probably hard for them to imagine, especially in their twenties, when they cursed their seniors and any form of conformism. But the Stones are still rolling and have no intention of stopping. Keith Richards confirmed it: "The Stones can still experience a very interesting golden age. The road we're taking has never been taken before." And if they don't feel like calling it quits, who's going to say otherwise? Not us, at any rate!
The Stones, past their due date? Some people call them the Strolling Bones, others the Groaning Bones... but how many rock bands do you know that get huge crowds on their feet on every single tour?

Keith Richards in Berlin in 2008 ©SIEBBI CCBY SA3.0

Berlin, 2008 ©Siebbi CCBY3.0

"NO BAND HAD EVER LASTED THAT LONG. I COULDN'T EVEN HAVE FANTASIZED ABOUT IT, BUT NOW IT'S BECOME A CHALLENGE. AS LONG AS THE BLOOD IS PUMPING, I NEED TO GO ALL THE WAY."

Keith Richards

In February 2006, they played before a million people at Copacabana Beach in Brazil. Not bad, eh? They may have become a part-time band, only reuniting for the space of a new album or a tour, but the heart is still beating. Theirs. And ours.

In March 2010, a major publishing event: after forty years of embargo on their archives, the Stones came out with a new, enhanced edition of *Exile on Main Street*, featuring a dozen previously unreleased titles from 1968–1972.

It's not every day you turn fifty! In August 2012, a three-CD Best Of was announced, soberly titled *GRRR*. The box set was released November 13, 2012, with two bonus new titles: "One More Shot" and "Doom and Gloom," recorded a few weeks earlier in Paris. They went on a five-concert mini-tour in late 2012, the first part of their "50 and Counting" tour: two shows in London and three in New York. In 2013, they were back at it, with nine shows from May to June in North America, followed by concerts at the Glastonbury Festival and London's legendary Hyde Park. The world tour came in 2014: "14 on Fire." The United Arab Emirates, Japan, China, Europe, Australia... all in all, over 782,000 people attended the Stones concerts. Then, another tour in 2015 and fans clamoring for a new album. Rumors grew stronger and Keith Richards eventually announced that the band would indeed be recording a new album in early 2016. In March 2016, the Rolling Stones made history once again by becoming the very first rock band to perform in concert in Cuba, an event that was both a cultural and political milestone. The Stones appeared at Havana's Ciudad Deportiva in front of 500,000 fans. And, as promised, the day before their fifty years as a band and eleven years after their last studio album, *Blue & Lonesome,* hit the stands, featuring reworked versions of their blues classics. In 2017, the Rolling Stones embarked on a new tour, a European one, titled "No Filter Tour." So... how long will the Stones keep rolling? Forever, perhaps..

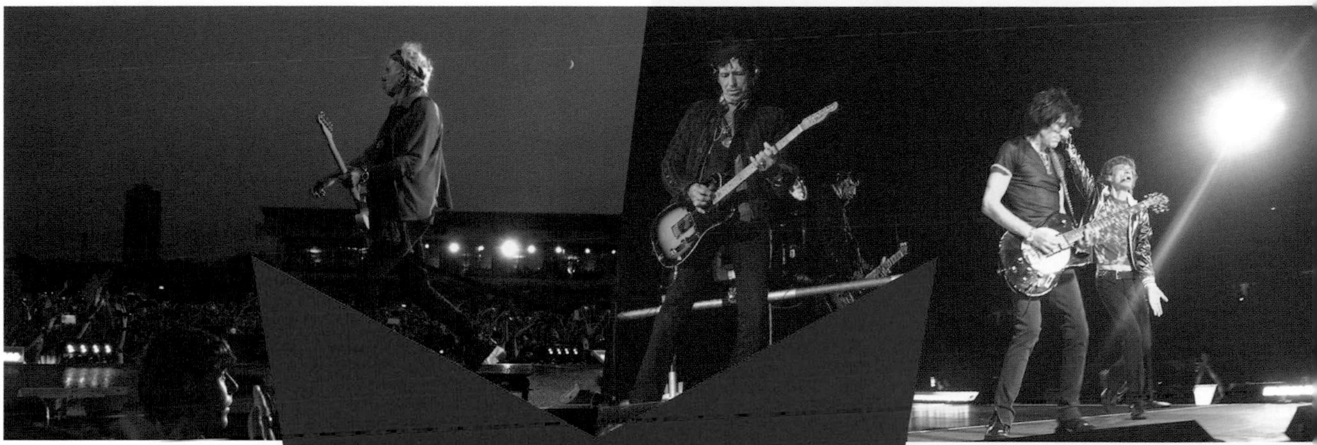

Hyde Park, 2013 ©Gorup De Besanez CC BY-SA 3.0

"I HAD COME THERE TO BURY THEM, BUT WHAT DO YOU DO WHEN THE CORPSE LEAPS OUT OF THE COFFIN AND STARTS DANCING ON THE GRAVE?"

Evening Standard

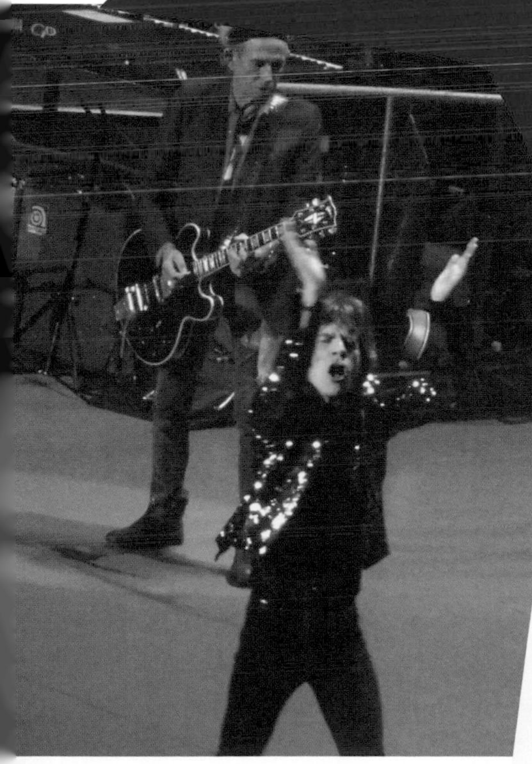

Concert in Boston, 2013 ©Michael Borkson CC BY SA 2

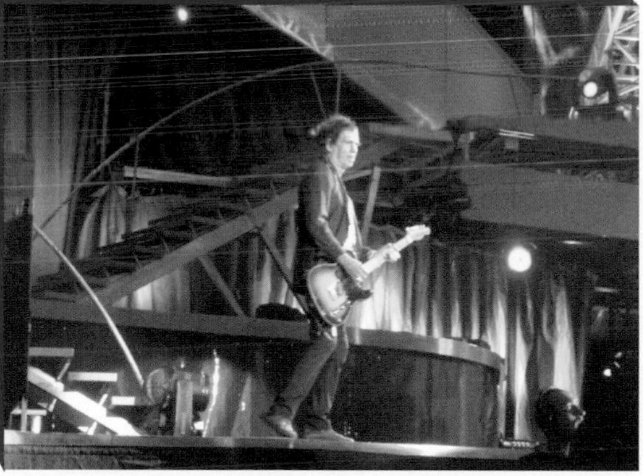

Stade de France, 2006 ©REGVARINOTCCBY2.0

Century Tour

Artist: Mao Suy-Heng

The Rolling Stones
Over Already?

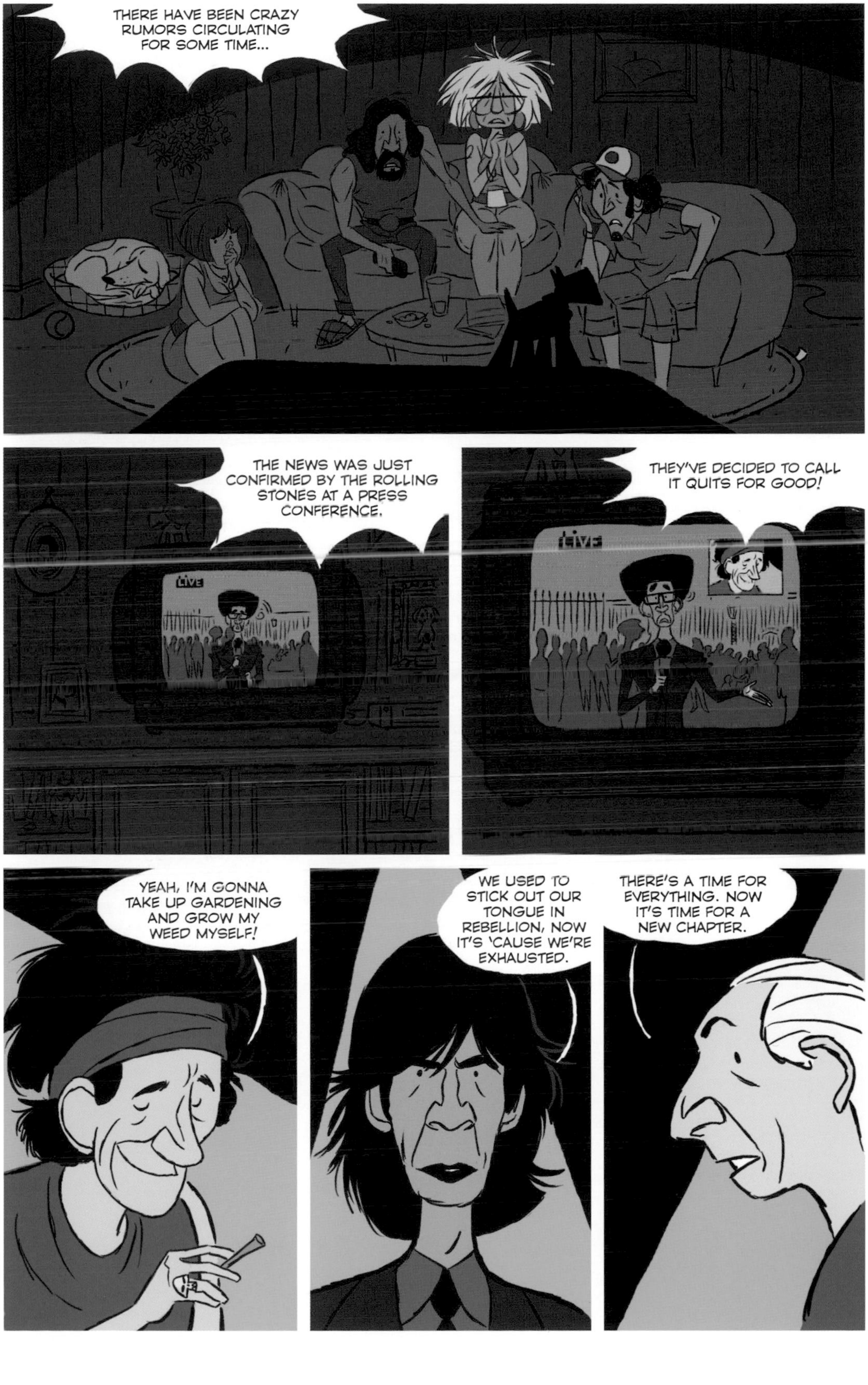
THERE HAVE BEEN CRAZY RUMORS CIRCULATING FOR SOME TIME...
THE NEWS WAS JUST CONFIRMED BY THE ROLLING STONES AT A PRESS CONFERENCE.
LIVE
THEY'VE DECIDED TO CALL IT QUITS FOR GOOD!
LIVE
YEAH, I'M GONNA TAKE UP GARDENING AND GROW MY WEED MYSELF!
WE USED TO STICK OUT OUR TONGUE IN REBELLION, NOW IT'S 'CAUSE WE'RE EXHAUSTED.
THERE'S A TIME FOR EVERYTHING. NOW IT'S TIME FOR A NEW CHAPTER.

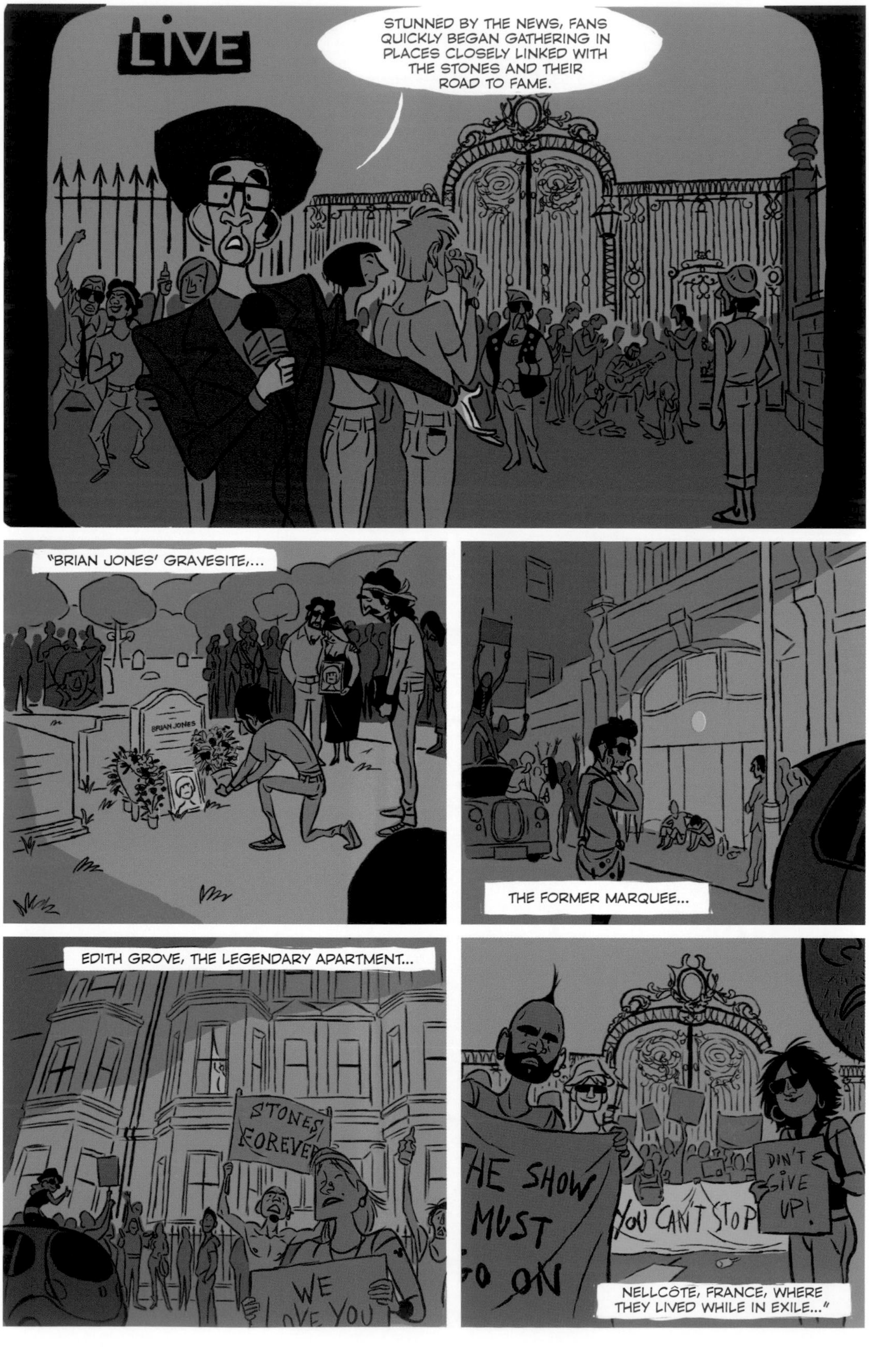
LIVE
STUNNED BY THE NEWS, FANS QUICKLY BEGAN GATHERING IN PLACES CLOSELY LINKED WITH THE STONES AND THEIR ROAD TO FAME.
"BRIAN JONES' GRAVESITE,...
BRIAN JONES
THE FORMER MARQUEE...
EDITH GROVE, THE LEGENDARY APARTMENT...
STONES FOREVER
WE LOVE YOU
THE SHOW MUST GO ON
YOU CAN'T STOP
DON'T GIVE UP!
NELLCÔTE, FRANCE, WHERE THEY LIVED WHILE IN EXILE..."

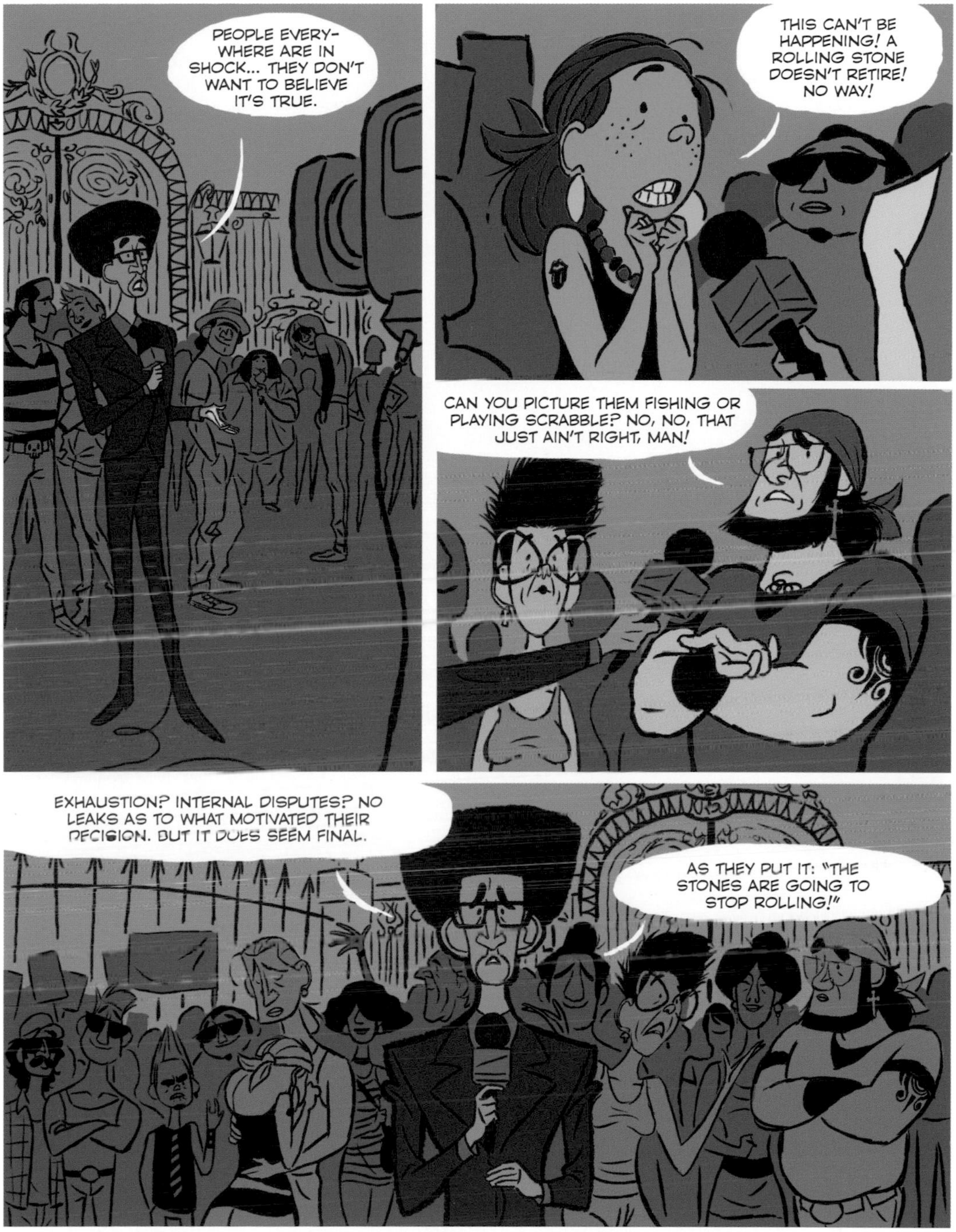
PEOPLE EVERY-WHERE ARE IN SHOCK... THEY DON'T WANT TO BELIEVE IT'S TRUE.
THIS CAN'T BE HAPPENING! A ROLLING STONE DOESN'T RETIRE! NO WAY!
CAN YOU PICTURE THEM FISHING OR PLAYING SCRABBLE? NO, NO, THAT JUST AIN'T RIGHT, MAN!
EXHAUSTION? INTERNAL DISPUTES? NO LEAKS AS TO WHAT MOTIVATED THEIR DECISION. BUT IT DOES SEEM FINAL.
AS THEY PUT IT: "THE STONES ARE GOING TO STOP ROLLING!"

SO WHAT DO YOU THINK ABOUT ALL THAT?

"REAL NEWS OR FAKE NEWS?"

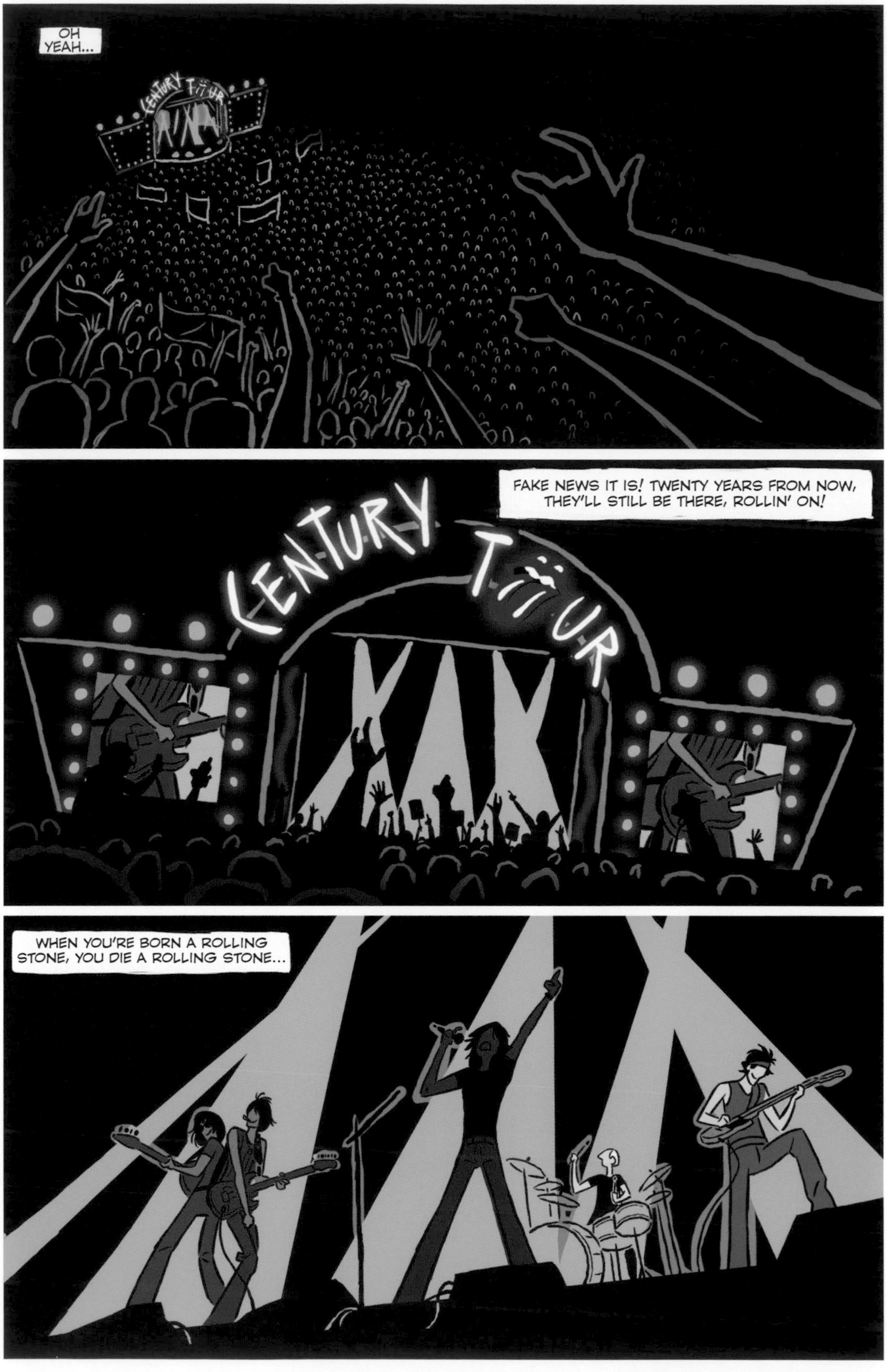
OH YEAH...
CENTURY TOUR
FAKE NEWS IT IS! TWENTY YEARS FROM NOW, THEY'LL STILL BE THERE, ROLLIN' ON!
CENTURY TOUR
WHEN YOU'RE BORN A ROLLING STONE, YOU DIE A ROLLING STONE...

Nine Fun Facts About This Legendary Band!

©Mr. Granger CC0

1. 1964 The Rolling Stones were approached by Kellogg's cereal to compose a jingle for a Rice Krispies commercial. Brian Jones wrote the song for 400 pounds.

2. June 1964 On their first U.S. tour, the Stones met their idol, Muddy Waters, in a Chicago recording studio. Legend has it that when they visited, he was busy repainting the ceilings.

3. 1965 Bill Wyman is said to have coined the term "groupie" during the Stones' Australian tour.

Muddy Waters ©Jean-Luc Ourlin CC BY-SA 2.0

1964

©Riksarkivet (National Archives of Norway)

©Riksarkivet (National Archives of Norway)

1965

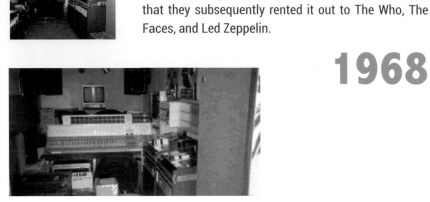

Inside the mobile studio © CantosMusicCC BY SA 2.0

4. 1968 Sick of having to rent studios by the hour, the Rolling Stones had the idea of building a mobile recording studio just for themselves. It worked so well that they subsequently rented it out to The Who, The Faces, and Led Zeppelin.

1968

5. 1972 The *Exile On Main Street* album was recorded on the French Riviera, where the Rolling Stones sought refuge for 21 months to avoid the taxman and various drug-related legal issues back home.

©gudrun from Berlin CC BY-SA 2.0

6. October 25, 2012 To prepare for their anniversary tour, the Rolling Stones rehearsed in a recording studio just outside Paris and gave a surprise concert at the Trabendo in Paris in front of 700 fans.

1972

2012

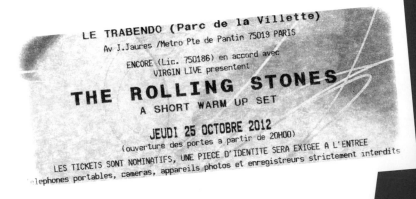

LE TRABENDO (Parc de la Villette)
Av J.Jaures /Metro Pte de Pantin 75019 PARIS
ENCORE (Lic. 750186) en accord avec
VIRGIN LIVE présentent
THE ROLLING STONES
A SHORT WARM UP SET
JEUDI 25 OCTOBRE 2012
(ouverture des portes a partir de 20H00)
LES TICKETS SONT NOMINATIFS, UNE PIECE D'IDENTITE SERA EXIGEE A L'ENTREE
Téléphones portables, cameras, appareils photos et enregistreurs strictement interdits

ENTRÉ KR 15:-

OBSI Fotografering förbjuden.

BILJETT

THE ROLLING STONES M. FL.

Arrangörer: Karusell Konsertbyrå och SBA

KUNGLIGA TENNISHALLEN
LIDINGÖVÄGEN 75

TORSDAGEN DEN 1 APRIL 1965 KL. 18.15

SEKTION **B**

BÄNK Nr. 4   PLATS   Nr   37
KÖPT BILJETT ÅTERTAGES EJ

7. In **1965** a ticket to a Rolling Stones concert cost just 3 dollars. Fifty years later, it was over 100 dollars!

1965

2008

Shine a Light World Premiere Berlinale ©Jli Schmidt CC BY 2.0

2006 ©Kelsey Tracey CC BY SA 3.0

8. American filmmaker Martin Scorsese used the song "Gimme Shelter" in four of his films, in addition to making the 2008 documentary about the Stones titled *Shine a Light*.

9. For many years, there was a rumor circulating that Keith Richards had undergone a full blood transfusion in an attempt to get off heroin. In 2010, he confessed to having started the rumor himself.

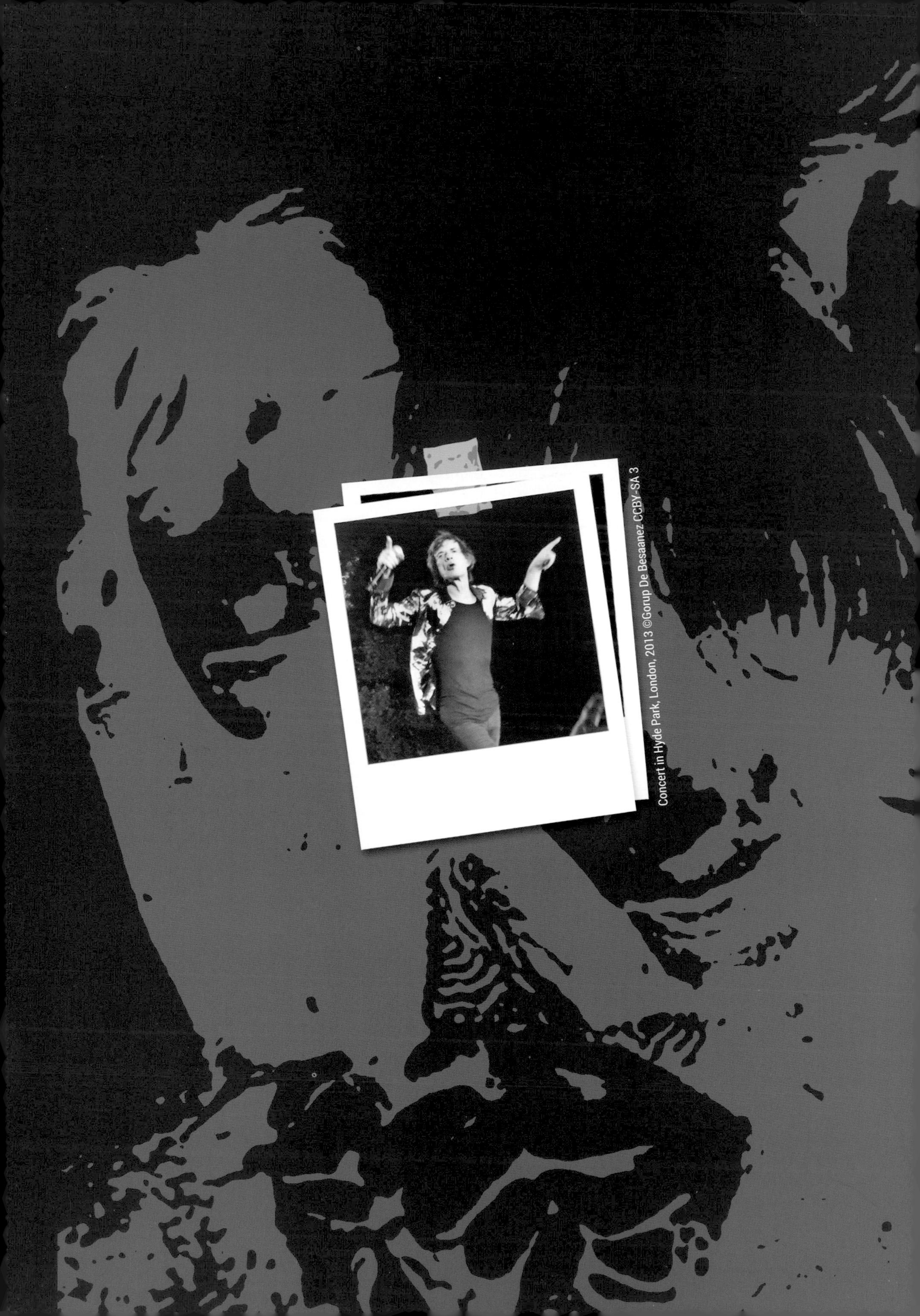

Concert in Hyde Park, London, 2013 ©Gorup De Besaanez CCBY-SA 3